Alfred John Church

Stories from the Greek comedians

Aristophanes, Philemon, Diphilus, Menander, Apollodorus

Alfred John Church

Stories from the Greek comedians
Aristophanes, Philemon, Diphilus, Menander, Apollodorus

ISBN/EAN: 9783337103040

Printed in Europe, USA, Canada, Australia, Japan

Cover: Foto ©Andreas Hilbeck / pixelio.de

More available books at **www.hansebooks.com**

STORIES

FROM THE

GREEK COMEDIANS

ARISTOPHANES, PHILEMON,

DIPHILUS, MENANDER, APOLLODORUS

BY THE

REV. ALFRED J. CHURCH, M.A.

LATELY PROFESSOR OF LATIN IN UNIVERSITY COLLEGE, LONDON

WITH SIXTEEN ILLUSTRATIONS
AFTER THE ANTIQUE

LONDON
SEELEY AND CO. LIMITED
ESSEX STREET, STRAND
1893

PREFACE.

IT has been said that the Greeks had three schools of comedy, — the old, the middle, and the new. The old was the "Comedy of Politics." It took the form of extravaganza or farce. The reader will find nine specimens of it in this volume, all taken from Aristophanes, who indeed is the only writer of this school that is left to us. With the middle we need not now concern ourselves. Possibly we may get some idea of what it was like from the *Women in Parliament* and the *Plutus*, two of Aristophanes's later plays. The new comedy was the "Comedy of Manners." It may be compared with the dramas that bear this name on the modern stage, and also with the ordinary novel. We have it only in the translations of Plautus and Terence.

I have dealt very freely with my originals, not indeed adding anything, but leaving out much, translating sometimes, and sometimes paraphrasing. Of the liberty which I have allowed myself, I may give an instance. In the *Acharnians* I have in one place translated "drachmas" by "guineas," though "shillings" would have been nearer the truth. But the context seemed to require it. It was necessary that the envoys should be thought overpaid, and the word "shillings" would not have given the impression.

I have many obligations to acknowledge. Perhaps my largest debt is to the translation of Mr. Hookham Frere. These I have even ventured to alter and compress, and to mingle with them some of my own renderings. I owe much to the admirable versions by Mr. B. B. Rogers of the *Wasps* and the *Peace*, and to the editions of Mr. Merry, one of the most ingenious and felicitous of Aristophanes's critics. I would mention also a translation of the *Acharnians* by Mr. Billson, and of the *Women in Parliament* by the Rev. R. Smith. Mr. Lucas Collins's excellent summaries in the "Ancient Classics for English Readers" I have also found useful.

ALFRED J. CHURCH.

CONTENTS.

PART I.

STORIES FROM THE OLD COMEDY.

PART II.

STORIES FROM THE NEW COMEDY.

LIST OF ILLUSTRATIONS.

Part I.

STORIES FROM THE OLD COMEDY.

ARISTOPHANES.

STORIES FROM THE GREEK COMEDIANS.

I.

THE ACHARNIANS.

The long struggle between Athens and Sparta which goes by the name of the Peloponnesian war broke out early in 431 B.C. Athens kept for a considerable time the command of the sea, but was unable to resist in the field the overwhelming forces of Sparta and her allies. Early in the summer of the first year of the war, Archidamus, one of the kings of Sparta, entered the Athenian territory at the head of an army of eighty thousand men. Pericles, who was then the leading statesman of Athens, had persuaded his countrymen to dismantle their country-houses and farms, and to bring all their movable and portable property within the walls. Still the sight of the ravages of the invading host, which, of course, could be plainly seen from the walls, roused the people almost to madness. The Athenians, though excelling in maritime pursuits, were passionately fond of a country life, and it was almost more than they could bear to see their farms and orchards and olive-yards wasted with fire. Inferior as they were in numbers, they loudly demanded to be led out against the invaders, and it was as much as Pericles could do to keep them within the walls. The inhabitants of the deme or township of Acharnæ were prominent among the malcontents. Acharnæ was the richest and most populous of the townships of Attica, contributing no less than ten thousand men to the total force (about twenty-nine thousand) which Athens could put into the field. The chief occupation of the place was charcoal-burning, the woods of Mount Parnes being conveniently near. No place was more interested in the question of peace and war, as it was here that the Spartan king pitched his camp. The invasion was repeated year after year, though on some few occasions various things happened to prevent it. Not only did the Athenians lose greatly by the desolation of their country, but they suffered much by being cooped up within the

3

walls of the city; a most fatal pestilence was thus caused in the second year of the war. And it was but a small satisfaction to retaliate by ravaging the coasts of the Peloponnesians, and by annually invading the territory of Megara, a city which had concluded an alliance with Sparta. There had always been a peace party in the state, and when Pericles died, early in the third year of the war, this party became more powerful. At the same time the war party conducted affairs less prudently. The cautious policy of Pericles was discarded for remote expeditions and out-of-the-way schemes. Aristophanes, in this play, exhibited in February, 425 (it is the earliest comedy that has come down to us), sets forth the views of the advocates of peace. He expresses the feeling of distress caused by the desolation of the country, and also the dislike felt by prudent politicians for the extravagant ideas of the war party. The play, or, as I may call it for my present purpose, the story, opens in the Athenian place of Assembly (Pnyx). Dicæopolis (Just-City), whose name I have Englished by " Mr. Honesty," is sitting alone on one of the empty benches, and begins by expressing his disgust at the indifference of his fellow-citizens.

"DEAR me!" said Mr. Honesty to himself, as he got up and walked about the empty place of Assembly at Athens, "how careless these people are about their country! Look at them there, lounging among the market stalls, and dodging the rope.[1] Even the magistrates are not here. As for peace — nobody gives a thought to it. For myself, I think of nothing else. I am here the first thing in the morning, and it is always 'peace,' 'peace' with me. How I hate the city! How I long to see the fields again, my own village, and my poor little farm! No fellows there bawling out, 'Buy my charcoal!' 'Buy my oil!' 'Buy my everything!' There was no

[1] A rope rubbed with red chalk, with which the police swept loiterers into the place of Assembly.

buying there. Everything came off the estate, and was to be had for nothing. Ah! here they come at last. Well, nobody shall say a word with my good-will, except he speaks for peace."

After various preliminaries the magistrates took their places, the people crowded in, and a herald opened the proceedings by shouting out, "Does any one wish to speak?"

"Yes; I do," cried out a strange-looking creature, dressed as if he had stepped down from a pedestal in a temple.

"What is your name?" asked the herald.

"Demigod," said the stranger. "I am directly descended from the goddess Demeter, and I am sent by the gods to arrange for a peace between this city and Sparta; only, unfortunately, I want a little ready money for my journey, and I can't get the magistrates to advance it."

"This is a very sensible man," said Mr. Honesty. The next moment he was amazed to see that the presiding magistrate was sending the archers[1] to turn the stranger out. "Hold!" he cried, "you insult the people. Don't you know that the man wants to give us peace?"

Just at this moment there was a diversion. The herald shouted out, "Silence there! Make way for the ambassadors from the Great King!"

"Gentlemen," said one of the ambassadors, coming

---

[1] "Archers" would be about equivalent to police.

forward, "you will remember that you sent us a few years ago on an embassy to the Great King with a poor allowance of a couple of guineas a day."

"Poor guineas!" muttered Mr. Honesty, "we shall never see them again."

The ambassadors went on : "You ought to know, gentlemen, that it was a very laborious service on which you sent us. All day we had to ride in carriages, lying on soft cushions, with an awning over our heads."

"Very laborious !" growled Honesty. "I was on guard all night, with nothing over me, and only a mat under me."

Ambassador. "Then the barbarians entertained us, and we were obliged to drink strong wine, without a drop of water in it, if you will believe us, out of cups of crystal or gold, for this, you must know, is the test with them ; the best man is he who can eat and drink most. At the end of four years we reached the royal palace, and found that His Majesty had gone to the hills for his health. There he stayed eight months, till the cure was complete. When he came home he gave us audience, and entertained us at a royal banquet, at which were served up oxen baked whole in crust."

Honesty. "Oxen baked whole in crust ! Did you ever hear such a lie ? "

Amb. " Also there was served up to us a big bird, as big as a man, that they call the Chousibus."

Hon. "Chousibus indeed! You have choused us out of our guineas."

Amb. "However, we did not go for nothing; we have brought back with us a great Persian noble-man. Sham-Artabas is his name; he is nothing less than the King's Eye. Come forward, Sham-Artabas, and explain to the people of Athens what the Great King means to do for them."

On this, a curious creature, wearing a mask which was all one big eye, came forward, followed by a train of attendants in Persian attire. He muttered something which sounded like —

"Artaman exarksam anapissonai satra."[1]

"There!" cried the ambassador, "didn't you hear him? Don't you understand him?"

"Understand him!" said Mr. Honesty, "no; not a syllable."

Amb. "Why, he said that the Great King means to send us some gold. Tell them" (*turning to Sham-Artabas*), "tell them about the gold; speak louder and more plainly."

The Eye spoke again.

"Gapey Greeks, gold a fooly jest."

Hon. "Ah, that is plain enough!"

Amb. "Well, what do you make of it?"

Hon. "Why, that it is a foolish jest for us Greeks to think that we shall get any gold."

---

[1] Supposed to resemble the words with which a Persian edict commenced. ·

Amb. "You're quite wrong; he didn't say 'jest,' but 'chest.' He told us that we should get chests full of gold."

Hon. "Chests indeed! You're nothing but a swindler. Stand off, now, and I will get the truth out of the fellow. Now listen to me, Mr. Sham-Artabas, and answer me plainly. You see this fist; if you don't want a bloody nose of right royal purple, speak the truth. Is the king going to send us any gold?"

The Eye shook his head.

"Are the ambassadors cheating us?"

The Eye nodded.

"Well, anyhow, the creature knows how to nod in Greek."

While saying this he closely scrutinized the strangers, and cried out, "I believe he comes from this very city; and, now I come to look, I see two scoundrels in his train whom I know as well as I know my own brother. Ho there, you rascal! what do you mean — ?"

"Silence!" shouted the herald; "the Senate invites the King's Eye to dine in the Town Hall."

Hon. "Is not that enough to make a man hang himself? These rascals are to dine in the Town Hall, and I am left outside here! But here comes Demigod. Now, my good fellow, take these two half-crowns, and make the best of your way to Sparta, and conclude a separate peace for me, my wife, my children, and my maid-servant. But whom have we here?"

"Silence!" cried the herald again, "for His Excellency, the ambassador, returned from Thrace!"

"Gentlemen," said the ambassador, "I should not have stayed so long —"

Hon. (*aside*). "If you had not been paid by the day."

Amb. "If it had not been for the snow, which covered all the country and froze up all the rivers. We passed the time drinking with King Sitalces, who is a very good friend of yours, gentlemen; he chalks up your name on the walls, for all the world like a lover.

> "Sweet Athens, fair
> Beyond compare.

As for his son, a citizen as you know, he is passionately fond of Athenian sausages, and would not be satisfied till his father promised to send an army to help us. The king swore that he would, aye, and so big a one that we should say when we saw it, 'Good heavens! what a tremendous flight of locusts!'"

Hon. "Well, you're right there. Locusts indeed!"

"These are the men," the ambassador went on, pushing forward as he spoke a troop of deplorable looking ragamuffins; "they are the fiercest fellows in Thrace. Give them a trifle of a couple of shillings a day, and they will worry the Bœotians out of their lives."

"What!" shouted Honesty, "a couple of shillings a day for these beggars! How about our brave sea-

men, the men who really keep us safe? What do
they get? Two shillings! What an iniquity! Yes,
and one of the scoundrels has stolen my garlic. Ho
·there, you magistrate, are you going to see a citizen
robbed before your eyes? Well, if you won't listen,
I will put a stop to this. I protest against going on
with business. I felt a drop of rain." [1]

Hereupon the herald proclaimed, "The Thracians
must attend again on the first of next month. The
Assembly is adjourned."

"That is all right," said Honesty, "but I have lost
my luncheon all the same. However, here comes my
friend Demigod back. Welcome, Demigod!"

"It's a very poor welcome that I've had," said the
man, who was panting for breath. "As I was coming
along, some wild fellows — charcoal-burners they
seemed to be — smelt out the treaties of peace.
'What!' they cried, 'you bring treaties of peace,
when our vines are cut down to the ground! Stone
him! Down with him!' And they filled their pockets with stones and ran howling after me."

Hon. "Let them howl. Have you brought the
treaties?"

"Yes, indeed," said Demigod, producing three
wine-skins, "I have three samples of them. Here is
a five years' specimen; what do you think of it?"

---

[1] This was the Greek form of parliamentary obstruction. The Assembly had to be adjourned for bad weather; that it had to be done if
a single member declared that he felt a drop of rain is doubtless an
exaggeration.

Hon. "I don't like it at all. It smells of rosin —
no, not exactly rosin, but pitch and ship-tar."

Dem. "Try this ten years' one, then; that may suit
you."

Hon. "That's not much better. There is a kind
of acidity about it; some sort of taste, it seems to me,
of ambassadors going about to quicken allies, and
allies hanging back."

Dem. "Well, here's the thirty years' sort. What
do you think of that?"

Hon. "Admirable! That's the kind for me. This
is pure nectar and ambrosia. No smack of 'every
man will provide himself with rations for three days'
here, but a 'go where you please' kind of taste in
one's mouth. I'll take this; no more wars for me,
but a jolly time on my own farm when the vintage
feast comes round again."

Dem. "Very good; but I must be off, or those
charcoal-burners will be down upon me."

Saying this, Demigod disappeared.

"And now," said Honesty, "for a little festival of
my own."

At this point the charcoal-burners rushed in, in
hot pursuit of Demigod, a set of stout old fellows, all
grimy and black with their work. While they were
looking about for the fugitive, cursing his impudence
for thinking of peace when their vines and fig-trees
were burnt-to the ground, and lamenting the burden
of years which had made them lag behind in the

race, they spied Honesty coming out with his household, prepared to celebrate the festival in the old
fashion. His daughter walked in front, bearing on
her head a basket with a long roll of bread in it;
Honesty himself carried a bowl of porridge, and two
slaves brought up the rear. The worthy man was
very anxious that everything should be done in order.
He cried "Silence!" to the spectators, told his wife to
go up to the roof and look on, and was very particular in his directions to his daughter. "Carry it
prettily, my dear," he said, "and look your primmest,
and mind no one filches your ornaments in the press.
You are a nice girl," he went on, as he saw how well
she behaved; "your husband will be a lucky man.
And now let me sing the song.

> "Leader of the revel rout,
>   Of the drunken war and shout;
>   Half a dozen years are past,
>   Here we meet in peace at last;
>   All my wars and fights are o'er,
>   Drinking contests please me more;
>   If a drunken head should ache,
>   Bones and crowns we never break;
>   If we quarrel overnight
>   At a full carousing soak,
>   In the morning all is right,
>   And the shield hung out of sight
>   In the chimney smoke."

Scarcely had he finished, when the charcoal-burners, who had been in hiding, burst in upon him,

crying, "This is the scoundrel with the treaties! Stone him! Stone him!"

Hon. "What is all this about? You'll break the bowl."

Charcoal-burners. "Stone him! Stone him!"

Hon. "But why, my venerable friends?"

C.-b. "You ask us why! You're a traitor. You have made peace on your own account."

Hon. "But you haven't heard why I made it."

C.-b. "No, and won't hear either. Stone him! Stone him!"

Hon. "How! hold!"

C.-b. "Why should we hold? You've made peace with the Spartans."

Hon. "You won't listen, then?"

C.-b. "Not to a word."

Hon. "Well, if you won't, I'll have my revenge. I've got a young townsman of yours here, and as sure as you throw a single stone, I'll run him through."

C.-b. "Good heavens! What does the fellow mean? Has he got one of our children there?"

Hon. "Throw, throw if you want to. But he dies the death."

So saying, he produced what looked like a baby in long clothes, but turned out to be — a coal scuttle. "Spare him! Spare him!" cried the charcoal-burners, and shook out all the stones from their pockets, while Honesty dropped his sword. After this he was allowed to plead his cause.

But to plead it effectively he had to make sure of
rousing the compassion of his judges, and this, it
occurred to him, could not be better done than by
donning some of the pitiable rags with which Euripides, the tragedian, was wont to clothe the heroes of
his dramas. "I must make my way to Euripides,"
he cried, and hurried off to the poet's house. After
a little difficulty in discovering whether the great
man was at home or not, — he was at home himself,
writing a play, the servant explained, but his mind
was out collecting verses, — the petitioner was allowed
an interview. Euripides, who was sitting in his gar-
ret, himself dressed in rags, that he might be more in
sympathy with his subject, which was, as usual, a
hero in reduced circumstances, demanded what his
visitor wanted.

Hon. "I implore you, my dear Euripides, to give
me some rags from that old play of yours. I have
to make my defence, and if I fail it means death."

Euripides. "What play? What rags? Do you
want those in which the luckless old Œneus[1] wres-
tled with fate?"

---

[1] The stories of these unfortunate heroes may be briefly told:

1. Œneus, father of Tydeus, was king of Ætolia. Artemis, whose
sacrifices he had neglected, sent the Calydonian boar to ravage his
country. He was expelled from his kingdom by the sons of Agrius.

2. Phœnix, the tutor of Achilles, blinded by his father (according to
one tradition, but not in Homer) on account of a false accusation.

3. Philoctetes, one of the chieftains who sailed to Troy. He was
bitten in the foot by an adder in the course of the voyage, and the
wound became so noisome that his companions could not endure his

Hon. " No, no ; it must be some one far more wretched than Œneus."

E. " The blind Phœnix, then ? "

Hon. " No, not Phœnix ; far worse off than he."

E. " What does the man want ? The rags of the beggar Philoctetes ? "

Hon. " No ; ten times more of a beggar than Philoctetes."

E. " Bellerophon, then, the blind Bellerophon ? "

Hon. " No, not Bellerophon, though it is true that he was a blind beggar and a terrible fellow to talk."

E. " I know the man you mean — Telephus of Mysia."

Hon. " Exactly ; it is Telephus's rags I want."

E. (*to his servant*). " Boy, give this gentleman the rags of Telephus. They are on the top of Thyestes's and below Ino's."

Hon. " You have been very kind, Euripides, but if you would give me also the Mysian hat."

E. " Here it is."

Hon. " And the beggar's staff."

E. " Take it, and vanish from my marble halls."

Hon. " O my soul ! see how hard he is on me, and

neighbourhood and put him ashore on the island of Lemnos, then uninhabited.

4. Bellerophon, exiled on account of a false accusation, and afterwards lamed by a fall from his winged horse Pegasus.

5. Telephus, Prince of Mysia, wounded by Achilles and afterwards cured by the rust from the spear which had pierced him. The circumstances under which he appeared clothed in rags are not known to us,

I want a number of other things. Do give me a
wicker lamp-shade with a hole burnt in it."

E.   "Know, fellow, that you bore me, and depart."
Hon. "Once more I ask — a cup with broken lip."
E.   "Take it and perish, trouble of my house!"
Hon. "And yet again a pitcher plugged with sponge."
E.   "Fellow, you rob me of my work; and yet
        I give it — go!"
Hon. "Oh! yet once more I beg
        One thing which lacking I am all undone;
        O dearest, sweetest singer, may the gods
        Destroy me, if I ask but one thing more,
        One only, single, solitary boon,
        A plant of chevril from your mother's store."[1]

E. "The man insults us; close the palace doors."

Thus clad, and laying his head on the chopping-
block, to be ready, if he failed to make out his case,
for instant execution, Honesty proceeded to defend
himself.

"You blame me for making peace," — this was the
substance of his argument, — "but what was the war
about? Why, the most trumpery thing in the world!
A girl is kidnapped from our neighbours of Megara.
Our neighbours kidnap two girls from us, and the
mighty Pericles, forsooth, must bring out his thunder
and lightning, for all the world like Olympian Zeus,
till all Greece was in a turmoil. Then came his
decree, short and sharp : ' No one from Megara shall

---

[1] Aristophanes is never weary of joking about the low extraction of
Euripides's mother, It was said that she had sold vegetables.

have any trade with Athens.' Our neighbours, being half starved, go to the Spartans and ask them to intercede. The Spartans beg us to repeal these decrees. Once, twice, thrice they ask, and we refuse. Then they go to war. But say, were these poor people so very wrong after all? Suppose the Spartans had manned a boat, and stolen a puppy-dog from one of the islands, would you have sat quietly down under the insult? Not so; you would have launched three hundred ships, and all the city would have been in an uproar with troops marching and crews clamouring for pay and rations, and we should have had newly gilt statues of the goddess carried about the street, and wineskins, and strings of onions and garlic in nets, and singing girls, and bloody noses. No, no; they only did just what we should have done."

Honesty's eloquence converted half his enemies; the other half called the darling of the war party, General Dobattle, to their aid. He came at once, in full armour, wearing a helmet with an enormously large crest, and declaiming in pompous tones,

> "Whence falls this sound of battle on mine ear?
> Who needs my help? The great Dobattle's here!
> Whose summons bids me to the field repair?
> Who wakes my slumbering Gorgon from her lair?"

" Dear me!" cried Honesty, pretending to be frightened; "what an awful plume! What kind of

bird does it come from? A white-feathered boastard
[bustard] by chance?"

Dobattle. "Fellow, thou diest!"

Hon. "You're not the man to do it."

Dobat. "Do you know you're speaking to a general, you beggar?"

Hon. "Beggar! Beggar in your teeth! You a
general! Only one of the draw-his-pay sort!"

Dobat. "I was duly elected."

Hon. "Elected! yes, by half a dozen cuckoos. I
am sick of the whole business; white-haired men
serving in the ranks, and you and your young sprigs
of nobility off on an embassy to Thrace or Sicily or
heaven knows where!—but always drawing pay."

Dobat. "We were duly elected."

Hon. "But why is it always you, and never honest
fellows such as he? Here, Coaldust, did you ever
go on an embassy? He shakes his head. And yet
he would have done admirably for it. Or you, Heart-
of-Oak? Or you, Bend-in-the-Shoulders? No, you
see, not one of them."

Dobat. "O sovereign people, shall I bear such
wrong?"

Hon. "All things are borne, so Dobattle is paid."

On this Dobattle marched off, finding that he could
make nothing of his antagonist. "Hereby I proclaim," he said, as he departed, "that I will harass
the men of the Peloponnesus night and day."

"And I," said Honesty, "hereby proclaim that I

GENERAL DOBATTLE.

open a market for the men of the Peloponnesus and
their allies, and that they may come and buy and sell
with me, but not with General Dobattle."

The other half of the charcoal-burners now proclaimed their conversion, and Honesty, encouraged
by their support, set about marking out the boun-
daries of his market, appointed constables to see that
the regulations were observed, and set up in the midst
a pillar with the terms of the treaty engraved upon it.

The first dealer that presented himself was one of
the neighbours from Megara. The poor fellow had
got nothing to sell but his two little girls; still he
was delighted to see an Athenian market again.

> "Market of Athens, hail! For as a child
> Longs for its mother, have I longed for thee!"

Then he turned to the children: "But you, the
luckless children of a luckless sire, what is to be done
with you? Would you sooner be sold or starve at
home?"

"Sell us, sell us, dear papa!" cried the two in
chorus.

"Yes; but who will buy you? It would be a
sheer loss. Hold! I have an idea. Put these pet-
titoes on and these little snouts, and mind you grunt
and whine and kick about like pigs. If you don't, I
shall have to carry you back home, and you will be
worse starved than ever. — Mr. Honesty, do you
want to buy some pigs?"

Hon. "What? Who is this? A man from Megara?"

Megarian. "Yes; I have come to market."

Hon. "And how are you getting on?"

Megar. "As hungry as thunder."

Hon. "And your government? What is that doing?"

Megar. "Doing its best to ruin us."

Hon. "Well, what have you got in your sack there? Salt?"

Megar. "Salt? How could it be salt, when you have got all our salt-pans?"

Hon. "Garlic, then?"

Megar. "Garlic indeed! How could it be garlic when you came and dug up the very roots, like so many field-mice?"

Hon. "What is it, then?"

Megar. "Pigs, pigs for sacrifice."

Hon. "Oh! indeed."

Megar. "Yes, pigs. Don't you hear them squeak?" (*Aside*) "Squeak, you little wretches, or it will be the worse for you."

"Wee, wee," squeaked the two daughters.

Hon. "Can they feed without their mother?"

Megar. "I should think they could, and without their father either."

Hon. "What do you want for them?" after some more chaffering.

Megar. "This I will sell for a rope of onions, and the other for a bushel of salt."

Hon. "Very good ; I'll take them. Stand there a moment."

"That's good business," said the man to himself. "I only wish I could sell my wife and mother at the same rate."

At this point one of the informers, who made a living out of denouncing contraband goods, made his appearance. "Who are you?" he said to the man from Megara.

"A man of Megara, come to sell pigs," was the answer.

"I denounce you and your goods as contraband of war. Here, hand them over."

"Mr. Honesty, Mr. Honesty," screamed the man, "I am being denounced!"

"Constable," said Honesty, "put the fellow out; no informers are allowed in this market. And here, my good friend, is the garlic and the salt. And now farewell."

"Farewell indeed," said the poor man ; "but it is not our way in Megara to fare well."

A dealer from Bœotia was the next to come. The man had a heavy basket on his back, and was followed by slaves similarly burdened. "That's a pretty load," he said, as he put the basket on the ground. "And now, my friend, what will you buy?"

"What have you got?"

"Got? Why, everything, as a body may say; all the good things of Thebes,— marjoram, penny-royal,

rush-mats, lamp-wicks, ducks, jackdaws, partridges,
coots, sandpipers, divers."

"Why, you are like a north wind in winter, with
all the birds you bring."

"Yes, and I've got geese, and hares, and foxes,
and moles, and hedgehogs, and weasels, and mountain cats, and — what do you think? — eels from
Copais!"

"What! Eels? Let me see the eels."

The Bœotian held out a fine eel in his hand, and
addressed it with profound respect : —

> "First-born of fifty daughters of the lake,
> Come forth and greet the stranger."

The Athenian answered in a similar strain : —

> "O my child,
> O long regretted and recovered late,
> Welcome, thrice welcome! Hark ye there, my man
> Prepare the stove, the bellows, and behold,
> At last behold her here, the best of eels,
> Loveliest and best, after six weary years
> Returned to bless us. Bear her gently in.
> O eel, so fair thou art, that e'en in death
> Still would I fain possess thee — stewed with beet!"

Bœotian. "Yes, very good; but what are you
going to give me for her?"

Hon. "Oh! I take this as a sort of perquisite; but
if you have anything else for sale I shall be glad to
buy."

Bœot. " Everything is for sale."

Hon. " Well, what do you say for the lot? I suppose you won't mind taking a return cargo?"

Bœot. "Certainly not; but what is there that you have in Athens and we haven't got in Bœotia?"

Hon. " Anchovies? Crockery?"

Bœot. " Anchovies and crockery we have in plenty. But surely there is something that you have, and we have not!"

Hon. "Ah! I have it. Ho there! Bring out the informer; pack him as so much crockery."

Bœot. " Excellent! excellent! I should make ever so much money by exhibiting him as a mischievous ape."

Hon. " See there; there is another of the same kind coming."

Bœot. " He is very small."

Hon. " Yes, but very bad."

Informer the second came in. " What goods are these," he said.

" Mine," replied the Bœotian. " We be come from Thebes."

Informer. " Then I denounce them. They come from the enemy's country."

Bœot. " What! denounce the birds and beasts? What harm have they done?"

Inf. " Yes, and I denounce you, too."

Bœot. " Me! What have you to say against me?"

Inf. " Just to satisfy the bystanders I will explain. You have brought in lamp-wicks. That means a plot to burn the arsenal."

Honesty interrupted at this point. " What in the
world do you mean ? Burn the arsenal with the
wick of a lamp ! "

Inf. " Certainly."

Hon. " But how ? "

Inf. " Listen ! This Bœotian rascal would catch a
water-spider, fasten the wick on its back, wait for a
strong north wind, light the wick, and send the
spider with it into the harbour. Let the fire once
catch a single vessel, and the whole place would be
in a blaze."

" Stop his mouth ! " cried Honesty. " Tie a hay-
band round him, and send him off."

The charcoal-burners, by this time thoroughly converted to peace views, were so delighted that they
burst out into song.

> " To preserve him safe and sound,
> You must have him fairly bound
> With a cordage nicely wound,
> Up and down and round and round ;
> Securely packed."

Honesty took up the strain : —

> " I shall have a special care ;
> He's a piece of paltry ware ;
> As you strike him here or there, [*strikes him*]
> Don't you hear his cries declare
> That he's partly cracked ? "

C.-b. " How, then, is he fit for use ? "

Hon. " As a stove-jar for abuse,
> Plots and lies he cooks and brews,
> Slander and seditious news."

C.-b. " Have you stowed him safe enough? "
Hon. " Never fear; he's hearty stuff;
　　Fit for usage hard and rough,
　　Fit to beat, and fit to cuff,
　　　To toss and fling.
　　You can hang him up or down,
　　By the heels or by the crown."

The Bœotian bade one of his servants take the package on his back and march off with it.

"Well," said Honesty, looking after the party, "you've got a queer piece of goods with you; if you do make anything of him, you will be the first person that ever got anything good out of an informer."

A slave now appeared with a message : "General Dobattle sends five shillings, and wishes to buy a dish of quails and a good-sized eel from Copais."

Hon. " General Dobattle! And who, pray, is General Dobattle ? "

Messenger. " The fierce and hardy warrior; he that wields The Gorgon shield and waves the triple plume."

Hon. "Let him wave his triple plume over a mess of salt fish; quite good enough for him."

By this time it was noised about that Honesty had got some of that precious commodity, peace, and he was overwhelmed with applications for it. A countryman came in groaning and lamenting.

" What's all this about ? " asked Honesty.

" Oh, my dear friend," said the man, "just a little drop of peace."

Hon. " What's the matter ? "

Countryman. " I'm ruined, I'm ruined ! The Bœotians came down this morning and carried off my
pair of plough oxen. They were all my living."

The lucky possessor would not part with a drop.
The only petitioner that succeeded was a bridesmaid
whom the bride had sent with a little bottle. " She
wanted," she said, "just a little drop to keep her husband at home." Mr. Honesty was willing to oblige
a lady, and sent her away with the bottle full, explaining that the bride must use it the next time there
was a ballot for recruits.

Meanwhile, General Dobattle had come in person
to try whether he could not succeed better than his
messenger. But before he could open his mouth, a
despatch from the War Office arrived. " You are
hereby directed to muster your men, and march to
the mountain passes. There you must ambush in the
snow, information having been received that a ma-
rauding party is coming from the Bœotian frontier."

Hardly had he read the despatch when a message
came for Honesty. It was to this effect : " You are
hereby requested to come with all your belongings to
the temple of Bacchus. The company are waiting
for you, and everything is ready, — plum cake and
plain, confectionery, fruits preserved and fresh,
savouries and sweets, flowers and perfumes." And
now began a bustle of preparation on either side.

The General. " Quick with my knapsack ! "

Hon. " Quick with my dinner and wine ! "

Gen. " Give me a bunch of leeks."

Hon. " Veal cutlets for me."

Gen. " Let me see the salt fish. It does not smell good."

Hon. " How fresh this mullet is ! Cook it on the spot."

Gen. " Bring me the lofty feather of my crest."

Hon. " Bring doves and quails ; I scarce know which is best."

Gen. " Behold this snowy plume of dazzling white ! "

Hon. " Behold this roasted dove, a savoury sight!"

This was past all bearing, and the General at-tempted to draw his sword, but found it rusted to the scabbard. On the other hand, Honesty was going to defend himself with the spit, but had first to disengage it from the roast meat. However, they didn't come to blows. The General contented himself with a threat : " Pour oil upon the shield. What do I see in it ? An old man frightened to death because he is going to be tried for cowardice."

"Ah!" said Honesty, "pour honey on the pancake. What do I see in it ? A jolly old fellow, who tells the Dobattles and the Gorgons to go and hang themselves."

The General marched off to the frontier, while Honesty went to the feast, the charcoal-burners bidding the two rivals farewell in the following stave : —

> " Go your ways in sundry wise,
> Each upon his enterprise.
> One determined to carouse,
> With a garland on his brows;
> T'other bound to pass the night
> In a military plight
>   Undelighted and alone;
>   Starving, wheezing,
>   Sneezing, breezing,
>   With his head upon a stone."

After a while a message arrived from the seat of war.   He said : —

> " Slaves of Dobattle, make the water hot;
> Make embrocations and emollients ready,
> And bandages and plasters for your Lord;
> His foot is maimed and crippled with a stake,
> Which pierced it as he leapt across a ditch;
> His ankle-bone is out, his head is broken,
> The Gorgon on his shield is smashed and spoilt;
> The cock's plume on his helmet soiled with dirt."

Immediately afterwards the General himself appeared in the sorriest plight, and at the same time Honesty, who had won the prize at the feast by finishing a gallon of wine, came in supported by his companions.

> *Dobat.* " Strip off th' encumbrance of this warlike gear
>   And take me to my bed."
> *Hon.*   " And for me,
>   My bed, I take it, is the fittest place."

Dobat. "O bear me to the public hospital!"

Hon. "Where is the ruler of the feast? The prize
Is mine, this empty gallon testifies."

C.-b. "Then take the wineskin as your due:
We triumph and rejoice with you."

II.

THE KNIGHTS.

The campaign which followed the production of the *Acharnians* greatly encouraged the war party, and dashed the hopes of the advocates of peace. The most important victory of the year is referred to in the story about to be told, and must be briefly described. As the result of a series of operations, which it is needless to relate in detail, a body of four hundred and twenty Spartan soldiers were blockaded in Sphacteria, an island close to Pylos on the western coast of the Peloponnesus (near the modern Navarino). For some time the siege dragged on, the Athenian generals seeming unable to bring it to a successful issue. The demagogue, Cleon, censured their incompetency in the Assembly at Athens, and declared that were he in command, he would bring the Spartans to Athens within a few days. He was taken at his word, almost compelled to go, and, strange to say, whether from trick, skill, or the audacity of ignorance, accomplished his task. Such a disaster had never before happened to Sparta. The men whose lives were in danger were a considerable part of the fighting power of the state. The Spartan authorities at once asked for an armistice, and to secure it consented to hand over their fleet to the Athenian admiral in command on the spot. This done, they sent an embassy to Athens and opened negotiations for peace, offering most favourable terms, all, in fact, that could reasonably have been expected. These, however, were rejected, and the war went on. Aristophanes exhibited the play of the *Knights* (so called from the chorus, which was supposed to consist of the " Gentlemen " of Athens, a class next to the wealthiest). We are told that Cleon was at this time so powerful and so much dreaded that the people who manufactured masks for the theatre refused to make one that would represent the demagogue's features. Aristophanes, who acted the character himself, possibly because he could not find an actor willing to undertake it, had to "make up" for the part by smearing his face with the lees of wine.

30

It is only fair to say that a view of Cleon's character and policy very different from that which we get from Aristophanes, and, it may be added, from Thucydides, may be found in some modern writers, notably in Mr. Grote and Sir George Cox. ("Greek Statesmen," second series.)

It should be explained that there are five characters in the story:

1. Demos (people), who is represented as a selfish old man, of a very uncertain and fickle temper, very hard on old servants who have done well for him for years, and taking up with new favourites who humour his caprices and minister to his appetites. The original of this is the Athenian people.

2 and 3. Two old servants whom I call Victor and Hearty. They are now out of favour with their master, thanks to the interference of a new-comer, Bluster (or the Tanner), and look about for some means of getting rid of their oppressor. The originals are two well-known Athenian soldiers and statesmen, Nicias (*niké*—victory) and Demosthenes (*sthenos*—strength, and *demos*—the people). These names nowhere occur in the play, but the characters were doubtless recognized at once by the resemblance of their masks to the features of the originals.

4. Bluster (or the Tanner) = Cleon.

5. The Sausage-seller, destined to be Demos's new favourite.

A body of "Knights" or "Gentlemen" is present, and takes the part of Bluster's enemies.

"WHAT a scandal and a shame it is!" cried Hearty, coming out of Demos's house, followed by Victor; "ever since Master brought home that scoundrel Bluster, not a day passes without his thrashing us unmercifully; confound him, I say!"

"And I say so, too," cried Victor, rubbing his arms and shoulders.

Hearty. "Well, it is no good cursing and crying. We must do something. What do you propose?"

Victor. "Can't you propose something yourself?"

H. "No, no! I look to you."

V. "Well, I have thought of something. Say 'run.'"

H. "Very good. I say it: 'run.'"

V. "Now say 'away.'"

H. "Quite so: 'away.'"

V. "Now both together very quick: first 'run,' then 'away.'"

H. "Here you have it: 'run away.'"

V. "Well, doesn't that sound sweet?"

H. "I don't know. I seem to hear the crack of a whip somewhere about."

V. "Then we must think of something else."

H. "Shall I tell the state of things to our friends here?" pointing to a little crowd of people that had gathered round.[1]

V. "You could not do better."

H. "Listen, then, my good friends. We have a master at home here, a rough, passionate old gentleman, and just a little deaf. The first of last month he bought a new slave, Bluster by name, who had worked in a tanner's yard. A more wicked, lying fellow there never was. Well, he got to know our master's ways, and flattered and wheedled him with this kind of thing — 'You'll take a bath, sir; you've done business enough for one day, and here's a little trifle of money that has just come in for you,'[2] and, 'Can I serve you with anything, sir?' And as sure

---

[1] In the play Hearty addresses the spectators.

[2] Lit. "Take your three *obols*." This was the sum which an Athenian citizen received for acting as a juror. The custom was introduced by Pericles.

as any one of us got something nice ready for the old gentleman, he would lay hands on it and give it to him. Why, this very morning I had made some Spartan pudding,[1] and he comes in the most rascally way and carries it off, and serves it up as his own. Yes, the pudding that I had made. He won't let one of us go near the old gentleman, but stands behind him with a great flap of his own leather, and keeps us all off like so many flies. Then he tells lies about us and we get flogged. Or he goes round among us and blackmails us. 'You know,' he says, 'what a beating Barker got the other day. It was all through me; and if you don't make it worth my while you'll catch it ten times worse.' If we say no, then old Demos knocks us down and tramples on us till we haven't any breath left in us. That's about the state of things — isn't it?" he went on, turning to Victor. "The question is — what are we to do?"

V. "I see nothing so good as the runaway trick."

H. "Run away! It is impossible. The fellow has his eyes everywhere."

V. "Then there is nothing left for it but to die. Only we must die like men."

H. "Well, what is your idea?"

V. "I think that we should drink bull's blood. We can't do better than follow Themistocles."

H. "Bull's blood indeed! the blood of the grape, I say! Then we might have some happy inspiration."

---

[1] See Introduction.

V. "What?　Do you think getting tipsy will help us?"

H. "Yes, I do, you poor water-pitcher.　Do you mean to doubt the inspiration of wine?　Where can you find anything more potent?　Is there anything that men can't do when they are drunk?　Wealth, prosperity, good luck, helping their friends, everything is easy to them.　Bring me a pitcher of wine. I'll moisten my understanding till the inspiration comes."

V. "You'll ruin us with your drink."

H. "Ruin you!　Nothing of the kind.　Off with you and bring the wine."

Victor ran off and in a few minutes reappeared carrying a pitcher of wine.　"Well!" he said, "it was lucky that I got it without any one seeing."

H. "Tell me, what was Bluster doing?"

V. "He had gorged himself with half-digested confiscations, and was lying fast asleep and snoring on a heap of his own hides."

Hearty went on drinking and thinking.　At last he started up, crying : —

"Thine is the thought, good Genius, not mine own."

V. "What is it?"

H. "That you go and steal the prophecies that Bluster keeps indoors."

This was not really to Victor's liking.　However, he went, and came back with them.　One he knew to be especially precious. Bluster, he explained, had been so fast asleep that he knew nothing of what was being done. Hearty took the writing and looked at it and asked for another cup of wine. "Well," said his companion after a pause, "what says the prophecy?"

H. "Another cup."

V. "Does it say 'another cup'?"

H. "O Bacis!"[1]

V. "What is it?"

H. "Quick with the cup!"

V. "Bacis seems to have been very fond of cups."

H. "O scoundrel of a Bluster! I don't wonder you kept this prophecy so close, for it shows how your fall will be brought about."

V. "Quick, tell me — what does it say?"

H. "It says that it is ordained that first of all a hemp-jobber shall rule the city."

V. "That's jobber number one. Go on."

H. "After him a calves-jobber."

V. "Jobber number two. But what is to happen to him?"

H. "He is to prosper till a greater scoundrel than he shall come, a daring, thieving rascal, a tanner by trade, and Bluster by name."

V. "And what of him? Is there another jobber to come?"

---

[1] Bacis was a well-known author of prophecies, the Nostradamus or Mother Shipton of those days.

H. "Yes; one with a noble business."

V. "What is it?"

H. "Must I tell you?"

V. "Certainly."

H. "Then listen. A sausage-seller shall drive out the man of hides."

V. "A sausage-seller! Good heavens! what a trade! where are we to find him?"

H. "We must look for him. And, as I am alive, there he comes just in the nick of time.

> "Blest sausage-seller, best and dearest, come,
> Saviour of Athens, saviour of thy friends!"

The sausage-seller, greatly astonished at this address, wanted to know what was meant, and was told to put down his tray and then kiss the earth, and make a reverence to the gods. Again he asked what they wanted, and was again addressed with profound respect : —

> "Thrice happy child of wealth, little to-day,
> To-morrow growing great beyond compare,
> Of Athens, dear to heaven, lord and chief."

Sausage-seller. "Come, come, don't make game of me; let me wash my paunches and sell my sausages."

H. "Paunches indeed, and sausages! Look here. Do you see these crowds of people?"

S.-s. "Yes, I see 'em."

H. "Well, you'll be their lord and master. Everything — Assembly, Senate, admirals, generals — will be under your heel."

S.-s. "What? *my* heel?"

H. "Yes; and that is not all. Get up on this stall and look at the islands."

The sausage-seller climbed on to the stall, which was supposed to command a view of the islands in the Ægean Sea, tributary to Athens, as members of the Delian Confederacy.[1] "Yes, I see them," he said.

H. "You see their ports and their merchant vessels?"

S.-s. "Yes."

H. "And are you not a lucky man? Now look a little further; look at Asia with your right eye, and Carthage with your left."

S.-s. "I don't see much happiness in squinting."

H. "All this is yours to buy and sell. So the prophecy says."

S.-s. "What! mine, and I a sausage-seller?"

H. "That's the very thing that makes your title, because you are a low-bred, vulgar, impudent fellow."

S.-s. "I don't see how I am fit for such a big thing."

H. "Not fit! What do you mean? I am afraid that you have something good on your conscience. Are you by any chance a gentleman by birth?"

[1] The Delian Confederacy was originally a league of Greek states, especially of the islands in the Ægean, formed after the Persian war to make a combined resistance to any future attack from the Persians. By degrees it became an Athenian empire. Many of the islands preferred making a money payment to furnishing ships and crews. They thus became entirely dependent on Athens.

S.-s. "A gentleman? Bless me, no. I am come of as poor a lot as any in the town."

H. "What luck! You could not have started better."

S.-s. "But I've got no education; just a little writing, and that very bad."

H. "Well, that's against you, that you can write at all. Greatness here, you must understand, is not for educated, respectable people. Dunces and black-guards get it. So don't you let the chance slip. Now listen to the prophecy: —

> "Whene'er the eagle in his pride,
> With crooked claws and leathern hide,
> Shall seize the black, blood-eating snake,
> Then shall great Bluster's tan-pits quake;
> And Zeus shall give high rule and place
> To men of sausage-selling race,
> Unless, perchance, it please them more
> To sell the sausage as before.

Do you understand all this? No? Well, listen: the leathern eagle is Bluster. His claws are his way of pouncing on people's money. The snake, of course, is a black pudding. Snakes are long and black, so are black puddings; snakes are full of blood, so are black puddings. There's a prophecy for you!"

S.-s. "Yes, it sounds fine. But how shall I be able to manage the people?"

H. "Manage the people? The easiest thing in

the world. Do just as you have been doing. Mangle
and mash everything. Flavour and spice to suit the
people's taste. You have got every qualification for a
demagogue. You have a vile voice, you are low-
born, you are ill-bred. Absolutely nothing is wanting, and here are the prophecies fitting in. So make
your prayer to the god of Boobydom, and tackle the
fellow."

S.-s. "Yes; but who will be on my side? The rich
are afraid of him, and as for the poor, they shake
in their shoes."

H. "Who will be on your side? Why, a thousand
gentlemen of Athens who scorn and detest him, aye,
and every honest man in the city."

At this point there was a terrified cry from behind,
"He's coming! he's coming!" and Bluster rushed
out of the house, vowing vengeance against everybody. The sausage-seller was about to take to his
heels, when Hearty entreated him to stand firm, as
his friends were at hand. The next moment the
promised host of gentlemen appeared on the scene,
and gaining confidence by their support, the sausage-
seller came forward and confronted his adversary.
A fierce contest followed, in which each combatant
sought to overpower his adversary with abuse and
threats.

Bluster. "I charge this man with treason. He
sells sausages to the Peloponnesian fleet."

S.-s. "I charge this man with worse than that.

He runs into the Town Hall with his belly empty,
and runs out with it full."

B.   "Dog and villain, you shall die."
S.-s. "I can scream ten times as high."
B.   "I'll o'erbear you and out-bawl you."
S.-s. "I'll out-scream you and out-squall you."
B.   "Stare at me without a wink."
S.-s. "Never do I blush or blink."
B.   " I can steal and own to stealing;
         That's a thing I know you dare not."
S.-s. "That is nothing; when I'm dealing,
         I can swear to things that are not,
         And, though hundreds saw, I care not."

Bluster was still unconvinced that he had found his
match and more; and the sausage-seller related for
the encouragement of his backers incidents in his
bringing up which fully justified their hopes. "It is
not for nothing," he said, "that ever since I was a
child I have been cuffed and beaten, that I have
been fed on scraps, and yet grown to the big creature that I am. Oh! I used to play rare tricks.
I would say to a cook, 'See, there's a swallow, the
spring is coming,' and when he looked away I stole
a bit of his meat. Mostly I got clear off; but in
case any one saw me, I swore that I had never taken
it. I remember a great politician in those days, who
saw me do it, saying, ' This child will be a great man
with the people some day.'"

After another fierce encounter of words, the two
fell to blows, Bluster getting the worst of it, espe-

cially when they closed, and the sausage-seller tripped him by a specially nasty trick. Enraged at being thus worsted, he rushed off to the Senate, threatening informations, charges of treason, and other dreadful things.

"He's gone to the Senate," said the sausage-seller's backers to him. "Now's your time to show your mettle, if you are the mighty thief and liar that you pretend to be."

"I'm after him," said the fellow, and off he went, having been duly rubbed with grease to make him slippery, and primed with garlic, like a fighting-cock, to give him courage. Before very long he was back, and told his backers, who had been getting a little anxious about him, the story of how he had fared.

"I followed him," he said, "close upon his heels to the Senate House. There he was storming and roaring, bellowing out words like thunderbolts, raving against the aristocrats, calling them traitors and what not, and the Senate sat listening, looking sharp as mustard. And when I saw they took in all his lies, and how he was cheating them, I muttered a prayer, 'Hear me, Powers of Fraud, and Boobydom, and ye Spirits of the Market and the Street, the places where I was bred, and thou, great Impudence, hear me, and help, giving me courage, and a ready tongue, and a shameless voice.' And when I had ended my prayer, I took courage, for I knew that the Great Spirits had heard me, and cried aloud, 'O Senators,

I have come with good news, for I was resolved that
none should hear them before you. Never since the
war broke upon us, no, never have I seen anchovies
cheaper.' Their faces changed in a moment; it
was like a calm after a storm. Then I moved that
they should lay hands on all the bowls in the town,
and go to buy the anchovies before the price went
up. At that they shouted and clapped their hands.
Then Bluster, seeing what a hit I had made, and
knowing of old how to deal with them, said, 'I propose, gentlemen, that in consideration of the happy
event that has been reported to the Senate, we have
a good-news sacrifice to the goddess of a hundred
oxen.' That took the Senate, you may be sure.
Well, I wasn't going to be outdone with his oxen;
so I bid over him. 'I propose,' I said, 'that the
sacrifice be of two hundred oxen! And furthermore,
that we sacrifice a thousand goats to Artemis, if
sprats should be fifty a penny.' That brought the
Senate round to me again. And when he saw it he
lost his head, and began to stammer out some nonsense, till the archers dragged him away. And what
did he, when the Senators were just off after their
anchovies, but try to keep them. 'Stop a moment,
gentlemen,' he said, 'to hear what the herald from
Sparta has got to say; he has come about peace.'
'Peace!' they all cried with one voice (that's because they knew that anchovies were cheap), 'we
don't want peace; let the war go on.' Then they

bellowed to the magistrate to dismiss the Senate, and leapt over the railings. But meanwhile I got down to the market and bought up all the fennel, and gave it to them for sauce, when they were at their wits' end where to find any. How much they made of me, to be sure! I bought the whole Senate, you may believe me, for three ha'porth of fennel!"

His backers, delighted at the story, greeted him with a song of triumph : —

> "You have managed our task on an excellent plan,
>   You certainly are a most fortunate man ;
>   Soon the villain shall meet
>   A more excellent cheat,
>   Of devices more various,
>   Of tricks more nefarious.
>   But gird up your loins for another endeavour,
>   And be sure you will find us as faithful as ever."

And, indeed, the man had need of all his courage ; for the next moment Bluster arrived, furious at his defeat, and swelling, as his adversaries said, like a wave of the sea. "Ah!" he cried, "you contrived to get the better of me in the Senate ; but come along to the Assembly, and you shall see. — Pray come out, my dear Demos," he went on, for they were just in front of Demos's house ; "pray come out for a moment." The sausage-seller joined in, "Yes, father, come out by all means." — "Come, dearest Demos," said Bluster, "come and see how they are insulting me."

The old man bounced out in a rage. "What is all this noise about? Get away with you! See what a disturbance you have made. Well, Bluster, who has been hurting you?"

B. "This fellow, with his young bloods, has been beating me."

D. "And why?"

B. "Only because I love you."

D. (*turning to the sausage-seller*). "And who are you, sir?"

S.-s. "One who loves you far better than this fellow. Aye, that I do, and so do other good men and true; only, unhappily, you won't have anything to do with them, but give yourself up to lamp-sellers, and cobblers, and tanners, and such low folk."

B. "But I have done Demos good service."

S.-s. "How, pray?"

B. "Did I not sail to Pylos, and come back bringing my Spartan prisoners?"

S.-s. "Yes; and I, on my walks the other day, saw a dish of meat that somebody else had cooked, and filched it."

B. "Well, Demos, call an assembly, and settle which is your best friend."

S.-s. "Settle it by all means, but not in the Pnyx."[1]

D. "I can't sit anywhere else."

S.-s. "Then I am a lost man. The old gentleman is sensible enough at home; but once let him settle

---

[1] The Pnyx was the place of Assembly at Athens.

himself on those stone seats, and he takes leave of his senses."

However, his friends encouraged him ; he plucked up spirit, and, when Demos had taken his seat in the Pnyx, boldly confronted his rival. " Demos," began Bluster, "now listen to me : —

"If I should despise you, or ever advise you
Against what is best for your comfort and rest,
Or neglect to attend you, defend you, befriend you,
May I perish and pine ; may this carcase of mine
Be withered and dried, and curried beside,
And straps for your harness cut out from the hide."

The sausage-seller was not behindhand. " Listen to me," he said : —

"O Demos, if I tell one word of a lie,
If any man more can dote or adore,
With so tender a care, then I make it my prayer,
My prayer and my wish to be stewed in a dish,
To be sliced and be slashed, to be minced and be hashed,
And like offal remains that are left by the cook,
To the place of the dead be dragged off on a hook."

B. " Demos, had you ever a better friend than I have been ? Haven't I piled up heaps of money in your treasury, torturing and squeezing and threatening, caring nothing for any man, as long as I could do you a good turn ? "

S.-s. " There is nothing wonderful about that. I can do all that for you. I can·filch another man's loaves and serve them up at your table. But I have

something better for you than that.   Is it not a fact
that you, who fought the Persians at Marathon and
conquered them so gloriously, have been sitting here
ever since with nothing between you and the hard
stone ?   Look at this cushion that I have stitched
together for you.   Get up, my dear sir; and now will
you sit down again ?   Never again will you have to
rub what you made so sore at Salamis."

D. "My dear sir, who are you ?   One of the family of Harmodius,[1] I fancy.   I never saw a more
truly patriotic thing."

B. "Well, that is a trumpery little thing to make
so much of."

S.-s. "I dare say; but you have trapped him with
baits five times smaller."

B. "Now, I'll wager my life that there never was
a man who loved Demos more than I."

S.-s. "You love him! and you have let him live
now for eight years in tubs[2] and crannies and turrets
on the wall!   Ah! you have shut him in, like bees in
a hive, and taken his honey, too.   And when the ambassadors brought proposals for peace, — and a very
good peace, too, — you kicked them out."

[1] Harmodius and Aristogeiton, two Athenian nobles, assassinated
Hipparchus, who was one of the sons of Peisistratus, and, along with
his brother Hippias, had succeeded to his despotic power.   Though
the assassins seem to have had no other motive than to avenge a private wrong, their memory was always honoured in Athens, as if they
had acted from the purest patriotism.

[2] The poor Athenians during the siege were driven to live in any
place where they could find shelter.

B. "And quite right, too. It has all been done to make him lord of Greece; for what do the prophecies say? Listen: —

> "If he still perseveres, for a period of years,
>   He shall sit in Arcadia, judging away,
>   In splendour and honour, for fivepence a day."

S.-s. Arcadia indeed! Much you thought about Arcadia! What you are thinking about is how to make a purse for yourself out of the tribute, while Demos — thanks to the dust that you kick up — can see nothing of what is going on. But let him once get back to his farm, and get up his courage with a dish of porridge, and tackle an olive cake, and he will make you pay for all your villainies."

B. "O my dear Demos! don't believe him. You have never had a better friend, or a more watchful. Haven't I kept you up? Haven't I watched night and day, and discovered treasons, plots, and conspiracies without end?"

S.-s. "Oh, yes; we all know what you mean by your treasons and plots. You are just like the fellows that fish for eels. When the water is clear, they catch nothing; when they stir up the mud, then they have excellent sport. You confound everything with your talk about treason, and, when nobody is looking, pocket your fees and your bribes. But come; answer me this: you with all your leather, have you ever given him a single skin to mend his old boots with?"

D. "That he hasn't, I swear."

S.-s. "Does not that show what sort of a fellow he is? Now, look here at this nice pair of shoes; I bought them on purpose for you to wear."

D. "This is the very best patriot I ever saw."

S.-s. "Look again. It's winter now, and this fellow knew that you were getting on in years, and yet he has never given you a tunic. Now, see this nice one with two sleeves [1] that I have bought you."

D. "Why, this is a better thing than even Themistocles ever thought of; not that the Peiræus [2] wasn't a good idea, but it wasn't so good as this warm tunic."

B. (offering a leather cloak). "Take this, my dear sir; it will keep you admirably warm."

D. (turning up his nose). "Take it away; it smells most abominably of hides."

S.-s. "Of course it does; this is part of a regular plan to choke you."

Demos had sat awhile, buried in thought, and weighing against each other the claims and services of the two rival candidates for his favour. At last he roused himself from his reverie and spoke.

"I have come to the conclusion that the sausage-seller is the best friend that the workingman has ever had. You, Bluster, have made great pretences,

---

[1] Slaves wore a tunic with one sleeve only.

[2] The great harbour of Athens, the importance of which, for the welfare of Athens, Themistocles was the first to see.

and done me nothing but mischief. Hand me over my ring. You shall not be my steward any longer."

B. "Take it; take it; if you will not let me be your steward, you will find a far worse."

Demos took the ring and examined it. "Why," he said, "this is not my ring. The device is not the same, or I have lost my eyesight."

S.-s. "What was the device?"

D. "A steak of beef ready cooked."

S.-s. "That is certainly not here."

D. "Not the steak? What is it, then?"

S.-s. "Why, a cormorant standing on a rock with his mouth wide open."

Demos was on the point of giving the sausage-seller another ring as the sign of his appointment, when Bluster entreated him to wait awhile, at least till he had heard the prophecies that he (Bluster) had got at home referring to him. There was a whole chestful, he declared, and they were full of the most delightful things that were to happen hereafter.

The sausage-seller was not to be outdone. He had prophecies, too, at home; a whole attic and two flats were full of them. Bluster boasted that his were by the famous prophet Bacis. "Mine," retorted the sausage-seller, "are by Bacis's elder brother, Glanis." Both of them went to fetch these precious documents, and both returned staggering under a load. "Now," said Demos to Bluster, "hand me

4

that one that I like so much, of how I shall become
an eagle in the clouds."
Bluster reads : —

> " Son of Erectheus, mark and ponder well
> This holy warning from Apollo's cell.
> He bids thee guard the sacred sharp-toothed whelp,
> Who for thy sake doth bite and bark and yelp ;
> Guard and protect him from the chattering jay,
> So shall thy juries all be kept in pay."[1]

D. "What is all this about? What is meant by
Erectheus and the dog and the jay?"
B. "I am the dog; I bark for you, and Apollo
says that you are to take care of me."
S.-s. "It is nothing of the kind. I have got the
true oracle about the dog. Listen to this : —

> "Son of Erectheus, ever at thy feast
> Beware the dog, the greedy, filching beast.
> He wags his tail, still fawning as you eat,
> But when you look away he steals the meat."

D. "That sounds much better, Glanis."
B. "Listen again to this : —

[1] The poorer class of Athenians depended very much on the pay of
three *oboli*, or half a drachma (represented by fourpence farthing in
English money, if measured by weight, but actually equivalent to
more) which they received for performing the office of jurymen. The
practice of making this payment is supposed to have been begun by
Pericles, but the pay was increased by Cleon. It may be compared,
not so much in itself, but in its political significance, to the distribution
of money and corn under the empire at Rome.

> "In sacred Athens shall a woman dwell;
> There shall she bear a lion fierce and fell;
> With many gnats the noble beast shall fight,
> Guarding, as dam her cubs, the people's right;
> Him must thou shelter, for the public good,
> With iron bulwarks and a wall of wood.

I am the lion; Apollo commands you to take care of me."

D. "You the lion? Why, a moment ago you were a dog."

S.-s. "Ah! sir, but he hides the true sense of the prophecy of the lion and the wooden wall in which Apollo says you are to keep him."

D. "What is it?"

S.-s. "Of course it is the stocks; you are to keep him in the stocks."

D. "Good! That is a prophecy that seems very likely to be fulfilled. But I have not heard about the eagle yet."

B. "Listen then:—

> "Soon shalt thou soar aloft on eagle's wings,
> Acknowledged lord of earth, and king of kings."

S.-s. "And now hear mine:—

> "Earth and the Red Sea shall your rule obey,
> While comfit cake you munch from day to day,
> Sitting on juries in Ecbatana."

D. "I think Glanis is a better prophet than Bacis. But now listen, you two. Have done with your

promises and prophecies. The man that serves me
up the best dinner I shall make manager-in-chief.
Away with you, and see what you can get for me."
The two competitors ran off in furious haste, and
the gentlemen who had been backing the sausage-
seller took the opportunity of reproaching the old
man with his easy surrender to unworthy favourites.

> "Worthy Demos, your estate
> Is a glorious thing and great;
> All men trembling bow them down,
> As before a despot's frown;
> But you're easy of belief,
> So that every rogue and thief
> Finds you ready to his hand.
> Flattery you can't withstand;
> What your last advisers say
> Ever will your judgment sway."

Demos makes reply : —

> "You're a fine set of sparks, but your wits are but weak ;
> What you think is a folly is only a freak;
> Believe me, my friends, I am not what I seem,
> I am quite wide awake, though you think that I dream ;
> I pamper these thieves, but I smash them to bits
> As soon as the right opportunity fits."

The Gentlemen.

> "If that's what you meant, we approve your intent ;
> If you keep them like beasts, fattened up for your feasts,
> Fed high in the stall, till occasion shall call,
> And a nice little vote puts a knife to their throat,
> And your cook serves them up when you dine or you sup."

At this point the two competitors returned and began their final struggle. Bluster put a chair for his master, but the sausage-seller outdid him by putting a table.

B. (*handing a dish*). "See, here's a pudding which I made at Pylos."

S.-s. (*handing another*). "Here are some cheese-cakes which the goddess has made with her own ivory hand."

D. "Mighty goddess, what a big hand you have!"

B. "Here's some pease-pudding."

S.-s. "Here's a fine mess of porridge."

B. "Here's a batter pudding, also from the goddess."

S.-s. "And here's a savoury stew with sippets that she sends you."

B. "Taste this pancake."

S.-s. "Try these fritters and this cup of wine."

D. "The wine is excellent."

S.-s. "So it should be, for she mixed it herself."

B. "Here, I have got a slice of cake for you."

S.-s. "And here, I have got a whole cake."

B. (*aside to the S.-s.*). "Here is hare pie. When will you get hare pie?"

S.-s. (*to himself*). "How shall I get hare pie. O my soul, invent some knavish trick!"

B. "Do you see the hare pie, you poor devil?"

S.-s. "Never mind (*pretending to look away*). They are coming to me."

B. "Who? Who?"

S.-s. "Some envoys with bags of silver."

B. (looking eagerly round). "Where? Where?"

S.-s. "Can't you let the strangers alone? (*Snatches at the hare pie while Bluster is looking about him, and offers it to Demos.*) See, my dear Demos, the hare pie I have got for you."

B. "Why, the villain has taken my dish."

S.-s. "Just what you did at Pylos, my friend."

D. "Tell me, how did you think of stealing it?"

S.-s. (piously). "The thought was born of heaven, the theft was mine."

B. "I took all the trouble."

S.-s. "But I served it up."

D. "Who hands it gets the thanks."

S.-s. "Come now, can't you decide, my dear sir, who treats you best?"

D. "How am I to judge?"

S.-s. "I will tell you. Look at my basket and see what is in it, and then look at his. That will decide."

This Demos did. The sausage-seller's was found to be practically empty. Bluster's had all kinds of good things in it, especially the rest of the cake, of which he had only served up a small slice to his master. This roused Demos's wrath to the utmost. "O villain!" he cried, "and this is the way you have been cheating me."

B. "I stole for my country's good."

D. "For your country's good indeed! Take away his crown."

Bluster, seeing that it was all over with him, took it off with a pathetic farewell : —

> "Farewell, my crown, farewell! I yield thee up
> Unwilling. Some new lord shall wear thee now,
> One not more thievish but more fortunate."[1]

S.-s. "O Zeus of Hellas, thine the victory!"
And now it turned out that Demos had indeed made a most fortunate choice in his new favourite. The sausage-seller retired with his master, and after a short interval appeared again, crying, "Silence! Have done with your litigation; close the courts; I bring good news."

Kn. "Oh, glory of Athens, the holy, and help of our island
    allies,
      For what happy event, thro' our streets, shall the
      steam of our sacrifice rise?"

S.-s. "I have given new youth to our Demos; I have
      made him all lovely and fair."

Kn. "O deviser of wondrous devices, now where may we
      see him, O where?"

S.-s. "'Tis the Athens of old where he dwelleth, the city
      with violets crowned."

Kn. "Oh, say how arrayed, with what aspect, henceforth
      shall our Demos be found?"

S.-s. "You shall see him again in his beauty, as he was
      when he sat at the board
      Of old with the just Aristides and Miltiades, Mara-
      thon's lord."

---

[1] A parody on the farewell which the dying Alcestis takes of her marriage chamber.

> Farewell; another wife shall own thee now,
> Some wife not purer but more fortunate.

. And so indeed it was. The old man came forward, changed to a handsome youth, and wearing in his hair the old-fashioned ornament of the grasshopper, symbol of the antiquity of the Athenian race. Not a little ashamed was he when his new adviser reminded him of the follies of the past; how he would listen to any unprincipled politician that proclaimed himself his friend; how he would spend the public money, not in equipping fleets, but in feeing the jurymen. But he is resolved to be wiser in the future. Orators who appeal to his selfish fears shall be tossed headlong into the pit.[1] The seamen shall have all their pay the very moment of their return to port. No one whose name stands on the roll for military service shall be permitted to evade the obligation.

"And now," said the new minister, when he had heard all these good resolutions, "see what I have got for you ! "

And he led out the lovely figure of Peace.

" Where did you find her ? " cried Demos.

" Bluster hid her away in his house," replied the minister, "that you might not catch sight of her. Take her; she is yours; and live henceforth in the country home where you are always so happy."

---

[1] The "barathron," into which criminals were hurled. We may compare the Tarpeian rock and the Tullianum at Rome.

III.

PEACE.

An interval of four years separated the production of the *Acharnians* from that of the play with which I am now dealing.

The successes achieved by Athens in the years 427–5 B.C., especially the capture of the Spartan garrison of Pylos, — an event to which frequent allusions are made in the *Knights*, — were succeeded in 423 by great disasters. The Athenians had long coveted the fertile country of their Bœotian neighbours, a country widely different from their own barren though picturesque and attractive land. They had once asserted their supremacy over it, and had maintained it for seven years, till dispossessed by the disastrous defeat of Coronea in B.C. 440. And now, again encouraged by a sense of immunity from invasion, — they had threatened to put all their prisoners to death if a Spartan army should again cross their frontiers, — they attempted to renew it. Their hopes were again crushed. The whole military force of the city, except a few small detachments that were serving elsewhere, was routed by the Bœotians at Delium. Another defeat, even more serious, at least as threatening more widely reaching consequences, followed. The reverse at Delium did nothing more than convince the Athenians that certain hopes which they had long entertained must be abandoned forever; but the losses which were sustained in the following year in Thrace deprived them of possessions which they had long regarded as their own, and threatened to bring down their whole empire in ruin. Brasidas, probably the ablest man that Sparta ever produced, succeeded, by a remarkable combination of military skill and attractive personal character, in detaching from Athens some of its most important dependencies on the northwest coast of the Ægean. Amphipolis and other cities of Thrace were now in the hands of the Spartans. Athens made a great effort to stay the tide of Spartan victory, despatching the largest force she could raise to attempt the recapture of Amphipolis. The effort failed totally and even disgracefully; the Athenian forces were routed under the walls of that city, — routed almost without making a struggle.

But this disaster had its compensations. The Spartans lost but eight killed in the battle, but among the eight was Brasidas; and Brasidas was not only a very able soldier, but he was vehemently opposed to peace. Among the slain on the Athenian side was Cleon, the notorious leader of the war party. And now came the triumph of the peace party in the two states. Aristophanes, conscious that he had the majority of his fellow-citizens on his side, again did his best to promote his favourite object. The *Peace* was exhibited in January, 321. About three months afterwards peace for the period of fifty years was made, and, a few days later, an alliance, offensive and defensive, between Sparta and Athens was concluded. (This is known in history as the " Peace of Nicias.")

"Now, my man," said the steward of Trygæus the Athenian to one of the under-slaves, "bring another cake for the beast." With much grumbling the man obeyed, and fetched first one, then another, and then, again, several more, till the creature was satisfied.

But what was the beast? Nothing less than an enormously large dung-beetle which Trygæus had contrived to catch, and which he kept in one of the courts of his house, and was feeding up till it should grow big enough and strong enough to help him in carrying out a certain purpose of his. The fact was, that Trygæus, like many another Athenian citizen, was heartily sick of the war, and had got the idea into his head that, if he could contrive to get up to the palace of Zeus, he might persuade the god to fulfil his wish, which was, to put it shortly, to secure Peace, — long-banished, long-desired Peace. His first plan was to get some very thin scaling-ladders made, and to scramble up to heaven by means of them. Unfortunately they broke, and brought him down with them to the ground. After this he got the beetle, and proposed to fly on its back up to the sky.

The animal having finished its meal, Trygæus mounted on its back, and was preparing to start, first giving his steed sundry cautions not to set off at too great a pace, or to put itself out of breath. The steward entreated his master to give up the idea, and after vainly endeavouring forcibly to stop him, called to the old gentleman's daughter to come and help him. Accordingly the girl came running out of the house into the court-yard, where Trygæus, who had now risen some way from the ground, was preparing to fly off. "Father," she said, "surely it isn't true that you are thinking of leaving us and going to the crows?[1] Tell me the truth, if you love me."

Trygæus. "Yes, it is true. The fact is, that I can't bear to hear you poor creatures saying to me, 'Papa, give us some bread,' when I haven't got a stiver of money in the house to buy it with. Only let me succeed in this plan of mine, and I will give you, not only bread, but the biggest buns that you ever saw."

---

[1] "Going to the crows" was the Greek equivalent for our "going to the dogs," as a proverbial expression for going to ruin.

Girl. "But, dear papa, how are you going? Ships can't carry you."

T. "I have got a winged horse. None of your sea-voyages for me."

G. "What! a beetle, papa? How can you get to heaven on a beetle?"

T. "'Tis the only living creature that ever got to heaven; so Æsop tells us."

G. "Oh, it's past all believing, that such a nasty, creeping creature should get so far!"

T. "Yes; but it did, when it went to break the eagle's eggs."[1]

G. "But why not mount Pegasus?"

T. "Far too expensive to feed, my dear."

G. "Well, if you must go, take care you don't fall off. If you should, the fall would be sure to lame you, and then Euripides would make you the hero of one of his tragedies. Think of that!"[2]

T. "I'll see to that. Good by, my dear."

Finally, not without running many risks, chiefly from the animal's inclination to descend in search of its favourite food, the rider reached his destination,

---

[1] Æsop's fable, according to the scholiasts (it is not found in the existing fables ascribed to him), was this: The eagle carried off the young beetles; thereupon the beetle flew to the eagle's nest and pushed the young birds out of it. The eagle went to Zeus to complain, who bade the bird build again in his own bosom. But when it had done so, and laid more eggs, the beetle came buzzing about the god's ears, and he, jumping up to scare it away, dropped and broke the eggs.

[2] For this compare the *Acharnians.*

and found himself outside the celestial palace. He at once called loudly for admittance. Hermes, who was acting as porter, opened accordingly, and was not a little astonished and disgusted at what he saw. "What is this?" he said. "A beetle-horse," said the visitor. "Away with you, then, you and your beetle-horse," cried the god. Trygæus, however, had come prepared to overcome this obstacle, and made his peace with a piece of flesh that he had brought with him. "And now," said he, "step in, and tell Zeus that I want to see him."

Hermes. "Oh! that's impossible. You can't see the gods; they are gone to the seventh heaven."

T. "But how come you to be here, then?"

H. "Oh, they left me to look after a few little matters, pots and pans, and so forth, that they left here."

T. "But why did they go away?"

H. "Because they were displeased with the Greeks. That is why they went away, and left War settled here for good. He is to do what he likes with you. They are not going to look at you with your everlasting fightings any more."

T. "Oh, but why is this? What have we done?"

H. "When they wanted Peace, you were always for War. First the Spartans would get a little the better of the fight, and then it was, 'These Athenian rascals shall suffer for it.' Then you had a turn of luck, and it was, 'No, no, we won't listen; as long as we keep Pylos, we shall always have them on their knees.'"

T. "Yes, yes; that is exactly what we said."

H. "The end of it all is that you will probably never see Peace again."

T. "What? Where is she gone, then?"

H. "War has thrown her into a deep pit."

T. "What pit?"

H. "The one you see down there. Just look at the heap of stones he has piled on the top to prevent you from getting her out."

T. "And what does he mean to do with us?"

H. "That I can't say. I only know that last night he brought a monstrously large mortar into the house."

T. "What can he want with a mortar?"

H. "He is thinking of pounding the cities up in it. But I must be going. I hear him making a noise inside, and I think that he is coming out."

The next moment, War, a fully armed figure, with a great nodding plume, came out of the palace of the gods, carrying in his hands a huge mortar, and muttering, as he went, about a bad time coming for men. He set the mortar on the ground, and began throwing in the ingredients for a salad. First came leeks. "You'll be nicely pounded up, my friends," said he, as he threw them in.[1]

---

[1] The joke cannot be translated. The explanation is this: The Greek word for a leek is *prason*. War accordingly throws in a town called Prasiæ. This was on the Spartan coast, and had been taken by Pericles early in the war. Hence the remark of Trygæus that follows.

"That doesn't matter to us," said Trygæus; "that's a blow for our friends the Spartans."

Garlic followed.

"That's a bad lookout for Megara," was Trygæus's comment.

After garlic came cheese.

Trygæus rubbed his hands. "Now for the Sicilians," he said.[1]

But the next ingredient did not find him so indifferent. It was honey, actual Attic honey from Hymettus.

"Hold!" he cried; "none of that. That costs sixpence a pound."

"Now," said War to his boy Hubbub, dealing him at the same time a sharp rap on the knuckles, "bring me a pestle."

"We haven't got one, master," said Hubbub. "We moved in only yesterday."

War. "Then run and borrow one from Athens."

Hubbub. "I'm off, or I shall catch it."

"This is a terrible thing," said Trygæus. "If that varlet brings back a pestle, there'll soon be nothing left of our cities."

In a short time Hubbub returned. The Athenian pestle had been lost.[2]

---

[1] Megara was famous for its garlic, and Sicily for its cheese.

[2] The Athenian pestle, as has been explained in the introduction, was Cleon, one of the chief advocates of the war; the Spartan pestle, of course, was Brasidas.

W. "Then fetch the Spartan pestle, and be quick about it."

T. "This is an anxious moment."

In a short time Hubbub returned empty-handed, and in a great state of dismay.

W. "How now? Why haven't you brought it?"

H. "The Spartan pestle is lost, master."

W. "How is that, you rascal?"

H. "They sent it to some folk somewhere Thrace-way,[1] and they lost it."

T. "And they did quite right, too. By the great Twin-brethren, all may be well yet!"

W. "Hubbub, take the things indoors. I will make another pestle for myself."

Overjoyed to see War depart, Trygæus shouted out, calling on all Greeks to take the opportunity of ridding themselves of their troubles by pulling Peace out of the cave in which she had been imprisoned.

A miscellaneous crowd of husbandmen, natives and foreigners, dwellers in the islands and dwellers on the mainland, answered to the call, and came hurrying in, furnished with crowbars and ropes, and loudly expressing their delight at accomplishing the rescue of Peace, best and greatest of goddesses.

"Hush!" cried Trygæus; "make less noise, or you'll rouse War, who is indoors there."

Husbandmen. "Oh, we were so glad to hear your

---

[1] Brasidas, as has been stated in the introduction, was killed at Amphipolis in Thrace.

proclamation! So different it was from that hateful 'Come with three days' rations apiece!'"

T. "Yes; but remember Cerberus down there. With his blustering and barking he may do what he did when he was up here, and hinder us from dragging the lovely goddess out of her cave."

Hus. "Hinder us! Nothing shall tear her from us, if we only once get hold of her."

T. "I tell you that you'll be the ruin of the whole business with your dancing and singing. Why can't you keep your tongues and your feet still?"

The husbandmen protested that they could not help themselves. Their legs *would* dance whether they wished or not. All Trygæus's cautions and exhortations were in vain. They begged for only one more turn with the right leg, and when this was granted, for only one turn with the left, and wound up with a vigorous movement of both. "Wait," cried Trygæus, "till you've got her safe. Then you may really rejoice." So delighted was he with the prospect that he broke out into a song : —

> " Oh, then you'll have time to laugh and to shout,
> To stop in your homes, or go sailing about,
> To feast and to sleep and the *kottabos*[1] play,
> To be merry all night, and be merry all day."

[1] A favourite game among the Greeks. There were various forms of it, the most easily described being one in which the object of the players was to sink a number of little saucers that were floating about in a bowl of water by throwing wine into them from a distance.

The husbandmen replied with another : —

"O thrice blessed day ! may I see it at last !
I've had trouble enough in the time that is past !
No more will you see me so stern and severe,
But tender and younger by many a year,
When our troubles are gone, and no more we appear
Day by day on parade with a shield and a spear.
Only tell us our work, and we'll do what we can,
For you are our master, most fortunate man."

Trygæus then began to inspect the stones that covered the pit in which Peace was immured, and to consider the best way of moving them. At this moment Hermes appeared, and loudly protested against the daring deed on which they were about to venture. Trygæus and his friends entreated him not to betray them. At first he absolutely refused to listen. The death penalty had been proclaimed by Zeus against all that presumed to dig in that place, and he could not but denounce the offenders. Prayers seemed in vain till Trygæus bethought him of working upon his fears. " I'll tell you," said he, "about a great and dreadful secret, no less than a plot against the gods."

Hermes. " Go on ; you may say something worth hearing."

T. " Well ; it is this. The Moon and that terrible rascal the Sun have been plotting against you now for many years ; they are intending, in short, to betray Greece to the barbarians."

H. " But why are they doing this ? "

T. " Why ? Because while we sacrifice to you, the barbarians sacrifice to them : so, of course, they want to get us out of the way, and then they will get all the sacrifices themselves."

H. " Oh ! I .see; and that, I suppose, is the reason why they have been filching part of our days, and nibbling off bits from their rounds." [1]

T. " Just so, my dear Hermes ; so lend us a hand, and help to pull Peace out of the cave ; and it is to you that we'll keep all the great feasts, — the feast of Athené, the feast of Zeus, and the feast of Adonis, and all the rest of them. Yes ; all the cities will sacrifice to you as Hermes the Saviour. And here, my dear Hermes, by way of earnest, is a gold cup." (*Produces a gold cup.*)

H. " Dear me! how very pitiful the sight of the gold makes me. Now, my men, it is for you to do the rest. Up with your shovels, and work away."

T. But let us first do our duty to the gods. Hermes, hold out the cup, and we'll begin with libations and prayers."

H. " Silence for the libation ! "

T.   " I pour and pray. Let this glad morn begin
         All joy to Greece ; and he who lends to-day
         A willing hand ne'er carry shield again."

---

[1] Among the terrors and calamities which preceded and accompanied the Peloponnesian war, Thucydides (1.23) mentions " eclipses of the sun more frequent than had ever been recorded before." One of these happened in the first year of the war (August 3, 431), and another in the eleventh (March 21, 421).

Hus. " Yea, let him spend his days in peace, and sit,
          His wife beside him, by a blazing hearth."
T.   " If any armourer, who would sell his arms,
          Love battle more than peace, a curse upon him ! "
Hus. " And whoso, greedy for a general's pay,
          Holds back and helps us not, a curse upon him ! "
T.   " Again I pour to Hermes, to the Hours,
          The sister Graces, and the Queen of Love,
          And fond Desire."
Hus.   " And shall we say to Ares ? "
T.   " To Ares ?   Heaven forbid it !   Name him not."
                    (*Spits on the ground in disgust.*)

This ceremony ended, all set to work, and pulled
away at the rope with which the prisoners, that is,
Peace and her attendants, were to be hauled out of
their dungeon.   Hermes encouraged them, and Trygæus watched to see that none shirked their task.
This, indeed, he soon found some inclined to do.
The Bœotians[1] were very lukewarm, and made only
a show of working.   Then some of his own countrymen, such as Lamachus,[2] did nothing but get in the
way, while the men of Argos made no effort at all,
but laughed at both sides, and took their profit from
each.   As for the men of Megara, they seemed eager

---

[1] The Bœotians were not anxious for peace.   They had suffered
little by the war, and they had gained great credit by the crushing
defeat which they had inflicted on the Athenian army at Delium.
As a matter of fact, they refused to join in the Peace of Nicias,
and would do nothing more than make a truce of indefinite length,
which might be terminated at ten days' notice, with their Athenian
neighbours.

[2] The General Dobattle of the *Charcoal-burners.*

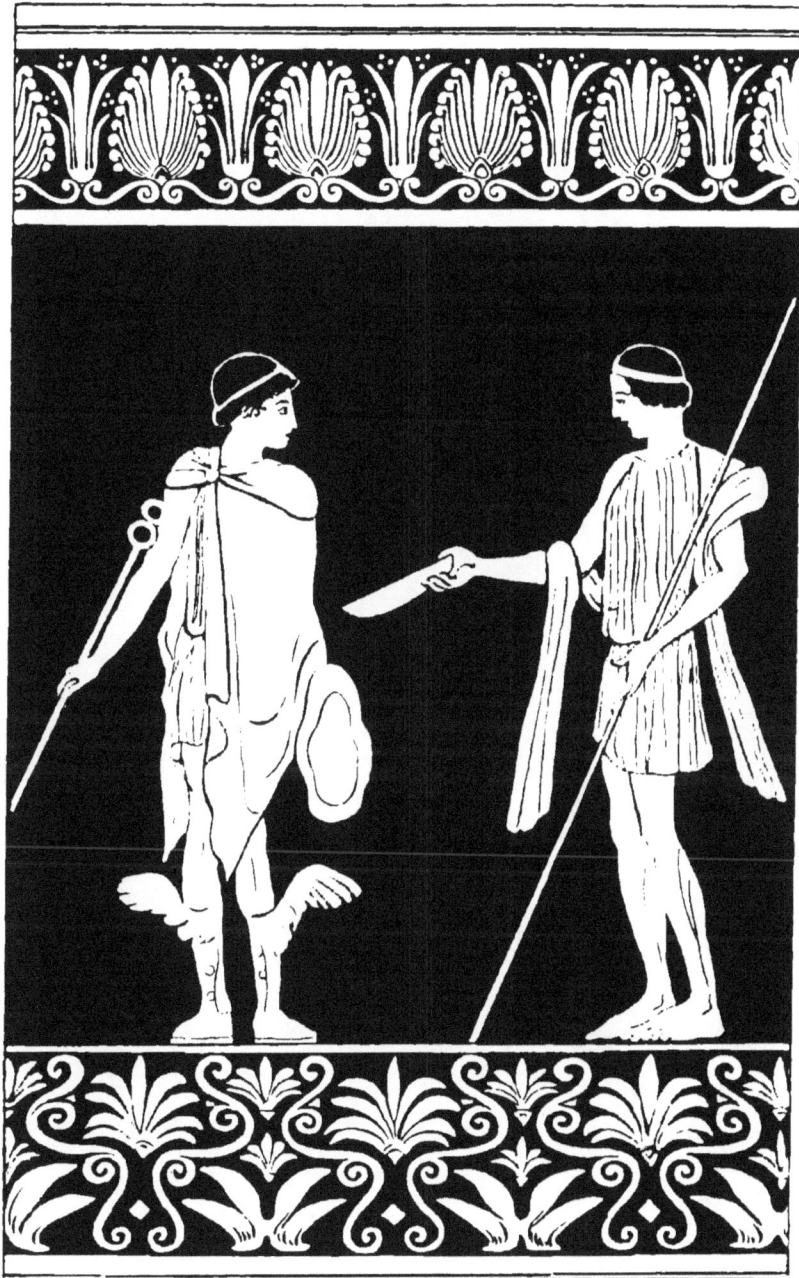

TRYGAEUS BRIBING HERMES WITH A GOLD CUP.

enough, but they were so weak with hunger that they gave no help. Sometimes it seemed as if no progress was being made. Still the work went on, and at last, with a long pull, and a strong pull, and a pull all together, the thing was done. Peace, with her two handmaids, Harvest-home and Mayfair, was lifted out of the pit. Trygæus was almost beside himself with delight. "Welcome, mighty mother of vintages!" he cried, "welcome, Harvest-home! welcome, Mayfair! O Mayfair, what a lovely face you have! and how sweet your breath! what a perfume!"

H. "Not the smell of a knapsack, eh?"

T. "A knapsack indeed! No such abomination as that, but a fragrance of harvests, and feasts, and flutes, and thrushes, and bleating of lambs, and empty flasks, and all kinds of good things."

Then he burst out into song again:—

> "Oh, think of the pleasures
>   Peace gave us of yore,
> Of her sweet country treasures,
>   Her bountiful store;
> Of the figs, and the vine,
> And the olives divine,
> And the myrtle-tree growing,
> And violets blowing,
> Where fountains were flowing.
> These are the joys for which long we've been yearning,
> For these we will welcome the goddess returning."

Hus. "Welcome, welcome, once more!

We have longed for thee sore.
Still desiring again,
With a passionate pain,
In the sweet country-side
Of our farms to abide,
We who follow the trade
Of the tillers of land,
For our labours are paid
By the gifts of thy hand.
Not a flower, not a fruit,
Not a tender young shoot
Of the fig or the vine,
But will fondly combine
Through the length and the breadth of our country to greet
The thrice welcome sound of thy home-coming feet."

"Now," said Hermes to the husbandmen, "I will explain to you the cause of all the mischief. Phidias began it by getting into trouble. Then Pericles, fearing lest he should be involved with him, and knowing your fierce temper, set the city in a blaze by his decree against Megara.[1] The smoke of that burning

---

[1] This has been mentioned in the *Charcoal-burners*. The first charge brought against Phidias was that he had embezzled some of the gold that was to be used for the statue of Athené. This he disproved by weighing the metal, and showing that the quantity was correct. Then he was accused of having introduced likenesses of himself and Pericles into the battle-scene pictured on the shield of Athené. This could not be denied, and the sculptor was thrown into prison, where he died. That these attacks on Phidias were made by enemies of Pericles, and with the idea of vexing and injuring him, is quite clear. That they influenced him in his policy of encouraging Athens to resist the Spartan demands, and so bringing on the Peloponnesian war, is another matter. It is stated by Diodorus Siculus and by Plutarch. But the causes of great political events are not to be found in personal matters of this kind.

drew tears from every eye in Greece. Not a vine
there was but groaned when it heard it, not a cask
but dashed itself against its neighbour. There was
nobody to stop the uproar, and Peace disappeared.
Then the subject cities, when they saw you snarling
at each other, thought that they could get rid of their
tribute, and bribed the great people at Sparta to help
them; so there was trouble abroad and trouble at
home, and the greatest mischiefmaker of all was a
certain tanner."

T. "Say no more about him, my dear Hermes; let
him rest where he is; he is one of your people now.
But, my dear lady (*turning to Peace*), why so silent?"

H. "She has been too much wronged to forgive
easily."

(*Peace, it should be said, was represented by a
colossal statue with a head which could turn round.
Hermes speaks to her and affects to listen to her
answers.*)

H. "Dearest lady, tell me your thought. Ah!
that is it, is it? She says that when she came, after
that affair at Pylos, with a chest full of treaties, she
was thrice rejected in full assembly."

T. "So she was; but our wits were covered up
with hides in those days."

H. "She wants to know who among you loves
Peace and hates War most."

T. "Cleonymus, of course."

H. "What about him?"

T. "He is not the son of the man whom he calls his father, and when he goes to battle, he throws away his shield and runs[1] away."

H. "Peace wants to know who is the first man in the Assembly now?"

T. "Hyperbolus,[2] of course. But, dear lady, why so disgusted?"

H. "She is disgusted with the people for choosing such a leader."

T. "Oh! he is only a make-shift. And besides, we thought that, as we were all groping in the dark, he might throw a little light on affairs."

H. "How so?"

T. "Because he makes lamps."

H. "She wants to know whether witty old Cratinus[3] is alive.

T. "No, poor fellow, he died when the Spartans invaded us. He saw a butt of wine staved in, and it broke his heart to see so much good liquor wasted."

In the end it was arranged that Trygæus should return home with Peace and her two handmaids, one

---

[1] Cleonymus, probably a political opponent of the poet, is continually attacked by him on account of alleged cowardice. Nothing is known of the circumstances.

[2] The successor of Cleon, and according to Thucydides, a worthless fellow.

[3] Cratinus, a writer of comedies, and one of the most formidable rivals of Aristophanes, was probably alive at the time. We find frequent jests at his fondness for wine.

of whom, Harvest-home, he should have for his own wife. He accordingly, after taking an affectionate leave of Hermes, called for the beetle. The beetle, however, was not available, having been harnessed to the car of Zeus; and Trygæus and his charges descended to earth by a staircase, which Hermes pointed out to him. "Dear me!" he said, when he felt his feet on firm ground again, "what a business it was to get up to the gods! How my legs ache! And how small you looked," he went on, speaking to the slaves, who had assembled to greet him, "from up there! I thought you seemed a bad lot, when I looked down on you, but now I see you closer, I find you very much worse."

A servant. "What have you got, master?"

T. "Got? A pain in my legs from travelling so far."

S. "And did you see anybody else wandering about up there?"

T. "Only a minor poet or two."

S. "And is it true that when we die we are turned into stars?"

T. "Of course it is."

S. "What are the shooting stars, then?"

T. "Rich stars going from dinner with lighted lanterns in their hands. But take the young lady; let her have a bath, and be dressed for our wedding. She is to be my bride."

S. "And is she to have anything to eat?"

T. " To eat ?   No.   She can't eat our food ; she's used to ambrosia."

Harvest-home being thus disposed of, Trygæus proceeded to make a sacrifice to Peace, to whom he and his servant, assisted by the husbandmen, addressed an ode of praise and thanksgiving : —

> " For thirteen long years we have longed to behold you,
> And now you are come we will steadfastly hold you.
> When our fightings are stayed and our tumults allayed,
> We will call you in future the war-ending maid ;
> We beseech thee to end all the whispers of doubt,
> All the clever suspicions we bandy about,
> All the Greeks with the solder of friendship to bind,
> Breathing into them thoughts that are honest and kind."

While the sacrifice was going on, a soothsayer approached, crowned with laurel, after the manner of his profession. Trygæus thought that he was going to interfere with the ratification of the treaties of Peace ; the servant, on the other hand, believed that he was attracted by the smell of the meat. Both turned out to be right, in a way. The sooth-sayer did wish to have a finger in the pie, and made sundry suggestions as to the treaties, which would be repaid, he hoped, by an invitation to share in the feast. But as his advances were rejected with very scant courtesy, he proceeded to quote prophecy after prophecy, foretelling a disastrous end to the pro-ceeding. Trygæus, however, had an answer ready to all his sinister suggestions, and when finally asked

to produce the prophecy in reliance on which he
had himself been acting, he bravely replied with
what was wanted. It came from Homer, he said,
but of course it was an impromptu of his own.

"When the sons of Greece had driven lowering clouds of war
  away,
Lovely Peace they gladly welcomed, making feast and holy day.
Flesh from thigh-bones duly burning, tasting duly, as is meet,
Savoury morsels from the inwards, pouring out libations sweet.
I, whom now you see before you, I the holy rites began,
But with bright gold goblet no one blessed the prophesying
  man."

Soothsayer. "Strange the words that thou hast
uttered; not the Sibyl's speech, are they?"

T. "Strange they may be, yet full wisely did the
mighty Homer say: —

"He who loves the savage strife that severs men of kindred
  race,
Motherhood he scorns and custom and the home life's kindly
  face."

The soothsayer continued to interrupt and intrude,
and in the end Trygæus and his servants drove him
away. The sacrifice ended, it became time to lay
out the wedding-supper, at which it was soon evident
there would be no lack of guests. Trygæus took
his helmet, and pulling out the crest, handed it to
the servant, with the remark that, as he had no more
use for it, it had better be used for wiping down
the tables. While this was being done, a sickle-

maker and a cooper made their appearance. Both were in the highest spirits. The first had sold sickles, for which for years past no one would give a farthing, for a couple of pounds; the latter had disposed of a lot of casks for country use at half-a-crown each. They offered Trygæus as many of both articles as he wanted, and gave him some money, too, by way of wedding present. The bridegroom invited them in to take part in the feast. The next moment a maker of crests appeared. He was as much depressed as the others had been elated. "What is the matter?" said the bridegroom, "A surfeit of crests? eh?"—"You have ruined my trade," replied the man; "and my neighbour's, too, who burnishes spears."

T. "Well, what shall I give you for these two crests?"

Crest-maker. "What will you give?"

T. "I hardly like to say. Well, as there is a good deal of work about them, say three quarts of raisins for the pair. They'll do to wipe my tables with."

C.-m. "Fetch the raisins; better that than nothing."

T. (handling them, when they came to pieces). "Take the rotten things away. The hairs are all coming out. Not a single raisin for the pair."

An armourer now appeared on the scene with a breastplate, which had cost, he said, forty pounds. Trygæus offered to buy it for a pan, but found it unsuitable, and packed the man off. A trumpeter followed, wanting to sell a trumpet, which had cost him, he said, two pounds ten. Trygæus could only suggest that he should fill it with lead, fasten a pair of scales at the top, and use it for weighing out rations of figs for the labourers at the farm. A helmet-maker was advised to take his helmets, which had cost him, he said, four pounds, to Egypt, where they might be used to measure medicines with, while the man that burnished spears had an offer made to him that if he would lop off the heads, and saw the shafts in two, Trygæus would buy them for vine poles, at twelve a penny. The men went off greatly insulted. Trygæus now espied some singing boys, whom the guests had brought with them by way of contribution to the feast. "Come," he said to one of them, "stand here by me, and let me hear you practise what you are going to sing."

The boy began : —

"Sing of heroes, sing the younger."

T. "None of that, boy; have done with your heroes. There is peace, and I want to hear nothing about them." [1]

[1] The word that excited Trygæus's wrath was that which stands for "younger." This is *hoploteroi*. It reminded him of *hopla*, the word for arms, and the association of ideas is odious to him. The words which the boy sings are the beginning of one of the poems of what is called the epic cycle (poems relating in heroic verse the events beginning with the Voyage of the Argo and ending with the Capture of Thebes). This last was the subject of the *Epigoni*.

Boy (singing again).

" When the armies met together, marching slow across the
   field,
Loudly buckler dashed on buckler, loudly round-bossed
   shield on shield."

T. " Buckler ! Boy, how dare you talk about buck-
lers ?"
Boy (singing).

" Vaunts of victors, groans of dying, rose together to the
   sky."

T. " Say another word about 'groans of dying'
and you shall repent it."
Boy. "But what am I to sing? Tell me the sort
of songs you like."

T. " Then on flesh of beeves they feasted, —

something of that sort."
Boy (singing).

" Then on flesh of beeves they feasted, first from off their
   sweating steeds
Loosing chariot yoke and traces, wearied sore of warlike
   deeds."

T. " That's good. They had had enough of war,
and then feasted. Sing again of how they had had
enough and feasted."
Boy (singing).

     " Rested well they called for casques."

T. " Yes, called for casks,[1] and very glad to do it." ·

Boy (singing).

" From the towers and walls descending rushed they to the fight again,
Till once more the roar of battle rose unceasing from the plain."

T. " Confound you, boy, you and your battles! You can't sing of anything but war. Who is your father ? "

Boy. " Lamachus."

T. " Ah! I thought when I heard you that you must be the son of some swash-buckler. Go and sing to the spearmen. Where is the son of Cleonymus? Here, sing us something before we go in. You won't sing of such things. Your father has too much of the better part of valour."

Second boy (singing).

" Some foeman I doubt not is proud of the shield,
The shield without blot that I left on the field."

T. " Good boy! Are you singing about your father ? "

Sec. boy. " But I saved my own life."

T. " And your parents you shamed. But go in, my boy. If you are your father's son, you won't for-

[1] The joke in the Greek is a play on a word which may mean " put on their breastplates," but which might be used to signify " fortified themselves with liquor." I am indebted for the English equivalent to Mr. B. B. Rogers; but I remember to have seen the pun in Mr. James Hannay's " Singleton Fontenoy."

get about the shield, I fancy. And you, my friends, set to ; there is plenty for all, and there is no good in having fine teeth if you don't use them."

Hus. " We will do our duty ; but you were quite right to mention it."

T. " Set to ; or you will be sorry for it some day."

Hus. " Now it's time that the bride and the torches you
        bring ;
And those that come with her shall dance and shall sing ;
And we'll pray to the gods to give plenty and peace
Forever henceforth to the children of Greece ;
Their fruit in abundance our fig-trees shall yield,
With the yard full of wine and of barley the field ;
With sons and with daughters our homes shall abound ;
By the side of our hearth shall the blessings be found,
That of late we have lost, though we had them before,
And the name of the sword shall be heard of no more."

IV.

THE WASPS.

Frequent reference is made in the plays of Aristophanes to the judicial system of Athens. The body of judges or jurymen — the second term is, on the whole, more descriptive of them than the first — consisted of six thousand citizens, chosen by lot out of the whole number. These six thousand were divided into ten bodies of five hundred each, who sat in different courts, dealing with different kinds of cases. The thousand that remained over were called upon to supply vacancies. Sometimes part only of a section would sit; sometimes two or more sections were combined. On very important occasions, it is said, the whole body was assembled. Each juryman received three *oboli*, or half a drachma, as a fee for his attendance; this sum having been increased, according to some authorities, by Cleon. The poet in this drama directs his satire against the characteristic faults of the courts thus constituted, faults which may be summed up in the phrase, "want of a judicial temper."

The Wasps was exhibited in the early part of 422 B.C., when Cleon was at the height of his power. A few months later he was killed. (See introduction to the *Peace*.)

THERE was an old gentleman at Athens who was afflicted with a very strange disease. It was a passion, not for the things that some of his contemporaries were devoted to, as drinking or gaming, but for the law courts. He was never happy except he was serving on a jury and trying a case. Such a hold had this passion got upon him that he could not sleep at night for thinking of his favourite em-

6

ployment, and if he ever did doze off for a moment
his soul seemed to flutter about the clock [1] by which
the advocates' speeches were timed. When he got
up in the morning, he always put his thumb and
two fingers together exactly as if he were holding a
voting pebble in them; and if a lover had written
on the walls,

> Pretty, pretty Goldilocks,

he would write underneath,

> Pretty, pretty Ballotbox.

When a cock happened to crow in the evening he
would cry : " That cock has been bribed to be late in
waking me by some officials who don't like the idea
of giving in their accounts." Supper was hardly
over before he clamoured for his shoes; and before
dawn he was off to the court, and went to sleep
leaning against the pillar on which the notices were
posted up. And when he was sitting, he was always
for severity. It was always the longest sentence
that pleased him most.[2] So afraid was he that

[1] A water-clock, or clepsydra; the water occupied a certain time in
running out, and a larger or smaller clepsydra, or, it may be, a clepsydra filled so many times, was granted to the speakers according to
the nature and importance of the case.

[2] Commonly, in an Athenian court, when a verdict had been given,
and (supposing that the prisoner had been found guilty) sentence had
to be passed, the prosecutor would first name the penalty which he
thought fit to meet the case, or which seemed to him such as the jury
would probably accept; and then the prisoner, on the other hand,
named some other punishment, as much milder as he could venture

he might perchance not have a pebble to vote with that he kept a private beach in his own house. The old gentleman's name was Philocleon;[1] and he had a son, Bdelycleon,[1] who strongly disliked his father's ways. At first this son did his best to persuade the old man to stop at home. Then he tried baths and purges; they did no good. Then he got him to join the worshippers of Cybele.[2] The old man rushed into court with a timbrel in his hand, and took his place as usual. Then he took him across the straits to Ægina, and made him sleep inside the temple of Æsculapius; but the very next morning he was standing at the court-rail. After that the only thing was to keep the old man at home. But he tried to get out through the water-pipes; when these were stopped up with rags, he drove perches into the wall and hopped down them like a jackdaw. Then his son surrounded the house

upon, having regard to the feelings of the court. (So when Socrates was found guilty, the prosecutor demanded the death-penalty, while the accused, after stating that, in his own opinion, he deserved the highest honours from the state, proposed, in deference to the judgment of his friends, a small money fine [£20]. This was practically a defiance to the court, and ensured the acceptance of the heavier penalty.) After this the jurors voted again; those who were for the severer sentence drew a long line on the wax tablet, those for the lighter a short one. The old man described in the text always drew a line as long as he could, and came home with his nails full of wax.

[1] The two words mean, respectively, "Cleon-lover" and "Cleon-loather."

[2] This consisted of wild orgies, celebrated with music and frantic dances.

with nets, putting a couple of slaves in charge of them. These two watchmen had been keeping guard all night and had dropped off to sleep, when they heard the voice of the young master crying out, " Run, run at once, one of you! my father has got into the kitchen-flue." Scarcely had he said this when he heard a voice from up above, and called out, " What's that noise in the chimney?"

Philocleon (who was trying to get out that way). "Only a little smoke escaping."

Bdelycleon. " Smoke? Of what wood, pray?"

Phil. " Fig-tree, to be sure."

Bdel. " The most biting kind there is." (*To the slaves*) " Run and clap a stone on the top of the chimney. You must try some other dodge, my dear sir."

Then the old man tried to make his way out by the door; finding that barred by the slaves, he screamed out, " I will gnaw the net."

" But you haven't any teeth, father," replied the son. Then he tried craft. It was market day, and he wanted to sell the donkey, and he was sure he would make a better bargain than his son. The son would not listen. He would take the donkey to market himself, and accordingly had the beast driven out. The creature seemed very loath to move, and Bdelycleon addressed it : —

" Why so sad, my ass? Because you are to be sold to-day? Move a little quicker. Why grunt and groan, unless you are carrying a new Ulysses?"

Slave. "And, by Zeus! there is a fellow hanging on underneath."

· *Bdel.* "What? Where?"

Slave. "Here, to be sure."

Bdel. "Who in the world are you?"

Phil. "No man."

Bdel. "No man, are you? Where do you come from?"

Phil. "From Ithaca, the son of Runaway."

Bdel. "Well, however you'll not get off in this way." (*To the slaves*)[1] "Drag him out."

The old man accordingly was dragged off, and pushed inside, and the door was bolted, barred, and still further fortified by stones and other things piled up against it. While the slaves were busy about this, one of them was startled by a clod of earth falling on his head. Philocleon had mounted on to the roof, and seemed to be intending to fly off. "Throw the net over him," cried his son. This done, the slaves ventured to suggest that a sleep would be welcome. Of this, however, their young master would not hear.

"Sleep!" he cried, "why, his fellow-juryman will

[1] Philocleon bethinks him of the device by which Ulysses and his men had escaped from the cave of the Cyclops. The hero had tied his companions under the bellies of rams, and he himself had clung in the same way to the biggest and strongest. The Cyclops, sitting at the mouth of the cave, and feeling the animals as they go out, asks this animal which was accustomed to lead the flock, why it is so long in coming out. The name "No man" is another reminiscence of the story.

be here very soon to call for him, and we shall have to deal with them."

"But, sir," said the slave, "it is only just twilight." — "Ah!" replied Bdelycleon, "then they are very late to-day; soon after midnight is their usual time for coming."

Slave. "Well, if they do come, we can easily pelt them with stones." .

Bdel. "Pelt them, indeed! You might as well stir up a wasps' nest as anger these old men. Every one of them wears a terrible sting, and they'd leap on you like live coals out of the fire."

Slave. "Don't be afraid. Give me some stones, and I'll scatter their wasps' nest, be it ever so big."

Sure enough, before many minutes had passed, the host of jurymen[1] appeared, a set of poorly dressed, hungry looking fellows. They came slowly on, picking their way, while their young sons carried lanterns by their side. They were greatly astonished, on arriving at Philocleon's house, to see no trace of their colleague, and sang a stave, in the hope of bringing him out: —

"Why doesn't he greet us in front of his hall?
Why doesn't he hear and reply to our call?
Perhaps he has had the misfortune to lose
The only one pair that was left him of shoes;
Or perhaps it may be he has injured his toe

---

[1] They were dressed in the play in garments striped with yellow and black, so as to resemble wasps, and each was furnished with a formidable looking sting.

With groping about in the dark; such a blow,
When a man is in years, very painful may grow.
He was ever the sharpest and keenest of all;
In vain on his ear all entreaties would fall;
If you sued for his grace, with an obstinate stoop
Of his head, he would mutter, 'Boil stones into soup.'
Can it be that, attempting in vain to forget
The fellow who yesterday slipped through our net,
Having cheated us all with detestable lies
About plots he had spied out among our allies,
He has sickened with fever? That's just like our friend.
But up with you now, for it's foolish to spend
Your time in these fruitless reproaches. We've got
From Thrace[1] a fat traitor to pop in our pot."

Philocleon replied in corresponding strains : —

"Friends, long have I wasted away with my woe,
As I heard through the chimney your voices below;
I am helpless; these will not allow me to go
With you as my spirit desires, for I burn
To do some one or other a mischievous turn,
If I only could get to the balloting urn.[2]
O Lord of the thunder, I pray that the stroke
Of thy lightning may speedily change me to smoke
Or to stone, if I only the table were made
To which for the counting the votes are conveyed."

[1] At the time when this play was acted, the struggle of Athens to retain her possessions in Thrace was going on. The meaning of the original is not that the traitor was a Thracian, or brought from Thrace, but that he had betrayed the interests of the city in reference to its Thracian possessions.

[2] The urns (one for acquittal, one for condemnation) in which the jurymen deposited their votes.

Colleague. "But who is it keeps you shut up, my friend?"

Phil. "My own son. But hush! he is asleep. Speak softly."

Coll. "But why? What reason does he give?"

Phil. "He wants to keep me from sitting on juries, and in fact from doing any mischief. He makes me comfortable enough, but I won't give in."

Coll. "Ah! I see; he's mixed up in some conspiracy, and afraid of what you might find out. But isn't there some way of giving him the slip?"

Phil. "How I wish there were! Can you think of anything?"

Coll. "You might dress yourself up in a beggar's rags, as Ulysses did, and creep out somehow."

Phil. "There is not a cranny that a gnat could get through. No, you must think of something better than that."

Coll. "Don't you remember how you stole the roast meat and let yourself down by the wall, when we were besieging Naxos?" [1]

Phil. "Ah! but I was a young man then and could go where I pleased; but now I am old, and, besides, they watch me too closely."

Coll. "Well, think of something; for the day is beginning to break, and time presses."

Finally Philocleon gnawed through one of the

[1] This was in 466 B.C. Naxos had seceded from the Delian Confederacy, and the Athenians blockaded and finally took the city.

nets with which all the outlets to the house were secured, and, tying round his body a rope, the other end of which he secured to a bar of the window, began to let himself down into the street, imploring his colleagues that if anything should happen to him — the rope breaking, for instance — they would pay him due honours, and bury him under the railings round the judges' seat. His friends encouraged him; and the thing was nearly done, when something chanced to rouse the slumbering Bdelycleon. The old man dropped, indeed, to the ground, but only to find himself in the hands of his keepers. In vain he appealed to his son's sense of filial duty, pathetically reminding him of how, long ago, catching him stealing grapes, he had tied him to an olive-tree and thrashed him, to the admiration of all beholders. In vain the old man's colleagues charged in the hope of rescuing him, using their stings freely. Bdelycleon and his slaves, first with sticks and then by means of smoke (always a thing which wasps detest), contrived to repel the attack. "Tyranny! Tyranny!" cried the assailants, as they found themselves beaten back. Bdelycleon suggested compromise; they would have none of it. "Tyranny! He's plotting to set up a tyranny!" they repeated.

"Ah!" said the young man, "that is what is always on your tongues now, — Tyranny! Conspiracy! You think of nothing else. For instance, I go into the fish-market and buy a bass, and don't buy pilchards. Immediately the fellow who is selling pilchards grumbles, 'A man who buys fish in this way must be thinking of being a tyrant.' Or, again, I want a leek as sauce to my anchovies. What does the girl that sells pot-herbs do but say, 'Ah! you buy pot-leeks. You would be a tyrant, I see.' Now this is the sort of thing that I want to get my father away from; and as soon as I try, then immediately I am an aristocrat, a tyrant."

Phil. "And quite right, too! Do you think that I would change those beloved courts for anything that you could give me? No, not for all the pigeon's milk in the world. Skates indeed, and eels! No; give me a nice little plea dished up with pettifogger's sauce."

Bdel. "Yes; that's the thing you have been so fond of all your life. Still, I think I can convince you that you have been wrong, if you will only sit still and listen."

Phil. "Wrong, do you say? I wrong to like sitting on juries?"

Bdel. "Yes; and scorned and mocked and cheated by the men you worship, — a slave without knowing it."

Phil. "You call me a slave? Why, I am lord of all."

Bdel. "Not you; you think that you are, but you are really a servant. Tell me now, father, what good you get out of your lordship."

CUR AND PINCHER.

Phil. "That I will gladly. We will argue the matter out, and let there be umpires to decide between us."

Bdel. "Very good." (*To the slaves*) "Let him go."

Phil. "And give me a sword; if I am worsted i.. this encounter I will fall upon it, and put an end to my troubles."

Philocleon, urged by his colleagues to do his best, lest their common employment should fall into disrepute, now proceeded to expound his view of the advantages of the juryman's profession. "Our kingdom," so ran his speech, "is inferior to none in the world. There is not a creature more blest, more petted, more feared, than the juryman. When I come trudging from my bed in the morning there are big fellows waiting for me at the bar. As soon as I come in, a delicate hand, that knows its way, I warrant you, into the public purse, is thrust into mine. How they bow, and scrape, and beg, and pray, lowering their voices to a whine, with a 'Pity me, sire, I beseech you, if you have ever made a little purse for yourself out of an office or a contract.' So they plead; fellows who would never have known that I existed, if they had not been acquitted before. So I take my seat, in excellent humour, as every one thinks; but I never think of keeping any of the promises that I have made. I listen to all that they say to persuade me to acquit them — and what will they not say? Some make a

moan over their poverty, — yes, actually try to make
themselves out as badly off as I am; and some tell
me fables, or quote something funny out of Æsop;
and some banter and jest to make me laugh, to put
me into a good temper. And if this doesn't move
me, then the man brings his children, boys and girls.
They huddle together, and bleat like so many lambs,
while their father beseeches me to pass his accounts
and let him go free.[1]   And I just let my wrath down
by a peg or two. Then if a player gets into trouble,
he has to give me one of his very best speeches; and
if a piper wins a suit, he plays us out of court with a
quick march. If a father leaves his daughter and
his fortune to a friend, what do we care for the will
with its big seal? Nothing at all; we do just what
we please with the girl and her money, and there is
nobody to call us to account. Then the government
takes care that we are not overworked. One suit a
day, they say, and then we may go home. Why, we
are the only people whom Cleon does not nibble at

[1] Every Athenian official, on reaching the term of his office, had to
submit his accounts to the public auditors. If any objection was made,
the matter in dispute was submitted to the judgment of the courts,
these tribunals being constituted as has been described in the introduction. The practice of the accused attempting to move the compassion
of his judges by bringing into court his children is frequently mentioned. One quotation will suffice. Socrates, at the conclusion of his
defence as given by Plato, says: " It may be that some one of you may
be indignant with me when he remembers that he himself, brought
before the court on a less serious charge than this, prayed and besought
the jury with many tears, and exhibited his children," etc.

and vex, but sits and keeps guard over us and brushes off the flies. What do you say to all this, you who would have it that I was a mere slave and dupe? And then, what is the most delightful thing of all, and yet I had almost forgotten it, when I get home with my day's pay in my pocket. How glad they all are to see me! First comes my daughter, and washes my feet, and anoints them, and kisses me. 'Dear papa,' she says, fishing out the money with her tongue ever so cleverly, pretty little creature! Then my wife is so kind, bringing me a little pudding she has made, and sitting by me and pressing me to eat, with a 'Do take a little more,' and 'Just another helping.' Oh! it is pleasant.

"As fine as the empire of Zeus is our sway;
  And indeed we are greatly alike, for they say,
  Great Zeus! what a terrible thunder they make,
  When we shout in our wrath,[1] and they tremble and shake,
  Though mighty and rich, when the wrath in our eye
  Flashes forth as the lightning that gleams through the sky."

Bdelycleon now addressed himself to the task of proving his point, and began by addressing the old man as "Son of Chronos, my father."

Phil. "Don't try to get round me with 'father, father.' Prove that I am a slave, or you die."

---

[1] Socrates in the defence (quoted above) says to his judges, "Do not make a noise," when some remark of his meets with the loudly expressed disapproval of his judges. The demeanour of the citizens sitting in court was very much like that of the Public Assembly.

Bdel. "Very well, dear papa; and don't look so stern. Just begin by reckoning — not exactly, of course, but roughly and in round numbers — the revenue that comes in from the subject states. Add to this the taxes, and the percentages, and the fees, and the fines, and the silver from the mines, and the market and harbour dues, and the sales. You will find the total not far off two thousand talents.[1] And now put down the jurymen's pay, reckoning how much the six thousand get in a year. Why, it will not come to much more than a hundred and fifty talents! And what is that among all the six thousand?"

Phil. "Then our pay is not a tenth part of the whole revenue?"

Bdel. "Certainly not."

Phil. "Pray tell me, then, where the rest of the money goes to."

Bdel. "Why, it goes to the gentlemen who 'will never betray the rabble of Athens,' who 'will always

---

[1] The talent valued by weight was worth £210 18s. 9d. (It should be observed, however, that this amount is arrived at by taking the price of silver at its coinage value, *i.e.* 5s. per ounce. Its market value is much less.) The total would be £421,875. What the purchasing power of this was it is impossible to say; but from the prices quoted for various articles, it may be supposed to be many times greater than the nominal equivalent in modern money. This would give £5 10s. apiece, possibly equivalent to £50, — a pittance quite worth struggling for, but not enough to raise the recipient above poverty. It must be supposed that all the courts (there were ten of them) did not sit every day.

fight for the people.'   And, O father, 'tis all your
fault.   It is you who make these men your masters,
cheated by their fine words.   And then they get
presents, fifty talents at a time, from the allies, by
means of threats of this kind, 'Hand over the *
tribute, or there will be an end of your city!'   And
you are content to gnaw away at the offal, while
they eat the meat.   Do you suppose that the allies
are not clever enough to see all this?   Of course
they do.   When they find you growing lanky and
lean, and your masters round and fat, it is to them
that they bring their presents, — their wine, their
cheeses, their jars of pickle, their pots of honey,
their caps, their mantles, their necklaces, and all
that a man wants to be healthy and wealthy.   And
you, from all the empire that you have won by toils
on land and toils on sea, you don't get a head of
garlic to flavour your boiled sprats with."

Phil. "Quite true; I had to send to the green-
grocer's yesterday for three heads.   But you take
a long time in proving that I am a slave."

Bdel. "Isn't it slavery when the men in power —
yes, and their toadies, too — get at the money, and
you are content with your miserable sixpence, —
money that you have earned yourselves on ship-
board, in battles, and in sieges?   Doesn't some
young fop come and bid you attend at the court
betimes?   Don't you lose your sixpence if you are
late, while he comes whenever he may choose and

pockets his shilling? And then if there's a bite going, do you get it? Not you; it goes to him and his partner. They work it between them, like two men at a saw, one pulling and one giving way."

Phil. "Is that what they do? This is terrible hearing."

Bdel. "Think how rich you might be, if it wasn't for these demagogues, — you, the master of I know not how many cities from the Black Sea to Sardinia, — and they dole you out this miserable pittance, just as if they were dropping oil from wool. The fact is, that they want you to be poor, and I'll tell you why. You must know your feeder's hand; and then if he sets you on any one that he wants to bring down, you fly at the wretch like a wild beast. Now listen to me. There are a thousand cities that are subject to us and pay us tribute. Allot twenty Athenian citizens to each to feed. Then you have twenty thousand citizens living like princes on hare and cream and all good things, with garlands on their heads, just as the men deserve to live who won the great fight at Marathon."

Coll. "Well, that was a wise man who said, ' Don't decide till you have heard both sides.' Bdelycleon, you have gained the day.

"And you, my old friend, you had better give in,
And be stubborn no more. If my own kith and kin
Would befriend me like this, oh, how thankful I'd be !
Some god, it is plain, sends this fortune to thee."

Bdel. "I'll give him, I'll solemnly vow and engage,
Whatever is good for a man of his age;
His pitcher shall ever of porridge be full,
And I'll wrap round his limbs a warm mantle of wool.
Why stands he so silent?"
    Coll.   "He is thinking how long,
Though you counselled him right, he has stuck to the wrong.
He'll be wiser hereafter."
    Phil.   "Woe is me! woe is me!"
    Bdel. "Why, what is the matter?"
    Phil.   .   "It is easy to see
All the things you have promised I scorn and despise.
It is there I would be, where the court-usher cries,
'If any one still has to vote, let him rise.'"

Bdelycleon besought his father to yield. The old
man would comply in everything but one. Death
would be better than not sitting as a juryman.

Bdel. "Well, if you are so bent on this, why not
stop here and judge your own household?"

Phil. "Judge my own household? What nonsense!"

Bdel. "Not at all. The porteress, for instance,
opens the door on the sly. You fine her a shilling.
Just what you did there. If the day is fine, you will
hold your court in the sun; if it snows, you will sit
by the fire. And the best of it will be that if you
choose to sleep till noon, no one will shut the door in
your face."

Phil. "An excellent idea."

Bdel. "Then again, however long-winded counsel

may be, you need not sit hungry, worrying yourself
and the prisoner as well."

Phil. " But do you think that I shall really be able
to judge and digest at the same time ? "

Bdel. " Why not ? You will do your judging all
the better. Don't they say when there is a good
deal of hard swearing in a case that the judge could
scarcely digest it ? "

Phil. " I can't resist you. But tell me true ; who
will give me my pay ? "

Bdel. " I will."

Phil. " Good ! then I shall always get my fee.
That joker played me a pretty trick the other day.
We had a drachma between us. He changed it in
the fish-market, and put down three fish scales for
my share. I popped them in my mouth, thinking
they were coins. Oh, the vile smell as I spat them
out ! "

Bdel. " You see, then, how much better you will
fare in this way."

Phil. " Yes, yes ; something considerable. But
make haste and do it."

Bdel. " Wait a bit. I will go and get the things."

Phil. " See how the oracle comes true. It ran
thus, I remember : —

> " Behold ! the days shall come, when every son
> Of Athens, sitting in his house, shall judge
> Causes of men, and at his door shall build
> A little court of justice for himself."

· The son now returned, bringing with him a number of judicial properties, such as red boxes to hold the votes and the like, and he set a basin of gruel by the fire, for the old man to refresh himself with. Everything being ready, Philocleon said, "Call the first case; I have been waiting a long time." This demand puzzled the son not a little. Who was to be tried? Who in the household had committed a fault? Well, the Thracian maid had burnt the pitcher. While he was meditating whether he should not begin with her, Philocleon discovered to his horror that the judges were not railed off from the rest of the court. To go on without the rails was impossible; he would go and find some for himself. Bdelycleon was meditating on the force of habit, when one of the slaves cried out, "Confound the dog! Why do they keep such a brute as that?"

Bdel. "Why, what has happened?"

Slave. "Pincher has got to the safe and stolen a rich Sicilian cheese."

Bdel. "Has he? Then that shall be the first case for my father to try. You shall be prosecutor."

Slave. "Not I, thank you. The other cur says he will prosecute with pleasure."

At this point the old man returned with some railings from the pigsty, two bowls for voting-urns, and everything at last was complete. So important a business, however, could not be inaugurated without sacrifice and prayer. Philocleon called for frankincense, a pan of coals on which to burn it, and some sprigs of myrtle.

The colleagues sang : —

> "O Phœbus, who dwell'st in the Delphian shrine,
> We beseech thee to favour this righteous design."

Bdelycleon took up the chant : —

> "Great master, who dwellest in front of my gate,
> His sternness of temper now somewhat abate.
> Let him not be so prompt with accusers to side,
> But inclined more to pity the wretch that is tried."

Phil. "Who is the accused in this case?" (*Aside*) "He'll not get off very easily."

Bdel. "Listen to the indictment : Cur, of the town of Cydathon, accuses Pincher of Ænone of having embezzled a Sicilian cheese and eaten it all himself.[1] Proposed sentence, a dog-collar of fig-wood."[2]

Phil. "A collar indeed! To be hanged like a dog, if he is found guilty."

Bdel. "The prisoner Pincher is here, and pleads not guilty."

Phil. "A manifest villain! What a thievish look he has! And how he grins! thinking, I suppose, to take me in. Where is the accuser, Cur of Cydathon?"

---

[1] There is probably an allusion to some proceedings which had taken place at Athens six years before. "Cur" represents the Greek *kuōn*, which is not unlike "Cleon." "Pincher" is a rendering of the Greek *labēs*, which by the change of a single letter becomes "Laches." Cleon had indicted Laches, in 426 B.C., for peculation committed when he was in command of an expedition sent by the Athenians to Sicily in 427 B.C.

[2] Meaning that he would have to be tied up.

Cur. " Bow, wow ! "

Bdel. " Silence in the court! Cur, go up into the box and state the charge."

Slave (as representing Cur, the prosecutor). " Gentlemen of this honourable court, you have heard the charge that I bring against the accused. I say that he played a most scandalous trick on me and my fellows. He ran off into a corner by himself, and gorged himself with the cheese."

Phil. " He is manifestly guilty. The rascal smells of cheese most vilely." [1]

Slave. " Yes; he devoured it, and would not give a morsel to me when I asked him. Mark this, he gave nothing to me, your favourite, Tear 'em."

Phil. " What! nothing to you? and nothing to me, either ! "

Bdel. " My dear father, for heaven's sake don't. decide the case before you have heard both sides ! "

Phil. " Why not, my boy? The thing is quite plain. It speaks for itself."

Slave. " Don't let him off. There never was such a keeping-all-to-himself dog. And, as you know, one bush is not big enough for two thieves." [2]

---

[1] Philocleon, it will be seen, manifests the most violent prejudice against the accused. This is doubtless a reflection on the want of a judicial temper among the citizen judges.

[2] An adaptation, it seems, of a proverb that " one bush never holds two robins." The pugnacious character of the robin redbreast and his intolerance of all intruders seem to have been known to the Greeks as they have been observed among us.

Phil. "Here is a string of charges. The creature is clearly a regular thief."

Bdel. (*to Pincher*)ₜ "Now, up with you, and make your defence! What! can't you speak?"

Phil. "Because he has got nothing to say for himself."

Bdel. "No, no, sir; I have seen it happen before in court." (*To the dog*) "Get down, and I'll plead your cause myself." (*To the court*) "It is not easy, gentlemen, to defend a dog that has got a bad name. Still, I will do my best. He is a good dog, and drives away wolves."

Phil. "A good dog indeed! I call him a thief and a traitor."

Bdel. "He is the best dog that we have got about the place. He is fit to take charge of any number of sheep."

Phil. "What is the good of that, if he steals cheeses and eats them?"

Bdel. "What good? He fights for you, he watches at your door; altogether, he is an excellent creature. And if he did steal a bit, well, you see that he has not been properly educated. But I have a witness."

The advocate now called a cheese-grater, which was directed to get into the box, and on examination testified that it had grated cheese for the accused, and that others had received a share. This disposed of the charge of having devoured the stolen property in solitude.[1] He then proceeded to say that Pincher was a hard-working animal, that lived on odds and ends, bones, gristle, anything, in short, that he could get, while Cur was a mere stay-at-home, always asking for a share of what was brought in, and biting if he did not get it. The next thing, following the regular course of proceeding, was to excite the compassion of the court. With this object, a litter of puppies was brought in, and made to whimper for mercy for their father.

Phil. " You can step down ; I am satisfied."

Bdel. " Step down I will ; though I don't quite trust you.   I have known many men taken in before this.[2]   Well, father, will he get off ? "

Phil. " 'Tis hard to say."

Bdel. " My dear father, I do beseech you to take the merciful side.   Here is the voting pebble.   Pray drop it in the ' Not guilty ' urn.   It is that far one, you know.   Shut your eyes while you are passing the other."

Phil. " No, no, my boy ; you see I have not been educated." [3]

Bdel. " Let me lead you, sir."

[1] This, of course, is a reference to the Sicilian affair. The paymaster of the expedition had been called, and had testified to the proper distribution of the funds.

[2] Meaning that accused persons were often deceived by an apparent softening in the demeanour of the judges.

[3] He retorts on his son the argument which had been used in defence of Pincher.

Phil. " Is this the ' Guilty ' urn ? "

Bdel. " Yes, sir."

Phil. " In she goes ! "

The fact was, that Bdelycleon, seeing that his father was resolved to condemn, deceived him, and pointed out the " Not guilty " as the " Guilty " urn. " I have taken him in," he said, as the vote was dropped in. "And now, sir," he went on, addressing his father, " I will count the votes." [1]

~~Phil. Bdel.~~ " How has it gone ? "

~~Bdel. Phil.~~ " Pincher is acquitted."

The old man was so overpowered by this unexpected result that he almost fainted, and had to ask for water. " Is he indeed acquitted ? " he inquired; and when assured that it was so, he broke out into a doleful strain : —

> " How shall I bear this load upon my conscience ?
> A man acquitted ! What dread penalty
> Awaits us in the future? O great gods !
> I ask your pardon ; for against my will,
> Nor in my own true mood, I did the deed."
>
> *Bdel.* " Take it not ill. My father, from henceforth
> I'll tend thee well, taking thee everywhere
> To feast, to banquet, to the public show;
> The years to be in pleasure thou shalt spend,
> And no one cheat thee. Let us go."
>
> *Phil.*   " I go ;
> After to-day my occupation's gone."

[1] The pretence that a numerous court of judges were present is kept up. Philocleon professes himself unable to say which way the voting would go.

And now it was proved that it is not always a good thing to change a man's habit of life, even though it may be a bad one ; for it is quite possible that he may turn to something worse. Philocleon went to the feast. At first it was not easy to make him enjoy himself. He did not know how to behave himself among gay company; his very attitude was ungainly; he could think of nothing to talk about but old experiences in the law-courts. But he learnt his lesson with amazing rapidity. Before the banquet was half finished he was the noisiest of the company, jumping and frisking about like a donkey that has had a feed of corn, bantering the guests, telling stories that were not in the least to the point, and at last, when the party broke up, beating every one that he met on his way home. The slave Xanthias, who had come in for a sound thrashing, had just time to give warning at home of what had happened when the old man appeared. "Dear me," he said, "it is hard for a young fellow like me to be kept so strict! There's my son, the most cross-grained guardian that could be, always afraid that I shall turn out badly; but then, I am his only father, you see!" While he was speaking, the people whom he had maltreated on his way came flocking in. A girl that sold bread[1] complained that the

---

[1] These girls were as notorious in Athens for their command of bad language as fish-sellers among ourselves. Bacchus in *The Frogs* tells the two rivals (Æschylus and Euripides) that two great poets ought not to stand abusing each other as if they were a couple of bread-sellers.

old man had knocked at least a dozen loaves off her tray with his torch. Philocleon had nothing to say to her except it was to tell some of the pleasant stories which his son had said would suit gay society. " My good girl," he said, " what do you think Æsop once said to a dog that barked at him as he was going home from dinner ? " — " I don't want to know," said the girl. — " Well," he went on, " it was something like this : ' Don't make all that noise, but — buy some more flour.' "¹ — " And you insult me, too," she cried. " I'll bring you before the clerk of the market." — " No, but listen," he replied ; " I may be able to satisfy you. Simonides and Lasus² once had a trial of skill ; and Lasus said, ' I don't care.' And that's just what I say." Next came a man complaining of having his head broken. " I'll make it all right with him," said Philocleon. The man was pleased. He did not want, he said, to go to law if he could help it. " Well, then, listen : a girl at Sybaris broke a jug — " — " Oh ! " cried the man, " if that's the way you are going to make it right with me, I shall call my witnesses." — " That's just what the jug said," the old man went on ; " and the girl told it that it would show more sense if it

¹ The joke lies in the unexpected end of the story. What Æsop's advice to the dog may have been we do not know; what is given to the girl is that, if she had lost her loaves, she had better buy the materials for making some more instead of wasting her time in talking.

² Simonides and Lasus were contemporary poets, writers chiefly of lyric verse, and rivals. The date of the former is given as 556–467 B.C.

left off calling witnesses, and bought a rivet to mend itself with." — "Ah! you may laugh," said the aggrieved man; " but it will be a different thing when the magistrate calls on the case." The son now lost all patience, and forcibly carried his father into the house, already probably wishing that he had been content to leave him in the enjoyment of his old occupation.

V.

THE CLOUDS.

It is difficult to write anything about this play without going into matters more serious than would be becoming in such a volume as this. Something, however, may be said, by way of explanation, of the object which the poet had in view. He was a strong conservative, as in politics, so in education. And a new school of teachers, to whom the name of sophists had been given, had in his time come into vogue at Athens. These men, of whom Protagoras of Abdera and Gorgias of Leontium were perhaps the most famous, were not at all to the liking of Aristophanes. He clung to the old faith (though this adherence did not prevent him from being on occasion exceedingly profane), while the sophists explained it away. He held with the old notions of right and wrong, and they, as Mr. Merry expresses it, "did not profess to believe in an absolute standard of morality, or in any positive truth." Their aim in teaching was to be practically useful, to make their pupils fit for life, especially public life. But success in public life largely depended on power in speaking. "Rhetoricians" was the name for Athenian politicians. Hence the sophists gave especial attention to the art of speaking. So far as they believed that there was no absolute right or wrong, so far they would teach their pupils to use the rhetorical art which they learnt without regard to these considerations. To judge from the account given of his teaching by Plato, Socrates did not approve of the sophists. Again and again he is represented as confuting them. Yet it was not unnatural that Aristophanes should confound him with them, or even pick him out for attack as their representative. In truth, however, he was nothing of the kind. These sophists were mainly foreigners; Socrates was an Athenian. They lectured in private, receiving only those who were willing and able to pay the high fees which they demanded; Socrates taught in the public streets and squares any one who chose to listen to him.

The attack could have had only a remote influence in bringing about the condemnation of the great philosopher by his countrymen.

This took place in 399 B.C., whereas the play was acted in 423. Still it helped in producing the great prejudice which undoubtedly existed and which resulted in his being put to death. To this fact Socrates is represented as referring in the defence or apology which Plato puts into his mouth. He says: —

"I have had many to accuse me to you. This they have done for many years, saying things about me, not one of which was true. And of these enemies I am more afraid than I am of Anytus and his fellow-accusers, though these, too, are formidable. But, gentlemen, these old enemies are more formidable. These have represented to you in your childhood a false story, how that there is a certain Socrates, or wise man, who speculates on things above the earth, and searches into things under the earth, and makes the worse appear the better reason. It is they, men of Athens, who by spreading about this report of me, have been my really dangerous accusers; for those who listen to them hold that they who busy themselves with such speculations do not even believe in the gods."

And a little later he says: "You yourselves have seen this in Aristophanes's comedy, in which a certain Socrates is introduced, saying that he 'walks in air,' and talking much other nonsense on subjects on which I do not profess to know much or little."

However much Aristophanes was mistaken in his estimate of Socrates's character and teaching, it was the estimate commonly held. Indeed, there is no reason to suppose that the story sometimes told of the Athenians having repented of their condemnation of their great countryman, is true.

STREPSIADES, once a wealthy Athenian land-owner, but now reduced by losses that followed the war and by his son's extravagance to great distress, was meditating sadly on his troubles as he lay awake in the early morning. "Will it never be light?" he said to himself; "and yet I'm sure I heard the cock crow a long time ago. All the slaves are snoring, and one can't thrash them now, thanks to that detestable war. And there's my son there; nothing

disturbs him. I can't sleep a wink for thinking
of my debts. What with his foppery, and his horse-
racing, and the rest of it, he ruins me." After
another vain effort to get a little more sleep, the old
gentleman gave it up, and, calling for a light, began
to make a doleful calculation of his debts. "Fifty
pounds to Prasias," he read over to himself. "When
did I borrow fifty pounds of Prasias? Oh! I remember. It was to buy that Corinthian hack. 'Hack,'
indeed. I wish that I had had my eye hacked out
before I saw him." At this point the son, Pheidippides, cried out in his sleep, "It's not fair, Philo;
keep to your own course." — "Ah!" said the old man,
"that is my ruin, always racing, even in his dreams."

Pheidippides (still asleep). "How many rounds do
the chariots run?"

Strepsiades. "You are running your father a pretty
round. But let me see. What was next to Prasias's
account? Ten pounds to Ameinias for a pair of
wheels and a body."

Phei. (still asleep). "Give the colt a roll on the
sand, and then take him home."

Strep. "Ah! you dog, you have rolled me out of
house and home."

Phei. (awaking). "Ah! my dear father, what makes
you so uncomfortable that you toss about all night?"

Strep. "I am being bitten, my dear boy, badly
bitten, by bailiffs."

Phei. "Well, do let me go to sleep."

PHEIDIPPIDES.

Strep. "Sleep away; but all this will fall on your own head some day. Now a plague on the matchmaker, I say, who made it up between your mother and me. I was living the jolliest life possible in the country, with my bee-hives, and my flocks, and my wine-vats. Then I married a niece of Megacles, son of Megacles, I a farmer, and she a fine city lady. Then our son was born, and my lady and I had some words about his name. She must have something horsey, of course, — Xanthippus, Charippus, or Callippides.[1] I was for Pheidonides, my own grandfather's name.[2] At last we compromised it, and he was called Pheidippides.[3] Then when he grew a big boy she would say, 'When you are a man, my dear, you shall drive a chariot to the citadel, as Megacles did, and wear a fine cloak';[4] and I used to say, 'When you're a man you shall drive the goats home with a leather jerkin on, as your father did.' But he did not heed me in the least, and he has brought on my estate a gallopping consumption, as I may call it. However, I have thought of an excellent way out of my difficulties, if I can persuade him to

[1] All names with "hippo," signifying "horse," in them.

[2] Here one of the component parts of the name is Pheido, "frugality."

[3] A name in which both characteristic words appear. The name, it may be mentioned, was borne by the famous Athenian runner, who hurried to Sparta from Athens in the course of twenty-four hours, to tell the news of the landing of the Persians at Marathon.

[4] This he would do after winning a prize at the Pan-Athenaic festival.

take it.   Now, how shall I wake him?   Pheidy, my boy!"

Phei. "What is it, father?"

Strep. "Kiss me, and give me your hand."

Phei. "Yes, yes; certainly."

Strep. "Now, do you love me?"

Phei. "By the god of horses, yes."

Strep. "None of that, none of that; the god of horses is the cause of all my trouble.   But if you love me, my son, do what I shall ask you."

Phei. "But what is it?"

Strep. "You'll do it, then?"

Phei. "By Bacchus, yes."

Strep. "Do you see that door over there?"

Phei. "Yes; what of it?"

Strep. "That is the Reflectory of wise souls. There live the men who can prove that the heaven is a fire-cover, and we are the sparks.   Give them money, and they'll teach you to prove anything you want, be it right or wrong."

Phei. "Well, who are they?"

Strep. "I don't rightly know what they call them. But they are very clever fellows."

Phei. "Oh! I know — the rascals!   You mean those pale, slipshod fellows, that wretched Socrates, and Chærephon, and their lot."

Strep. "Hush! don't say anything foolish.   If you love your father, cut your horse-racing and take up with them."

Phei. " I take up with them ! No, not for Leago-ras's thoroughbreds."

Strep. " My dear son, I do entreat you to go and learn of them."

Phei. " What am I to learn ? "

Strep. " They say that these people keep two arguments, whatever they may be,— the Better and the Worse ; and that anybody who uses the Worse gets the upper hand, even when he has a bad case. You go and learn this, and then I sha'n't have to pay a shilling to any one of the debts which I have run up on your account."

Phei. " I could not think of it. You don't sup-pose I could meet the gentlemen who are on the Turf without a scrap of colour on my face ! "

Strep. " Well, if you won't, not another mouthful shall you have from me, you or your shaft-horse, or your leader. Out you go, bag and baggage."

Phei. " As you please. My great-uncle Megacles, I am sure, won't let me want for a horse."

The old man, however, was not going to be beaten by this refusal. If his son wouldn't learn, he would learn himself, though he doubted whether he was clever enough to acquire these subtleties. However, he took his courage in his hands, and knocked at the door of the Reflectory. The knock was answered by a disciple, who rebuked the visitor for the unman-nerly loudness of his kick. " You made," he said, " such a fine thing of mine to miscarry."

Strep. "Pardon me; I live a long way off in the country. Tell me, pray, what it was that I injured."

Disciple. "But these things are told only to disciples."

Strep. "Never mind; I am come to be a disciple."

Dis. "Very well; but remember these things are secret. The other day Socrates asked Chærephon how many of its own feet a flea could jump. One had been biting Chærephon's eyebrow, you must understand, and jumped on to Socrates's head."

Strep. "How did he measure it?"

Dis. "In the cleverest way possible. He melted some wax; then he took the flea and dipped its feet into the wax. When this was cold, the flea had slippers on; these he undid, and measured the distance."

Strep. "What a clever thing!"

Dis. "I can tell you something else. Yesterday evening we had nothing for dinner. So Socrates sprinkled a thin coat of ashes on the carving-board,[1] bent a spit, and making it into a compass, stole a piece of meat from the sacrifice."

Strep. "Wonderful! and we talk about Thales! Let me into the Reflectory. Show me Socrates, for I am bent on becoming a disciple."

Accordingly the door was thrown open.

"Good heavens!" cried the visitor, as soon as he was admitted, seeing the disciples scattered about

---

[1] This would be the carving-board of the altar of Hermes, which stood in the Gymnasium.

in various attitudes, "what kind of creatures are these? What are they looking on the ground for?"

Dis. "They are investigating things that are under the earth."

Strep. "Looking for truffles, eh? No use here; but I can tell them where they can find some very fine ones. And these who are bent double there — what are they doing?"

Dis. "In sub-Tartarean realms of night · they grope."

Strep. "And why is their other end turned up in that fashion?"

Dis. "It is learning astronomy on its own account."

Strep. "Stay a moment; what is this?"

Dis. "That is Geometry."

Strep. "What do you use it for?"

Dis. "Measuring the countries."

Strep. "I see, the countries where we have allotments."

Dis. "No, no; the countries generally, the whole earth."

Strep. "Splendid! What a patriotic notion! Dividing the whole earth among us Athenians."

Dis. "Look here; this is a map of the earth. Here is Athens."

Strep. "That Athens? I don't believe it. I don't see the courts sitting anywhere."

Dis. "Ah, but it is! And that's Eubœa stretching along there."

Strep. "Yes ; we stretched it, we did, Pericles and the rest of us.[1] But where's Sparta ? "

Dis. "There."

Strep. "Oh! but how near! See if you can't contrive to put it further off."

Dis. "Quite impossible."

Strep. "So much the worse for you. But who is the man in the basket there ? "

Dis. "That is He."

Strep. "What he ? "

Dis. "SOCRATES."

After two or three fruitless attempts, Strepsiades succeeded in attracting the great man's attention. "What want you, creature of a day?" he asked.

> " I walk in air, and fix a lofty thought
> Down on the sun."

Strep. "Oh, you look down on the gods from a basket, do you ? "

Socrates. " I never could have found out aerial things had I not detached my thoughts, bringing

---

[1] The original has a pun which can be given only imperfectly. The disciple speaks of the position of Eubœa stretching along the coast; Strepsiades takes the word in the sense of "straining," "stretching," and so "torturing." Pericles commanded the expedition which conquered Eubœa in 440 B.C. Thirty thousand allotments of the conquered country were distributed on the occasion among Athenian citizens.

them into the kindred air. Had I stayed on earth it would have been impossible, for the earth forcibly draws to itself the moisture of the intellect. Just the same thing happens to cress."

Strep. "What is it? Intellect attracts moisture to cress; is that it? But descend a while, and teach me that which I came here to learn."

Soc. "What is that?"

Strep. "I want to learn to speak. I am being cheated and plundered by the cruelest set of creditors."

Soc. "But how did you get into debt without knowing it?"

Strep. "A plague of horses has eaten me up. Now I want you to teach me one of the two arguments you keep; the not-paying-your-creditors argument, I mean. Teach me, and I will swear by the gods to pay you your fee."

Soc. "What gods? Gods don't pass current here."

Strep. "What does pass, then? Pieces of iron, such as they have at Byzantium?"

Soc. "Do you want to know the truth about gods and such things?"

Strep. "Yes, by Zeus!—if there is a Zeus."

Soc. "And make acquaintance with the clouds? They are what we worship, you understand."

Strep. "By all means."

Socrates then descended from his basket, seated the old man on a pallet-bed, put a chaplet on his

head, and sprinkled him with flour, — proceedings
which somewhat dismayed him, as they suggested
the idea that he was going to be sacrificed.[1]   But he
was assured that all who desired to become disciples
had to do it, and that, once initiated, he would learn
the art of clever speech, would become, in fact, the
flower (flour) of advocates.   " Well, that's true in
a way," said Strepsiades ; " there's a good deal of
flour about me now."   Socrates then proceeded to
invoke the clouds, while the new disciple folded his
cloak over him, lest, as he said, he should be
drenched.

" O ye Clouds, honoured much of the wise, your forms to this
     mortal disclose!
   Come, come from the height of Olympus, god-haunted and
     covered with snows,
   Or where in the garden of ocean the dance of the nymphs
     ye behold,
   Or where from the fountains of Nilus ye draw in your
     pitchers of gold;
   Or come from the lake of Mæotis, or snow-covered moun-
     tains of Thrace,
   Come, hark to our prayers, and our worship accept, of your
     bountiful grace."

Presently an answering voice was heard, accompanied by the noise of rolling thunder that seemed
to come nearer and nearer : —

[1] A victim was crowned with a garland and had meal sprinkled on
its head.

" Bringers of rain, a maiden band,
   We seek Athené's gracious land,
   The fair heaven-favoured dwelling-place
   Of ancient Cecrops' noble race,
   Where in their awful mansion dwell
   The mysteries inscrutable ;
   Nor miss the gods on high their right
   Of honour due, the pillared height
   Of stately fane, and shapely grace
   Of sculptured form, the solemn pace
   Of pomps that move through gazing streets,
   The festive flower-crowned throng that meets
   At feast or ritual, while the years
   Pass through the seasons' ordered way,
   And when the gladsome Spring appears,
   Our joyous Bacchic holiday,
   The while the dancers' twinkling feet
   Time to the flute's clear music beat."

Strep. " Tell me, Socrates, who are these that sing this very solemn strain ?   Are they heroines ? "

Soc. " Not at all ; they are the Clouds of heaven. It is they who give us wise maxims, and logic, and circumlocution, and cheating."

Strep. " Yes ; and when I hear them my soul is all agog for all kinds of subtleties and chatterings. But I should like to see them plainly, if it is possible."

Soc. " Look towards Mount Parnes, then ; I see them plainly coming down from it."

Strep. " Where ? where ? "

Soc. " There, down through the glens and thickets."

Strep. " I can't see them."

Soc. " Surely you must see them now, unless you are as blind as a bat."

Strep. " Now I do; indeed, they are everywhere."

Soc. " And didn't you know that they were goddesses ? "

Strep. " Not I; I thought that they were dew and mist. But tell me, if they are clouds, why they are like women. For the real clouds are not."

Soc. " What are they, then ? "

Strep. " Why, they are like fleeces floating about, but not in the least like women. Those clouds there have noses." [1]

Soc. " Now answer me a few questions. Have you ever looked up into the sky and seen a cloud that was like a centaur, or a panther, or a wolf, or a bull ? "

Strep. " Often; what then ? "

Soc. " They become whatever they like. When they see a minor poet with his hair all long about his shoulders, they mock at his folly, and make themselves into centaurs."

Strep. " What do they do when they see Simon, who stole the public money ? "

Soc. " They become wolves, to be sure."

Strep. " And so, when they see Cleonymus the coward, they turn into deer, I suppose."

The Clouds now greeted the sage who had invoked their presence : —

[1] Probably the masks had noses of comic size.

" High priest of all trumpery nonsense, we greet thee, old hunter
of words that are clever and fine!
Now tell us the thing about which you have called us; to no
voice do we listen so soon as to thine;
So solemn your gait, and so fierce are your glances, as we look
at you strutting along in the ways
Barefooted and wretched, while up to the heavens a look of
majestical greatness you raise."

Soc. " You see, my friend, that these are the only
divinities. All the others are mere moonshine."

Strep. " Stop! isn't Olympian Zeus a divinity,
then ?"

Soc. " What Zeus ? Don't talk nonsense. There
is no Zeus."

Strep. " What ? Who is it that rains, then?"

Soc. " Why, these, of course. Did you ever see it
rain without clouds? Zeus ought to rain from a clear
sky, if he did it."

Strep. " Well, but who is it that thunders?"

Soc. " These; they thunder as they roll along.
They are laden with water, and come crashing together, and so make a great noise."

Strep. " But who makes them move ? It must be
Zeus."

Soc. " No; it isn't Zeus: it is Whirl."

Strep. " So Whirl is king instead of Zeus. Well,
I didn't know it. But tell me about the lightning.
Doesn't Zeus strike perjurers with it?"

Soc. " Well, you are an antiquated old fool. If
Zeus strikes the perjurers, why doesn't he strike Si-

mon, and Cleonymus, and Theorus? Why does he strike his own temples, and the cliffs of Sunium,[1] and the oaks? The oaks don't perjure themselves."

Strep. "There is something in what you say." The Clouds now addressed Strepsiades: —

> "As you come our most excellent wisdom to seek,
> There is not an Athenian, no, nor a Greek,
> Shall be happy as you, if you only remember,
> And think, and endure in your soul, and disdain
> To feel heat in the summer, or cold in December,
> Or weariness walking or standing, or pain
> Of hunger, when others are wishing to dine,
> And care nothing at all for amusement or wine,
> But claim to be first all our speakers among
> In business and counsel and fence of the tongue."

Strep. "Well, you'll find me as hard as an anvil."

Soc. "And you won't believe in any gods besides ours — Clouds, Chaos, and Tongue — these three?"

Strep. "I won't even speak to the rest, if I should meet them."

The Clouds. "Tell us plainly what you want."

Strep. "I want to be miles away the cleverest speaker in Greece."

Clouds. "So you shall; no man shall carry more resolutions in the Assembly than you."

Strep. "I don't care about resolutions in the Assembly; I want to slip through my creditors' hands."

---

[1] The promontory at the southeastern corner of Attica.

Clouds. "Oh, that's a very little matter. Hand your accounts to our attendants, and fear nothing."

Strep. "I will trust you to the uttermost. What with my debts and my extravagant wife, I have no other choice. Hunger, thirst, cold, torture, anything that you please, so long as you make me a real clever speaker."

Clouds. "The man has a bold temper. Well, if you learn all this from me, you will be the most fortunate of men. You will have clients always sitting at your door to get your advice in heavy cases. And now, Socrates, take him and teach him."

Soc. "Well, my friend, have you got a good memory?"

Strep. "A very long memory when money is owing to me; a very short one, when I owe it myself."

Soc. "How will you be able to learn?"

Strep. "Well enough; don't be afraid."

Soc. "Can you speak?"

Strep. "I can't speak, but I can cheat."

Soc. "If I let drop a bit of the higher wisdom, you must snatch it up at once."

Strep. "What? Grab wisdom like a dog?"

Soc. "This is a very ignorant, barbarous creature. Old man, I am afraid you'll want a good beating. Come, take off your coat."

Strep. "Why, what have I done wrong?"

Soc. "Nothing; but it is our custom to come in without our coats."

Strep. "Well, give me a honey-cake. I feel as if I was going down into the cave of Trophonius."

After a while Socrates came out again, loudly complaining of the ignorance, stupidity, and forgetfulness of his new pupil. He had no sooner learnt a little subtlety than he forgot it. However, he was willing to try once more. Accordingly he proceeded to instruct him in various questions of prosody and grammar. All, however, was to no purpose. The old man remained hopelessly dense. As a last resource the teacher ordered him to lie down on a couch with which he had been provided, wrap himself closely up, and proceed to think. "If you get anywhere," he said, "whence you can't get out, then lightly leap to some other notion of the soul."

Strep. "Oh! oh!"

Clouds. "What is the matter?"

Strep. "Oh, the fleas are coming out of the mattress and biting me."

Clouds. "Don't trouble."

Strep. "How can I help it? My money is gone, and my skin is gone, and my life is gone, yes, and my shoes, too."

Soc. "Are you not thinking?"

Strep. "Yes; indeed I am."

Soc. "What about?"

Strep. "Whether the fleas will leave anything of me."

Soc. "Don't be a coward; wrap yourself up and think."

Strep. (*after a pause*). "My dear Socrates, I have a device for escaping interest."

Soc. "Explain it."

Strep. "I should buy a witch from Thessaly; she would bring down the moon out of the sky for me. I should shut it up in a round crest case, and keep it."

Soc. "How would that help you?"

Strep. "How? Why, if the moon was never to rise, of course I should not pay interest."

Soc. "Why not?"

Strep. "Because it is due at the new moon."

Soc. "Very good; but answer me this: An action is brought against you for five talents; how would it get rid of it?"

Strep. "How? how? I don't know, but I will consider."

Soc. "Don't keep your mind always going round and round yourself. Let it fly about like a cock-chafer tied by a string."

Strep. "I have found the very cleverest way of getting rid of a suit. You have seen at the druggist's that pretty transparent stone with which they light fires?"

Soc. "A burning glass, I suppose you mean."

Strep. "Just so. Well, might not I take this, and while the registrar was writing down the case, turn the sun on to it, and melt the wax?"

Soc. "By the Graces! a clever thought."

Strep. " I should really like having a suit for five talents brought against me."

Soc. " Now, turn your mind to this : You are defendant in a case, you are going to be cast, you have no witnesses, — how would you get out of it ? "

Strep. " In the easiest way in the world."

Soc. "Tell me."

Strep. "Why, when the last case was on, before mine was called, I should go and hang myself."

Soc. "You are a fool. I will have nothing more to do with you. There never was an old man so stupid and so forgetful. Away with you ! "

Strep. " Dear me ! What shall I do ? Dear, worshipful Clouds, advise me ! "

Clouds. " If you have a grown-up son, we recommend you to send him to learn in your place."

Strep. " Well, I have a son, but he won't learn."

Clouds. " And you allow him ? "

Strep. " You see, he is a sturdy fellow, and his mother is a fine lady. However, I'll go after him, and if he still refuses I'll turn him out of my house."

Pheidippides was not easy to persuade. " Father, what is it ? " he said. " By Zeus ! you are out of your senses."

Strep. " There you are with your Zeus — how silly ! "

Phci. " What is there to laugh at ? "

Strep. " Your talking about Zeus ; there is no Zeus."

Phei. " Who told you this nonsense ? "

Strep. " Socrates."

Phei. " And you believe these lunatics ? "

Strep. " Hush ! say nothing against these clever, sensible men. They are so economical that they never shave themselves or go to the bath. As for you, you wash away my property, just as if I were dead. But do go and learn what they have to teach you."

Phei. "Very clever, indeed ; and that is the reason, perhaps, why you have lost your cloak."

Strep. " I haven't lost it; I thought it away."

Phei. " And your shoes — what of them ? "

Strep. " Lost them, like Pericles, for a necessary purpose.[1] But go, I beseech you."

Phei. "Yes, I'll go ; but you'll be sorry for it some day."

The two Arguments, the Just and the Unjust, now appeared, and immediately engaged in a battle royal over the new pupil. " I'll be too much for you," cried the Just Argument. " How ? " replied the Unjust.

Just. " By saying what is right."

Unjust. " There is no such thing as right."

[1] Pericles, in 445 B.C., entered in the accounts which he rendered to the people of public moneys spent, " ten talents for a necessary purpose." This item passed without question. The money had been given, it was said, to Pleistoanax, king of Sparta, and Cleandridas, his " chief of the staff," to induce them to evacuate the Athenian territory which had been invaded by a Spartan army.

Just. "You say that there is no such thing?"
Unjust. "Where is it?"
Just. "With the gods."
Unjust. "Why, then, did Zeus put his father in prison?"
Just. "This gets worse and worse; it makes me sick."
Unjust. "What an ignorant fellow!"
Just. "You're a shameless beast."
Unjust. "Your lips drop roses."
Just. "You are a ribald jester."
Unjust. "This is praise!"
Clouds. "Well, make an end of this quarrelling. Plead each of you his cause. You, Just Argument, tell us what you used to teach the last generation. You, Unjust, explain to us the new education. This young man shall choose between you. Now, you shall speak first."
Unjust. "He may, if he chooses. I'll make short work with him when he has done."
Just. "Listen to me, when I tell you what the old-fashioned education was. Then a boy was never allowed to say so much as a word. He walked in an orderly fashion to his music-master's, without a cloak, mark you, though the snow might be as thick as meal. And the music was of the good old sort, none of your modern twists and twirls. Let a lad try one of those, and he would be well thrashed for his pains. And woe betide him if at table he took

a radish or a sprig of parsley before his elders, or showed a taste for dainty dishes."

Unjust. "What old-fashioned nonsense!"

Just. "Ah, but that is the way I bred the men who conquered at Marathon! Choose me, my young friend, and you will learn to be ashamed of what is base, and to blush if they banter you, and to rise up from your seat when your elders come in, and to mould yourself after the model of honour, keeping yourself from bad companions, and never contradicting your father, or making game of the nest in which you were hatched."

Unjust. "Yes; and they'll say that you're tied to your mother's apron-strings."

> *Just.* "In the ring of the wrestlers all blooming and strong
> You will stand, nor chatter away to the throng
> That meets in the market your far-fetched conceits;
> To the Academeia[1] you'll often repair,
> And you'll run in the shade of the olive-trees there,
> With a chaplet of reed on your head, while a friend
> As honest as you on your steps shall attend;
> In the joy of a leisure unblamed, in the time
> Of the spring, when the plane whispers soft to the lime.

Yes, young man, if you want a chest well filled out, broad shoulders, a clear complexion, and a short tongue, come to me. Go to my adversary, and follow in the ways that are fashionable now, and your

---

[1] The grove of Academus, in the outskirts of Athens, where there was a gymnasium, afterwards celebrated as the place where Plato and his successors taught.

complexion will be pale, your shoulders narrow, your chest thin, and your tongue long. Good will be evil to you, and evil good."

The Unjust Argument now opened his case, proceeding by cross-examination. "You say," he said to his adversary, "that the hot bath is not a good thing. What is your reason for finding fault with it?"

Just. "Because it is a very bad thing, and turns a man into a coward."

Unjust. "Hold! now I have you. Tell me, which of the sons of Zeus was the bravest and performed most valiant deeds?"

Just. "No one was superior to Hercules."

Unjust. "Well, did you ever see a cold bath called after Hercules?[1] And yet who was braver than he?"

Just. "Ah! this is the sort of argument which our young men chatter all day, and which make the bath-houses full and the gymnasia empty."

Unjust. "Then again you speak against the Assembly, but I speak well of it. If it had been a bad thing, Homer would never have made Nestor a great speaker in the Assembly. Then about the tongue. You say that young men ought not to cultivate it; I say that they ought. You say that they ought to be temperate; I say that they ought not. Tell me

---

[1] The hot baths at Thermopylæ (Hot-Gate) were called after Hercules.

now, when did you ever hear of a man getting good
by temperance?"

Just. "Many. Peleus got a sword by it."

Unjust. "A sword indeed! and a nice thing it was
to him! And how many talents did Hyperbolus the
lamp-maker make by his villany? Plenty, to be sure,
but certainly not a sword."

Just. "Then Peleus married the goddess Thetis."

Unjust. "Who left him. No, no; this is the way
to lose all the pleasures of life; and without them is
life worth living?"

Just. "But how about the disgrace that will fall
upon you, if you follow these profligate ways?"

Unjust. "Nothing at all. Tell me, who are the
great advocates?"

Just. "The profligate."

Unjust. "And the successful tragedians?"

Just. "The profligate."

Unjust. "And the political leaders?"

Just. "The profligate."

Unjust. "Well, what have you got to say?"

Just. "Nothing, but that I am beaten, and that
I come over to your side."

After this, of course, Strepsiades could do nothing
but hand over his son to Socrates to be instructed
by him, receiving the assurance that he would be
returned to him an accomplished rhetorician, always
able to make the worse appear the better reason.

Meanwhile the time grew near when these powers

would be wanted. "Four days," he said to himself,
"and then comes that day which I hate to think of.
All my creditors swear that they will give me no
mercy. I make the most reasonable propositions to
them. I say, 'Would you mind postponing part of
the debt, and cancelling part, and not receiving the
rest?' and they won't listen to me. However, it will
be all right if Pheidippides has learnt his lesson
properly. I must go over to the Reflectory and see
how he has got on." This he did, and had the
pleasure of having his son handed over to him,
changed into a pale-faced, cunning-looking fellow,
who gave promise of being exactly what he wanted.
He at once appealed to him for his help, explaining
that he was terribly afraid of the last day of the
month, when his creditors had declared that they
would sue him for the money which he owed to
them. Pheidippides explained to him that his fears
were groundless. He had a device which would
upset the creditors' calculations. These gentlemen
did not understand that this last day had been pur-
posely called the "old and the new "[1] by Solon, and
so made into two days, in order to give debtors a
loophole of escape. Relying on this new interpreta-
tion the old man received the threatenings of trades-
men, who called with requests for payment, with the

---

[1] The Athenian month was divided into three decades, and the last
day of the third was called " the old and the new " as belonging partly
to the month that was ending, and partly to that which was beginning.

greatest coolness. One claimed fifty pounds for a
dappled horse. He was met first with the objection
about the day, then with the argument that it was
very unlikely that he, Strepsiades, notoriously hating
all that had to do with horses, should have incurred
such a debt, and then, when reminded that he had
sworn to pay at the proper time, with ridicule of the
gods whom he had named in his oath, and finally by
questions of grammar. It was quite preposterous,
he said, that a man who did not know the gender
of nouns should presume to ask for payment of a
debt.

Another was asked a problem in physics. "Is the
rain always new water, or does the sun draw up the
same over and over again?"—"I don't know and I
don't care," said the man.—"Then," replied Strepsiades, "you are not fit to have your money."—
"Well," the man went on, "if you are short of
money and cannot let me have the capital, pay me the
interest."—"Interest!" replied Strepsiades, "what
kind of monster is that? Tell me, does the sea
grow bigger, or always remain the same?"—"Remains the same, I suppose," said the man.—"Well,"
Strepsiades went on, "if the sea does not grow
bigger though all the rivers flow into it, how can you
expect your capital to grow bigger? Out of the
house with you!" This was all very well; but
Strepsiades found before long that there was another
side to the affair. He asked his son to sing a song

of Simonides. The young man refused; Æschylus did not please him any better: he was an empty, bombastic old creature. Pheidippides would repeat nothing but Euripides. The father strongly objected, and the affair ended by the young man giving the old one a sound thrashing. In vain did Strepsiades remonstrate. "Shameless creature," he cried, "don't you know that I attended to all your wants in your infancy, and see how you treat me now!"

Phei. "Once upon a time I gave all my thoughts to horses, and then I could not say three words without making some blunder. My father made me give up these ways, and turn my thoughts to clever, sophistical speeches. Thanks to him, I can prove quite convincingly that it is quite right for a son to beat his father."

Strep. "For heaven's sake, go on with your horse-racing! That isn't as bad as beating me."

Phei. "I shall return to the point at which you interrupted me. Answer me this question: Did you beat me when I was a child?"

Strep. "Certainly, for your good."

Phei. "And shouldn't I beat you for your good, as it seems that beating does a person good? Why, too, should you go scot-free and I not? I am free born just as you. You say that it is right that a child should be beaten. But an old man is a child twice over. And an old man deserves to be beaten far more than a child, as he has less excuse for doing wrong."

Strep. " But it is usual everywhere for children to be beaten."

Phei. " It was a man that made the law; and why should not I make a new one ? Thé old scores we will wipe out; but hereafter the law is, that the sons beat their fathers. Consider, too, the cock and other animals. They punish their fathers, and there is no difference between them and us, except that they don't propose bills in the Assembly."

Strep. " Well, if you are going to imitate the cock in all things, why don't you eat dung and sleep on a perch ? "

Phei. " The argument does not apply. Socrates would not say that it did."

Strep. " But some day you will repent of it, for your son will beat you."

Phei. " But if I have no son, what then ? "

Strep. " I am afraid you have me there."

Phei. " Well, listen again. I shall beat my mother just as I beat you."

Strep. " Why, that's worse than ever. You and your Unjust Argument and Socrates with you ought to be thrown into the pit. Clouds, do you hear what he says ? "

Clouds. " It serves you right. You led the lad into wicked ways."

Strep. " Yes, but you encouraged me, a poor, ignorant old man."

Clouds. " Because you were dishonest. That is

our way. We always do this to those whom we
know to be disposed to evil, that they may learn to
fear the gods.")

Strep. " Well, it is very bad, but it is just. But
come, my son, let us destroy these scoundrels who
have deceived both you and me."

Strepsiades accordingly, with the help of his slaves,
for his son refused to lend a hand, proceeded to attack the Reflectory. The slaves set a ladder against
the wall, mounted it, and plied a pick-axe on the roof.
The old man himself caught up a lighted torch and set
fire to the lower story. " What are you doing ?" cried
one disciple. — " Chopping logic with the beams,"
said the assailant. — " Who are you?" shouted another. — " The man whose cloak you stole." — " What
are you after ?" asked Socrates himself. — "I walk in
air, and contemplate the sun," was the answer. — " I
shall be suffocated," cried Socrates. — " I shall be
burnt alive," said Chærephon. But the Clouds appeared. " Strike, and spare not," they said; "you
have many good reasons, and the best is this, — that
they blasphemed the gods."

VI.

THE BIRDS.

This play was exhibited at the Great or City Festival of Bacchus in the year 414 B.C. The struggle in Sicily, which was to end so disastrously for Athens in the following year, was then going on; and it has been suggested that the poet's purpose was to warn his countrymen against wild and hare-brained expeditions and schemes of conquest. This suggestion is scarcely probable, for the expedition had hitherto had a fair measure of success, and was still greatly popular at Athens. The question, however, need not be here discussed; but it may be well to mention, for the benefit of readers not familiar with the history of the time, an important incident connected with it. Alcibiades had been one of the chief advocates of the expedition, and had been appointed one of the three generals in command, Nicias and Lamachus being his colleagues. On the eve of embarkation an extraordinary outrage was committed in the city. This was the simultaneous mutilation of all the pedestal statues of Hermes that stood in the streets and public places of Athens. Suspicion at once fell on Alcibiades and the riotous young aristocrats in whose society he lived. The fact that almost the only statue spared was one that stood near his house was thought to point to his guilt, though to us it suggests that the affair was the work of his enemies. Alcibiades begged that the matter should be inquired into at once. This he could not bring about; but he was permitted, even compelled, to accompany the expedition. Not long afterwards he was recalled to take his trial, and one of the state galleys was sent to fetch him. He obeyed the summons, but escaped on his way home, and took refuge at Sparta. There he exerted himself to do all the injury possible to his country.

Two citizens of Athens, of whom one had the name of Plausible, and the other of Hopeful, Plausible being the leader, set out from Athens in search

of some country where they might live at peace,
being free from the troubles of law-suits and debts.
Plausible had bought a raven and Hopeful a jackdaw, hoping that they might be useful to them as
guides. They had a notion of finding King Tereus,
who many years before had married an Athenian
princess, and had been changed into a hoopoe, or, as
some said, a hawk; and a bird-seller in the city had.
persuaded them that these creatures would help
them to do so. Tereus, if they could light upon
him, would tell them of some country or other that
he had seen in his migrations. After many wanderings, in which their guides, as far as they could
make out, did nothing but contradict each other and
bite their masters' fingers, they came to a great rock,
where their guides behaved in such a way as to
make them believe that they had reached their journey's end. Hopeful gave a kick to the rock, calling
out at the same time, "Hoopoe! Hoopoe!"

"Who wants the master?" said the porter, who
turned out to be a sandpiper. The visitors did not
by any means please him. "A couple of bird-catch-
ing villains," he said, when he had taken a look at
them. "You shall both be put to death." They
roundly denied that they were men. Hopeful
declared that he was a bird from Africa; Plausible
professed to come from the river Phasis.[1] With
some unwillingness the porter consented to call his

---

[1] The region from which we get the pheasant.

master who was having a sleep after his midday meal of myrtle-berries and winged ants.

Before long King Hoopoe appeared, a majestic creature with a triple crest, and inquired of the strangers what they wanted. They replied that they had come to consult him.

King Hoopoe. "Consult me? About what?"

Hopeful. "You were once a man, as we are; you owed money, as we do; you were glad to get off paying it, as we are; after this you were changed into a bird; you have flown over lands and seas, and have all the feelings both of a bird and of a man; we have come therefore to you, hoping that if you have seen in your journeyings any snug country where we might find a comfortable place to lie down in, you would tell us of it."

K. H. "Do you want a finer city than Athens?"

Hope. "Not a finer one certainly, but one that would suit us better."

K. H. "What kind of a place are you thinking of?"

Hope. "Why, a place where the most important business they do is of this kind. Your friend comes to your door the first thing in the morning and says, 'Mind you come, you and your children, dressed in your best, for I am to give a wedding feast.'"

K. H. "Well, I know of a place that might suit you near the Red Sea."

Hope. "No; that won't do. It must not be anywhere near the sea, or else I shall have the state galley coming after me some fine morning, with an order for my arrest.[1] But tell me, what kind of a life do you lead among the birds here? Of course you know all about it."

K. H. "Not a bad one, on the whole. You can get on without money."

Hope. "Then you get rid of a vast amount of trouble."

At this point Plausible broke in with an idea of his own. "I see a great future," he said, "for the race of birds, if you will only listen to me."

K. H. "Listen to you, — about what?"

Plausible. "Do you ask about what? First, you mustn't go gaping about everywhere with open bills. It is quite an undignified thing to do. Among us, when we see any one particularly apt to change, we say, 'He is a flighty, volatile creature.'"

K. H. "By Bacchus! you are right. Well, what do you advise?"

Plaus. "Found a city, I say, a city of birds."

K. H. "How could we birds possibly found a city?"

Plaus. "How can you ask? Nothing could be easier. Look down."

K. H. "I am looking down."

Plaus. "Now look up."

---

[1] There were two state galleys belonging to Athens. One of these, called the *Salaminia*, had been sent, some months before the performance of this play, to arrest Alcibiades.

K. H. "I am looking up."

Plaus. "Now turn your neck round."

K. H. "What good shall I get by ricking my neck?"

Plaus. "Did you see anything?"

K. H. "I saw the clouds and the sky."

Plaus. "Well, that is the 'pole' of the birds."

K. H. "'Pole of the birds'! What do you mean?"

Plaus. "I mean that the birds will there get a polity. Make a city of this, and men will be as much in your power as if they were so many locusts; and as for the gods, you will starve them out just as we starved the poor wretches in Melos."[1]

K. H. "How is that to be managed?"

Plaus. "Don't you see? The air is between the gods and the earth; so, just as we, when we want to send to Delphi, have to ask the Bœotians for a passage, the gods will have to come to you, and unless they pay you a proper tribute, you won't let the smell of the sacrifices go through your territory."

K. H. "Good! good! Earth and clouds! springs and nooses! I never heard a cleverer thing in my life. I am quite ready to help you found the city you talk of; that is, if the other birds agree."

Plaus. "But who is to explain the matter to them?"

---

[1] The island of Melos, in the Ægean Sea, was blockaded in 416–15 B.C. by the Athenians, and reduced to the greatest extremity of starvation. "Melian hunger" became a proverbial expression.

K. H. "You. They know Greek now; before I came among them they had only their own foreign lingo, but I have taught them the language."

Plaus. "And how can you collect them?"

K. H. "I will just step into the thicket here and call the nightingale. They'll come fast enough when they hear her voice."

The king then summoned his herald by a song: —

> "Come, gentle mate, from sleep awake;
> Begin again
> The sacred strain
> With which, O minstrel bird, you make
> For Itys lost complaint so sweet,
> That through the woodland to the feet
> Of Zeus above, the song ascends,
> Where golden-haired Apollo lends,
> Touching his ivory-pedalled lyre,
> Such answering music that the choir
> Of all the blessed gods who throng
> The courts of heaven join the song."

This was answered by a burst of music, as of the most exquisitely played flute, from the neighbouring thicket: —

> "Epopopopopopopopopopoi
> Io io, ito ito, tio tio, tiu."

Then the king began again: —

> "Now come at my call,
> Now come one and all,
> From ploughland and plain,
> Ye feeders on grain;

Tio tio tio tio fio tio tio tio;
From garden and glade,
Where a shelter is made
By the ivy's deep shade;
From mountain and hill,
Ye on berries that feed;
From marsh and from mead
Well watered and flat
Where the trumpet sounds shrill
Of your quarry, the gnat.
You, who on the swell
Of the wide-rolling sea
With the kingfisher dwell,
Come, obedient to me.
Torotorotorotorotix,
Kikkabau, kikkabau,
Torotorotorotorolililix."

Before long a vast crowd of birds had assembled.
The king told them the business on which he had
called them together — two ambassadors from mankind had come to make a proposal of great importance to the bird-nation. This announcement was
not received with any favour. Their king, the birds
declared, had betrayed them, and broken their laws.
He had introduced into their country two creatures
of a race which from its birth was hostile to the bird-
nation. For this he would have to answer at some
future time; the first thing to be done was to put the
intruders to death. Accordingly the birds proceeded
to put themselves in battle array, the strangers meanwhile arming themselves with the first things that

came ready to their hands, the lid of a pot for a shield and a spit for a spear. The two parties were about to come to blows, when King Hoopoe made another effort to preserve the peace.

K. H. "Vilest of all creatures, do you intend to kill, for no reason at all, two strangers who are my wife's countrymen and kinsmen?"

Birds. "Why should we spare them? They are the worst enemies we have."

K. H. "Enemies, perhaps, by nature, but friends in intention and come hither to teach us something very useful."

Birds. "How can they teach us anything useful? They were our grandfathers' enemies, and they are ours."

K. H. "Still, the wise learn even from their enemies, caution, for instance; your friends don't teach you that. Isn't it from their enemies that men learn to build lofty walls, and ships of war, and so keep themselves and their belongings safe?"

These arguments prevailed so far that a truce was called. The birds gave up their hostile attitude, and the men laid down their arms.

Plausible then proceeded to address them with much solemnity, having first washed his hands and put a chaplet on his head. "My friends," he began, "I am sorely troubled when I consider your present condition, you who were kings in old time."

Birds. "We kings! Kings of what?"

Plaus. "Kings of everything and everybody. You were older, you must understand, than Chronos and the Titans and the earth."

Birds. "We older than the earth!"

Plaus. "Yes; it is so."

Birds. "Well, that I never knew before."

Plaus. "Of course not; because you have not been properly educated. You have not read what Æsop tells about the Lark; how his father died, and he did not know where to bury him, because as yet there was no earth; so he buried him in his own head. As for the fact that birds were kings in old time, there is an abundance of proof. Take the Cock: he was king of Persia once, long before the time of Darius. Isn't he called the 'Persian bird' to this day? And isn't it a proof of his old power, that even now, as soon as his voice is heard in the morning, all sorts of people — brass-workers, potters, cobblers, and the rest of them — jump up, put on their shoes, and go about their business, even though it is still dark? Then the Kite was once king of the Greeks."

Birds. "The Kite king of the Greeks!"

Plaus. "Yes; don't people make a bow to him to this day?[1] Then the Cuckoo was king of Egypt and all Phœnicia. Even now, when he cries 'cuckoo' these people begin to cut their corn. Again, not so very long ago, in our own cities,

---

[1] Just as people take off their hats to a magpie.

kings such as Agamemnon or Menelaus had a bird
sitting on their sceptres who had his share of all
the dues that they received. Zeus — and this, mark
you, is the weightiest proof of all — has an eagle
on his head, by way of token of his kingship; and
his daughter Athené has an owl, and Apollo a
hawk. What do you suppose to be the meaning
of all this? Why, that when any sacrifice was
made to the god, the bird. had his share first, —
yes, before the god himself. Yes; in old time men
thought you holy and venerable; how do they treat
you now?

" Why, they pelt you with stones, and they trap you with
    snares,
And the branches on which you may light unawares
With bird-lime they smear, and all this in the pale
Of the temples they do, and they hawk you for sale,
Heaped together in baskets, and those who would buy
In most impudent fashion your plumpness will try;
And when they would cook you, it is not enough
Just to roast, but they mingle some horrible stuff
With garlic and oil and a dozen things more,
For a sauce on your delicate members to pour."
    Birds. "Oh, sad is the story you bring to our ears,
Dear stranger, I heard it with shame and with tears;
To think of our glory so sadly decayed,
The rule of our fathers so weakly betrayed;
'Tis surely the happiest fortune that brings
Such a friend to our help. For if once we were kings,
'Tis a shame and disgrace not to be so again;
And this is the point we would have you explain."

Plaus. " To begin with, you birds must build one great city and surround it with a wall of baked bricks, just as if it were another Babylon. Then you must send an embassy to Zeus and require him to surrender the kingdom to you. If he refuses, or makes any difficulty, you must forbid him and his gods to pass through your domain on any errand or pretext whatsoever. After this you must send a herald to men, and bid them make their sacrifices in future to you and not to the gods."

K. H. " But will men really look upon us as gods when they see us flying about and having wings?"

Plaus. "Why not? Does not Hermes use wings? Hasn't Victory pinions of gold? And Eros,[1] too? And doesn't Homer say that Iris flew like a ring-dove?"

K. H. " But suppose Zeus should send his thunder, what then?"

Plaus. " Oh! we'll soon teach them that we and not the gods are the people to be feared. We will send a flock of sparrows to eat up the grain in their fields; and the ravens to pick out the eyes of their sheep and their plough-oxen. Let Demeter feed the men and Apollo heal the beasts — if they can!"

Hope. (*interrupting*). "Very good; but I should like to sell my two bullocks before we try this."

Plaus. " But if, on the other hand, men have the good sense to give you the honours that really belong

[1] Cupid.

to you, they will get all kinds of blessings. Say that a flock of locusts comes when the vines are in bloom, a troop of owls or hawks will eat them up; then as for the maggots which spoil their figs, a flock of thrushes will dispose of them."

K. H. "But how shall we make them rich? That is the thing they really care about."

Plaus. "Easily enough. You will show them profitable mines, and good places for trade, and will take care that no seaman be lost."

K. H. "How shall we manage that?"

Plaus. "When they consult the oracle about a voyage some bird will give them information. ' Don't sail now,' it will say, ' there is going to be a storm '; or, ' Sail now; you will make a good thing of it.' "

Hope. (interrupting). "I am not going to stop with you. I shall buy a merchantman, and make a fortune by trade."

Plaus. "Then the birds will show them treasures that have been buried in former times. They know all about such things. Don't people say, ' Nobody knows of the hoard, except it may be a bird ' ? "

Hope. "I shall sell my merchantman, buy a mattock, and dig up pots full of money."

K. H. "How shall we give them health? Health is a gift of the gods."

Hope. "That won't matter much. Depend upon it that a man is never ill if his affairs go well, and never well if they go ill."

K. H. " How about long life ? That again is a gift of heaven. Must they die in their youth ? "

Plaus. " Certainly not. The birds will add three hundred years or so to their span."

K. H. "Where will they get them to add ? "

Plaus. "Where will they get them ? Why, from their own store to be sure. Don't you know that the crow outlives five generations of men ? "

Hope. " It is quite clear that the birds will make much better kings than Zeus."

Plaus. " Yes; and men will no longer have to build temples of stone with gold-plated doors. The birds will be quite content to live in trees; an ilex will do for the commoner sort, and the most exalted will have an olive-tree. There will be no more need to go to Delphi or Ammon; men will stand in a shrubbery with a pennyworth of barley in their hands, — that will be sacrifice enough for these easy-going deities."

King Hoopoe now proceeded to invite the two friends to come into his nesting-place, as he called it; they should be enrolled, he said, in the bird-nation. The difficulty of their having no wings wherewith to fly would be easily got over. There was a root he knew of which would make wings grow without any loss of time. While they were gone to go through the ceremony of becoming naturalized citizens, and to fit themselves out with feathers, the assembled birds sang a ditty in which they set forth the superiority of their race over men.

" Ye children of man ! whose life is a span,
Protracted with sorrow from day to day,
Naked and featherless, feeble and querulous,
Sickly, calamitous creatures of clay!
Attend to the words of the Sovereign Birds,
Immortal, illustrious, lords of the air,
Who survey from on high, with a merciful eye,
Your struggle of misery, labour, and care.
All lessons of primary, daily concern
You have learnt from the Birds and continue to learn.
When the crane flies away to the Libyan sands,
The farmer bethinks him of sowing his lands,
And the seaman his rudder unships, for no more
Can he venture to sail, till the winter is o'er;
Then the spring is at hand, when the hawk reappears,
And the shepherd who sees him gets ready his shears;
When the swallow comes back, then your cloak you may sell,
A light, summer vest will do perfectly well;
For all matters of moment it clearly appears
The Birds are your oracles, prophets, and seers;
We give counsel and aid when a marriage is made,
A purchase, a bargain, a venture in trade;
An ox or an ass that may happen to pass;
A voice in the street or a slave that you meet;
A name or a word that by chance you have heard,
If you think it an omen you call it a bird.[1]
If you'll make us your gods, at all seasons you'll find
We are equally helpful and equally kind;
We sha'n't hurry off, sitting scornful and proud,
In the fashion of Zeus, on the top of a cloud.
We shall ever be near you to help and to bless;

[1] The word for "bird" signifies "omen" also. The flight of birds was, both with the Greeks and Romans, a common method of divining the future.

To you and your children we'll give to possess
All things that are good, — life, happiness, health,
Peace, plenty, and laughter, and feasting and wealth;
For, what is the most unattainable thing?
' Pigeons' milk ' — and that in abundance we'll bring,
Till the general plenty among you be such
That your only complaint will be having too much."

By this time the two friends had come back, equipped for the functions which they would have in future to perform. The first thing to be done was to give the new city a name. " Cloud Cuckoo Land "[1] was finally settled upon, and the tutelary deity was to be a gamecock. The builders were set to work, and an inaugurating sacrifice was performed to the new deities. This had scarcely been done when a poet appeared on the scene, with a ready-made ode.

" Muse, prepare a noble ditty,
    Hymning with your choicest lay,
    This the new-built, happy city,
    Nephelo-Coccugia."

Plaus. " What have we got here ? Who are you, sir ? "

Poet.   " Singer of melodious strain,
        Servant in the Muses' train."

Plaus. " A servant with long hair ! "

Poet. " All who teach the art of song are ' servants of the Muses,' as Homer puts it."

Plaus. " Well, what have you come here for ? "

[1] The Greek word is " Nephelo-Coccugia."

Poet. "I have brought an assortment of verses, —
some epic poems, songs for a chorus of girls, and a
trifle in Simonides's manner."

Plaus. "But when did you make all these?"

Poet. "Long have I named this city's noble name."

Plaus. "Well, that is odd, for I've only just given
it."

> *Poet.* "Faster than steed to the Muses' court
> Ever is carried the swift report.
> But thou who hast founded this noble state
> Haste to my needs to dedicate
> Some kindly gift, be it small or great."

Plaus. "This fellow will give us a lot of trouble
unless we get rid of him. You there (*speaking to a
slave*) — you have got a jerkin as well as a tunic.
Give him the jerkin. So clever a poet well deserves
it. There, poet, take the jerkin. You seem very cold."

> *Poet.* "My patron, thanks! The friendly Muse
> This little boon will not refuse,
> Yet hath another lay for thee,
> A strain of Pindar's minstrelsy."

Plaus. "We are not going to get rid of him just
yet, I see."

> *Poet.* "Among the wandering tribes that stray
> O'er Scythian plains he makes his way,
> A bard ill-clad and all alone,
> No woven garment doth he own;
> Harken! my meaning canst thou guess,
> He wears a jerkin tunic-less."

Plaus. "I guess that you want the tunic. Here, fellow; off with it. You ought to help a poor poet."

The next visitor was a dealer in prophecies. "Stop the sacrifice," he cried, as soon as he appeared; "I have a prophecy of Bacis that speaks expressly about Cloud Cuckoo Land."

Plaus. "But why did we not hear of it before the city was founded?"

Soothsayer. "The divine voice forbade me."

Plaus. "Well, there is nothing like having the words."

> *Sooth.* "In the days when the jackdaws and crows shall unite,
> Midway between Corinth and Sicyon's height,
> A fair city to build —"

Plaus. "But what have I got to do with Corinth?"

Sooth. "Oh! Bacis meant the air under the figure of Corinth, —

> "A fair city to build, you must offer a goat
> Milk-white to Pandora, presenting a coat
> Without spot, and of sandals a handsome new pair,
> To the man who this prophecy first shall declare."

Plaus. "Does he mention the sandals?"

Sooth. "Yes; look at the book. But listen again : —

> "And a cup he must have and some flesh for his share."

Plaus. "Does he mention the flesh?"

Sooth. " Yes ; look at the book. But he goes on : —

> " My bidding obey, noble youth, and you fly,
> To an eagle transformed, through the realms of the sky ;
> Refuse, neither eagle nor dove will you be,
> Nor even a woodpecker tapping a tree."

Plaus. " Does he say all that ? "

Sooth. " Yes ; look at the book."

Plaus. " Do you know that the prophecy that I have got — and I wrote it down from the very lips of Apollo — is quite different. Listen : —

> " When you sacrifice first, should some vagabond dare,
> Whom you have not invited, to ask for a share,
> Smite him hard in the ribs, I command you, nor care
> For his eagles that fly in the regions of air."

Sooth. " That is nonsense."

" Look at the book ! " cried Plausible ; and, producing a stout cudgel, he drove the fellow away.

The next arrival was an astronomer, carrying some mathematical instruments, with which he proposed to measure out and survey the territory of the new state. He was no more welcome than his predecessor. Plausible professed to respect him, and indeed to see in him another Thales ; but gave him some friendly advice to the effect that he had better be going about his business. There was trouble brewing, he said ; it was likely that all strangers would be expelled from the country, especially strangers of the impostor kind. This was a hint that the astronomer could not but take. " I am off," he said. — " Very good," said Plausible ; " but you are scarcely in time. The trouble is come," he added, administering a sound cuff. " There," he said, "you can measure your way back, I suppose."

Next came an inspector from Athens. " Where is the consul ? " [1] he asked, as he strutted in.

Plaus. " Who is this Sardanapalus ? " [2]

Insp. " I am the duly appointed inspector to the city of Cloud Cuckoo Land."

Plaus. " An inspector, are you ? Well, don't you think you might take your fees at once, and go back without giving us any trouble ? "

Insp. " A good idea that ! I did want to stop at home, and propose something in the Assembly. I have some business in hand for the Persians."

Plaus. (*striking him*). " Here is your pay ; take it, and off with you ! "

Insp. " I protest that I, an inspector from Athens, am being assaulted."

Plaus. " Off with you, ballot-boxes and all. The idea of sending an inspector before we have even sacrificed ! "

---

[1] The word in the original may be translated " Public Entertainer." In the Greek cities there were officials whose business it was to entertain envoys and other visitors who came in a public capacity. Each important state would have its own. Our consuls in foreign towns are, perhaps, the nearest approach that we can find.

[2] The last king of Assyria, whose name had passed into a proverb for luxury.

The next interruption came from a merchant who had a brand-new constitution to sell. Plausible treated him with as little ceremony as the others, and then, despairing of quiet, resolved to finish the sacrifice indoors. When everything had been duly performed, with, as it appeared, the happiest omens for the future, a messenger appeared, to announce the completion of the wall. So broad it was that two chariots could be driven on it side by side, while it was no less than a hundred fathoms high. The speed with which so vast a work had been completed astonished Plausible, and he demanded particulars. " Who had done it ? "

First Messenger. " Do you ask who did it ? The birds, and nobody else. There wasn't an Egyptian bricklayer, or mason, or carpenter. They did it all themselves. I was amazed to see it. About thirty thousand Cranes [1] came from Africa. They had swallowed the stones with which to build the fortifications. These the Water-rails worked up with their beaks. Ten thousand Storks laid the bricks, and the Curlews and River-birds brought water. The Herons carried the mud, and the Geese trod it with their broad feet. The Ducks were the bricklayers' labourers, and the Woodpeckers did the carpentering. And now the work is finished, — gates, and staples, and bars ; the sentries are set, the beacons are in the towers ; in fact, everything is ready."

[1] Cranes were supposed to swallow stones to steady their flight.

A second messenger now arrived, but his news was less satisfactory. One of the gods had bolted through the gates, in spite of the Jackdaws on guard. What god he was, no one knew, but only that he had wings. However, a squadron of thirty thousand Hawks had been sent after him. He could not have gone far. Indeed, almost before the messenger had finished, the intruder came flying back. It was Iris, the messenger of Zeus, clad in the colours of the rainbow.

Plaus. "What is your name, may I ask?"

Iris. "Iris of the swift foot."

Plaus. "Why does not some one take her into custody?"

Iris. "Take me into custody! What madness is this?"

Plaus. "You will repent of this."

Iris. "This is really too absurd."

Plaus. "Tell me which gate you came in by."

Iris. "I know nothing about your gates."

Plaus. "See how she pretends to be ignorant. Did you go to the General of the Jackdaws? or can you show the seal of the Storks?"

Iris. "Is the man in his senses?"

Plaus. "Then I understand that none of the bird-commanders gave you a pass."

Iris. "Gave me a pass indeed!"

Plaus. "How dare you then come quietly flying through other people's city, through the air, in fact?"

Iris. "What other way can we fly from heaven to earth?"

Plaus. "That I can't say; you are not going to fly this way. Do you know that it would serve you right if you were put to death?"

Iris. "Put to death! But I am an Immortal."

Plaus. "That makes no difference. It would be a terrible state of things, if, while everybody else submits to us, you gods are rebellious, and won't understand that we are your masters. But tell me, where were you flying to?"

Iris. "I? I was flying from Father Zeus to tell men that they must sacrifice sheep and oxen as usual to the Olympian gods."

Plaus. "What gods do you say?"

Iris. "What gods? The gods in heaven, of course."

Plaus. "Do you call yourselves gods?"

Iris. "What others are there?"

Plaus. "The birds are now gods. It is to them that sacrifice must be made, not, by Zeus! to Zeus."

Iris. "Fool, fool, stir not the gods' most awful wrath,
Lest Justice, wielding Zeus's strong pickaxe, smite
Thy race to utter ruin, and the bolt,
Descending in the lightnings' lurid flame,
Thee and thy dwelling's last recess consume."

Plaus. "Listen thyself. Cease now thy vaporous threats;
Be silent; think not that in me thou seest   ·
Some Lydian slave or Phrygian whom the sound
Of bombast hyperbolical may scare.

IRIS.

For if thy Zeus shall vex me more, I send
My eagles armed with firebrands who shall lay
The towers of heaven in ashes. And for thee,
Madam, depart in haste and shun thy fate."

Iris. " My father shall speak to you."

Plaus. " No, no, my dear; you must find some younger man."[1]

Iris immediately flew off skywards.

A herald now arrived with the news of the extraordinary popularity of the birds among mankind. Everybody was devoted to them. Before the new city was founded Spartan ways were all the fashion. Men walked about the streets with their hair long, half-starved themselves, and did as little washing as Socrates. Now, birds were the rage — men rose with the lark, hatched plots against each other, in fact did their best to make themselves like winged creatures. The new city must therefore prepare for a great immigration. There would be at least ten thousand applications for citizenship, and all the new-comers would of course want wings. Of these the authorities of Cloud Cuckoo Land at once set themselves to lay in a store. While they were thus engaged the new arrivals began to drop in. The first was a young fellow who sang as he came : —

> " I'd fain be an eagle who soars on high,
>   O'er the land and the rolling sea to fly."

[1] He affects to understand her as referring him to her father, as a girl might refer a suitor who aspired to her hand.

Plaus. " The news was true.   Here comes a fellow singing about eagles."

Young Man. "Of all things flying is the most delightful.   I am in love with your laws, my dear birds, and want to live under them."

Plaus. "What law in particular are you so fond of ?"

Y. M. " The one that makes it lawful for a young bird to kick his father."

Plaus. "Yes; we do think it a fine thing for a chicken to get the better of his father."

Y. M. "That is why I want to migrate.   My idea is to strangle my father and take possession of his property."

Plaus. " But, sir, we have a law that the young cranes must support their father."

Y. M. "Support my father indeed!   That would not suit me at all."

Plaus. "Well, my young friend, I will give you a piece of advice.   You seem fond of fighting.   Go off to Thrace, and have your fill of it there.   But you will hardly do for us."

The next arrival was a lyric poet, who wanted wings, that he might mount into the clouds, and search among them for fine ideas.   After him came an informer, who thought it would be very convenient if he could fly from place to place in search of victims, without any of the dangers of travel.   All that he got was what Plausible called a slashing pair of wings, but was really a cowhide whip very vigorously applied.

But now came a more important visitor, Prometheus, wrapped up in a close disguise and in a terrible fright lest Zeus should see him. At last, finding from his inquiries that all was safe, he came out from his concealment and was heartily welcomed.

Plaus. "My dear Prometheus!"

Prometheus. "Hush! hush! Don't make a noise."

Plaus. "What is the matter?"

Pro. "Don't mention my name. I am undone if Zeus sees me. Here, hold this umbrella over me while we talk."

Plaus. "Very good; an excellent idea of yours. It is all safe; talk away."

Pro. "Zeus is ruined."

Plaus. "Since when?"

Pro. "Since you built your city. From that time we have not had the smell of a single sacrifice from earth. We are simply starving; and the end of it is that the barbarian gods vow that they will invade the realm of Zeus, unless he consents to open the ports and to let sacrifice smoke enter free."

Plaus. "Barbarian gods! I did not know that there were such beings. What is their name?"

Pro. "Triballi. But listen. You will have an embassy coming here very soon from Zeus and the Triballi. But don't you make peace unless Zeus restores the sovereignty to the birds, and gives you the lady Queenship to wife."

Plaus. "Who is the lady Queenship?"

Pro. "The prettiest girl in the world. She keeps Zeus's thunderbolts for him, and, in fact, everything that he has got, — order, temperance, the navy, and the jurymen's fees."

Plaus. "She's his general steward, you mean."

Pro. "Just so. Get her, and you get everything. This is what I came to tell you. I was always partial to men, you know."

Plaus. "Very true. It is only you we have to thank for being able to cook our victuals."

Pro. "Yes; and I hate the gods."

Plaus. "Very true again; that was always your way."

Pro. "Yes. I am a regular Timon.[1] But now hold the umbrella over me. If Zeus should see me he'll only think I am walking in a procession."[2]

Prometheus had scarcely gone, when the embassy arrived. There were three envoys, Poseidon, Hercules, and a Triballian god.

Poseidon (addressing the Triballian). "What are you doing there? Is that the way to wear your

---

[1] The story was that Prometheus stole fire from heaven, and by this gift civilized man. For this Zeus punished him by chaining him to a rock in Caucasus. Timon, the famous misanthrope, was a contemporary of Aristophanes. He is spoken of in another of the comedies of Aristophanes, as well as in fragments of plays by other writers.

[2] The daughters of aliens resident in Athens (*metoeci*) used to carry umbrellas over the Athenian maidens that walked in procession at the great festival of Athené.

cloak? Not on the left like that; on the right side always. Democracy, what are you bringing us to, when a fellow like that is put on an embassy?"

Triballian (to Poseidon, who is trying to arrange his cloak). "Hands off, will you?"

Pos. "Confound you! — the most barbarous god I ever saw! Well, Hercules, what are we to do?"

Hercules. "You heard my opinion. Throttle the villain."

Pos. "But we came to treat for a peace."

Her. "I don't care. I say, throttle the villain."

Plausible took no notice whatever of the new arrivals. "Give me the cheese-grater," he said to his assistant. "Now a little cheese; now a blast with the bellows."

Her. "·Man, we three gods greet you heartily."

Plaus. "Grate the cheese."

Hercules, always a great eater, and now furiously hungry, was profoundly interested in the cooking, and could not help showing it. "What meat is this?"

Plaus. "Certain birds rebelled against the bird-state, and were condemned to death."

Her. "And you are grating cheese over them."

Plaus. "O my dear Hercules, how are you? What brings you here?"

Her. "We have come from the gods to treat for peace."

A slave. "There is no oil in the flask, sir."

Plaus. "Get some, my man; bird-meat must have plenty of oil with it."

Her. " The war brings us no good. As for you, by being on good terms with us you can always have rain in your cisterns, and always fine weather. We have come, you will understand, with full powers to treat."

Plaus. " Well, we did not begin the war, you know, and we are quite ready to make peace, if you are willing to do the right thing. Give back to the birds the power which they once possessed, and the matter is settled. On these terms I invite the ambassadors to breakfast."

Her. " These terms satisfy me; I vote for accepting them."

Pos. " You are a fool and a glutton. Are you going to rob your father of his kingdom?"

Plaus. " Don't you think that you gods will be all the more powerful if we birds rule the lower region ? As things are now, men take your name in vain, because you can't see them for the clouds. Call the birds to help you, and as soon as any rascal forswears himself, a crow will have his eye out in a trice."

Pos. " That is well put."

Her. " And so I think."

Pos. (*to the Triballian*). "And what is your opinion ? "

Trib. " Say true." [1]

---

[1] The jargon which is put into the Triballian's mouth is *nabaisatreu.* The last six letters, as Frere remarks, make the English words " say true."

HERCULES AND POSEIDON.

Plaus. "He agrees, you see. Then, again, men make vows, and are a long time in paying them. 'The gods are easy creditors,' they say. Well, we will set that right for you."

Pos. "How?"

Plaus. "When the man is counting out his money, a hawk will fly down, snatch the price of a couple of sheep, and carry it off."

Her. "I vote to give back the kingdom to the birds."

Plaus. "Ask the Triballian what he thinks."

Her. (*showing his fist to the Triballian*). "Vote yes, or you shall suffer for it."

Trib. "Ya, ya, goot, goot."

Pos. "Well, if you think so, I agree."

Plaus. "There is another little matter which I have just remembered. Zeus may keep Heré, but I must have the lady Queenship to wife."

Pos. "I see you don't really want peace; we shall go."

Plaus. "I don't care. Cook, take care to make the sauce sweet enough."

Her. "My good Poseidon, are we to have war just about a mere woman?"

Pos. "What are we to do then?"

Her. "Make peace, I say."

Pos. "Don't you see, you silly fellow, how you are being cheated? Supposing Zeus should die, when he has handed over the kingdom to this fellow here, you would be a beggar. Otherwise, of course, all the property he may leave will come to you."

Plaus. " Now, Hercules, listen to me. Your uncle is cheating you; you are not a legitimate son, and you would have nothing. Your father couldn't leave you his property even if he wished to do it. 'Failing legitimate children, to the testator's brother,' that is how the law runs. Your uncle would have it all. Now, put in your lot with us, and I'll make it worth your while."

Her. " You are quite right about the girl. I'm for giving her up."

Pos. " I vote against the proposition."

Plaus. " The matter rests with the Triballian. Triballian, what do you say ? "

Trib. " Pitty girli and great Queendi I give to Birdi."

Pos. " Well, have your own way; I shall say nothing now."

Plausible, accordingly, departed to heaven to fetch his bride, Hercules staying behind to look after the cooking. In a very short time he returned, bringing the fair lady with him, and was greeted with a song of welcome from his subjects : —

> " Stand aside and clear the ground,
> Spreading in a circle round
> With a wor hy welcoming ;
> To salute our noble king,

In his splendour and his pride,
Coming hither, side by side,
With his lovely, happy bride.
Oh, the fair, delightful face!
What a figure! what a grace!
What a presence! what a carriage!
What a noble, worthy marriage!
Let the birds rejoice and sing
At the wedding of their king,
Raising to the vanquished sky
Sound of lyre and pæan high."

VII.

THE FROGS.

This play was exhibited at the Lenæan festival in 405 B.C. Its main purpose may be described as critical, *i.e.* it is intended to satirize the dramatic art, the style, and the morality of Euripides. This poet, as well as his great rival Sophocles, had died in the preceding year; and Bacchus, finding Athens without any tolerable tragedian at all, — Aristophanes is willing to concede that there might be worse poets even than Euripides, — proposes to make a journey to the regions of the dead to bring him back.

ONCE upon a time two travellers, a master and his slave, might have been seen making their way across the market-place of Thebes. The master was attired in the saffron-coloured robe commonly worn at the festivals of Bacchus, and had on his legs the buskins used by the actors in tragedy to give them additional height; but these garments contrasted oddly enough with the lion's skin which was wrapped round his shoulders and the heavy club which he carried in his hand. This was, in fact, Bacchus. We shall soon learn why he had thus disguised himself, and what he had come for. Behind him came his slave Xanthias, riding on a donkey, and carrying on his shoulders a heavy knapsack, which contained his master's luggage. This burden seemed to distress the poor fellow very much, and he grumbled greatly at its

168

weight, not being much consoled by his master's assurance that it was really the donkey that carried both him and it. "All the same, I feel it on my shoulders," said the man. — "Well," replied the master, "if you say the donkey is no use to you, why don't you get down and take a turn at carrying the donkey?"

They had reached by this time the house for which they were bound. It was that in which Hercules lived; and Bacchus, who assumed a certain swagger, as being suitable to his equipment, kicked loudly at the door. "Who's that?" cried Hercules from within. "It might have been a centaur kicking."—"You see how afraid of me he is," said Bacchus in an aside to his slave. — "Afraid!" replied Xanthias; "he was only afraid you were mad." And indeed Hercules did seem to think that his visitor was out of his mind. So queer was his appearance that he could not help laughing. "What do you want?" he said; "what do you mean by your buskins and your club?"

Bacchus. "Now, brother, don't laugh at me; I am really suffering a great deal. I do want Euripides so. He is dead, you know, and I have made up my mind to go and look for him."

Hercules. "What? down to Hades?"

Bac. "Yes, and further too, if need be."

Her. "What do you want?"

Bac. "A good poet. The good poets are dead, and those who are alive are not good."

Her. " But you have got Iophon."

Bac. " Yes; he's the only one, and I don't feel certain about him."

Her. " If you must bring back a poet, why not Sophocles, who is much to be preferred to Euripides ? "

Bac. " Ah ! but, you see, I want to get Iophon by himself, and see what he can do without his father.[1] And then, Euripides is just the rascal who would be ready to run away. As for Sophocles, he is sure to be contented there, as he was here."

Her. " How about Agathon ? "

Bac. " He has gone. An excellent poet he was, and his friends miss him very much."

Her. " But where has he gone ? "

Bac. " Oh ! to a better country."[2]

Her. " But surely you have ten thousand and more young fellows that write tragedies, who could give Euripides more than a furlong in chattering and beat him."

Bac. " O yes, I know them ! the last leavings of

---

[1] Iophon was the son of Sophocles, and gained some brilliant successes during his father's lifetime; but, as Aristophanes hints, it was possible that he might have been assisted. Only a few lines of his tragedies survive.

[2] This might mean that Agathon was dead. It is probable, however, that it alludes to a visit paid by Agathon about this time to the court of Archelaus, king of Macedonia (413–399). He is supposed to have died in 400. Elsewhere Aristophanes speaks less favourably of him. It was in Agathon's house that Plato laid the scene of his famous dialogue called *The Banquet.* The occasion is supposed to have been the first victory won by him in the competition of tragedies. This was in 416 B.C.

the vintage, the poorest chatterboxes in the world.
They try one play, and then we see no more of
them. But I know no one who dares venture on
a really fine thing."

Her. " What do you mean ? "

Bac. " Well, something of this kind : —

      ' High heaven, residence of Zeus,'

or   ▲

      ' Time's viewless foot,'

or

      ' A soul that reverenced the oaths of heaven,
      A tongue still perjured, from the soul apart.' "

Her. " And you like that sort of thing ? "

Bac. " I am simply crazy for it."

Her. " I call it abominable rubbish."

Bac. " Indeed ; now if you were to give us your
opinion about dining it might be worth having.
However, I will explain why I have come dressed
up in this fashion like you. ⌐I want you to tell me
what friends you stayed with when you went down
after Cerberus, and all about the provision shops,
and the harbours, and the roads, and the springs,
and the inns where there were fewest fleas."

Her. " Are you really thinking of going ? "

Bac. " Yes ; on that point I want to hear nothing
more. But tell me the shortest way down. Mind,
it must not be too hot or too cold."

Her. " Well, let me think. Which is the best ?
There is a good road by the Rope and Noose. You
hang yourself, you know."   •

Bac. "Too choky by far."

Her. "Then there is a very short cut by the Pestle and Mortar."

Bac. "Do you mean the hemlock road?"

Her. "Certainly."

Bac. "Too cold and wintry for me. One's hands and feet get so numb."

Her. "Come, shall I tell you the quickest and most direct of all?"

Bac. "Yes, yes; I am but a poor traveller."

Her. "Stroll down, then, to the Potter's Quarter;[1] climb to the top of the tower, and watch till the torch race begins, and when the people say, 'They're off!' off with you."

Bac. "Off where?"

Her. "Why, down to the bottom."

Bac. "Yes, and lose two platefuls of brain? Not that way for me, thank you."

Her. "How do you intend to go, then?"

Bac. "By the way that you went, to be sure."

Her. "But that's a long journey. First, you will come to a very big lake without any bottom."

Bac. "How am I to get over?"

Her. "Oh! there's an old sailor with a tiny boat, just so big (*spans a length of five or six feet*), will ferry you over for a groat."

Bac. "Ah! a groat means something everywhere."

---

[1] The Ceramicus, where the bodies of Athenian citizens killed in battle were buried.

Her. "After this, you will find a great slough of mire and filth in which lie all sorts of villains, men who have robbed their friends, or boxed their father's ears, or perjured themselves, or copied out one of Morsimus's speeches.[1] This once passed, your ears will be greeted with the soft breathing of flutes, and you will see a very lovely light, and happy troops of men and women, who will tell you all you want to know; and now good by, brother."

Bac. "Good by. Xanthias, take up the baggage."

Xanthias. "Take it up! I have never put it down."

Bac. "No nonsense! Take it up at once."

Xan. "But won't you hire one of the dead people who are going this way to carry it?"

Bac. "A good idea! Ho! you dead man there, will you carry some baggage to Hades?"

Dead Man. "How much is there?"

Bac. "What you see there."

D. M. "Down with a couple of shillings, if we are to have a deal."

Bac. "Won't you take eighteen pence?"

D. M. "I'd sooner come to life again."

Xan. "What airs the fellow puts on! I'll go."

Bac. "You are a really good fellow. Come along."

In course of time they came to the lake of which Hercules had spoken. The old sailor was there,

---

[1] Morsimus was an indifferent tragic poet.

calling out, "Any one for Happy Despatch, or the Pig-shearers, or Cerberus Reach, or the Isle of Dogs?" Bacchus stepped on board with many entreaties to the boatman to be careful; but Xanthias was not allowed to follow. "I take no slaves," said the old man, "except they are volunteers."[1] Accordingly he had to run round and wait for his master on the other side.

"In with you," said Charon to his passenger. "Anybody else for the further side? Now to your oar."

Every one was expected to work his passage.

"What are you after there?" cried the ferryman; for the passenger was sitting on the oar, not at it.

"Wasn't this what you told me to do?" replied the god.

"Sit on the bench there, Corpulence, and forward with your hands."

Bacchus stretched his hands out, but without the oar.

"No more nonsense," cried Charon; "but set to, and row with a will."

Bac. "How can I, when I have never been to sea in my life?"

[1] When the Athenians made a supreme effort and manned at a few days' notice a large fleet to relieve Conon, who was blockaded by the Spartans in the harbour of Mitylene, slaves were permitted to volunteer, and received their freedom. The victory of Argimone, the last success gained by Athens in the Peloponnesian war, was the result of this effort.

Charon. "You will do it easily enough. Just dip your oar in, and you'll hear the sweetest singing you ever heard in your life."

And, indeed, the next moment the frogs in the lake began a strain : —

> "Brekekex, koax, koax,
> Brekekex, koax, koax,
> All ye children' of the lake,
> Join your voices till you make
> Sweetest harmony of song
> For the revellers' merry throng.
> Brekekex, koax, koax."

Bac. "But I'm getting very sore
As I labour with the oar
Now have done there with your noise."

Frogs. "Brekekex, koax, koax."

Bac. "Oh, confound you with your koax."

Frogs. "But the minstrel Pan enjoys
The sweet music of our voices,
And the Muses' tuneful choir
In our singing much rejoices,
And Apollo with his lyre.
Brekekex, koax, koax."

Bac. "But I've blisters on my hands,
O ye music-loving crew;
'Tis the god himself commands
That ye make no more ado."

Frogs. "But our voices we will raise
All the louder, while we sing,
How in sunny summer days
Through the reed and rush we spring.
Brekekex, koax, koax."

Bac. "I forbid you to proceed."

Frogs.	" No; that would be hard indeed."
Bac.	" Yes; but I should suffer more
	Overstraining with the oar."
Frogs.	" Brekekex, koax, koax."
Bac.	" Have you nothing else to say ? "
Frogs.	" We'll make music all the day,
	And as loudly as we may.
	Brekekex, koax, koax."
Bac.	" But I'll beat you at your game."
Frogs.	" We shall go on all the same."
Bac.	" Will you, then ? But I will shout,
	If 'tis needful, all the day,
	Till I beat your noisy rout,
	And your dismal music stay."
Frogs.	" Brekekex, koax, koax."

In due course the boat reached the further shore. Bacchus paid his fare, and, stepping out, began calling for his slave. Xanthias appeared, and congratulated his master on his safe arrival.

Bac. " What is that before us ? "

Xan. " The darkness and mire that Hercules told us of."

Bac. " Have you seen any of the parricides and murderers ? "

Xan. " Have not you ? "

Bac. " Certainly I have, and do at this moment; and not very far off, either." [1]

Xan. " Well, master, I think that we had better be going on, for this is the place where he said the dreadful monsters were."

[1] This was said with a glance at the spectators. Aristophanes frequently banters them with this somewhat savage playfulness.

Bac. " Oh, that's all nonsense! The fact is, Hercules was jealous of me. He knew what a plucky fellow I was, and wanted to frighten me. I do really wish to have some little adventure that might make it worth while for me to have come so far."

Xan. " O master! I hear a noise."

Bac. " Where, where ? "

Xan. " Just behind us."

Bac. " Get behind then, can't you ? "

Xan. " Oh! now I seem to hear it just in front."

Bac. " Get in front."

Xan. " Dear me, I see a monster."

Bac. " What is it like ? "

Xan. " All sorts of things. Now it's an ox, and now it's a mule, and now it's a woman, and now it's a dog."

Bac. " It must be the Vampyre."

Xan. " Its face is all ablaze with fire."

Bac. " Has it one leg of brass ? "

Xan. " Yes; and the other of cow-dung. Oh! we are lost, King Hercules."

Bac. " For heaven's sake, don't call me that! "

Xan. " Bacchus, then."

Bac. " Oh! that's still worse. Dear me, what shall I do ? "

Xan. " Courage, master; all's well; the Vampyre's gone."

The two travellers now proceeded on their way till they found themselves in front of a building

which they were assured was the palace of Pluto.
"How shall I knock?" Bacchus inquired. "How
do people knock in these parts?"—"Knock away,
master," the slave replied, "just as Hercules would."
—"Who is there?" called out Æacus the porter
from within. — "The mighty Hercules," was the
reply. The result was unexpected. The door was
flung open, and the porter overwhelmed the visitor
with a torrent of abuse.

> "O wretch audacious, shameless, horrible,
> O villain trebly dyed and far beyond
> All possible counting, you that stole away
> Our watch-dog Cerberus, my special charge,
> Half-strangled in your grasp. Now, villain, now
> We have you fast. For these high Stygian cliffs,
> Black-hearted, and the gory-dropping rock
> Of Acheron hem thee in, with those fell hounds
> That haunt Cocytus; and about thee raves
> The hundred-headed Hydra that shall tear
> Thy vitals, while the monstrous snake that haunts
> The Western seas shall strangle in her grasp
> Midriff and heart — and even now I lift
> A hasty foot to fetch them."

Bac. "Oh, what a terrible noise! Xanthias,
weren't you frightened?"

Xan. "Not a bit; never gave a thought to them."

Bac. "Well, you are a brave fellow. Come now,
you shall be me. Take the lion's skin and the club,
and I'll carry the baggage."

Xan. "Now mark the Xanthias-Hercules, and see
if he shows the white feather."

The transformation had hardly been effected when a maid-servant from Proserpine's palace appeared upon the scene, with a warm invitation for Hercules. "As soon as she knew of your coming," said the girl, "her Majesty set to work making fresh loaves, boiled two or three pots of porridge, roasted an ox whole, and cooked a quantity of cheese-cakes. Come in, if you please."

Xan. "Thank your mistress very much, but—"

Servant. "Oh, we can't excuse you — we have boiled fowl, and sweetmeats, and the best wine that can be got."

Xan. "Well, as you are so pressing. Come after me, my man, with the bundles."

Bac. "Oh, nonsense, man! You did not think I was in earnest about this changing clothes? Come, you'll carry the baggage again."

Xan. "Surely you are not going to take away the lion's skin and the club?"

Bac. "Oh, but I am! down with them this moment."

Xan. "I make appeal to the high gods in heaven."

Bac. "Gods indeed! How could you fancy that you could pass for the son of Alcmena, a mere man, a mere slave?"

Xan. "Very well, take the things, but you may want me after all."

Two women who kept eating-houses in those regions now appeared.

" Plathané, Plathané," cried one to the other, " here's that villain come again who ate those sixteen loaves!"

Second Woman. "Yes, by Zeus! it is the very man."

Xan. " Some one is in a scrape."

First Woman. "Aye, and he ate besides twenty cutlets at threepence each."

Xan. " Some one is in for it."

First W. " And a whole lot of garlic."

Bac. " Nonsense, woman! I don't know what you are talking about."

First W. " Ah! you thought I should not know you because you had buskins on. And I haven't mentioned the salt fish."

Second W. " No; nor the green cheese which the fellow ate up, baskets and all, and when I asked him for the money he looked so fierce, and bellowed so."

Xan. " Just like him. That's his way everywhere."

Second W. " And he out with his sword, just like a madman, but I scrambled up into the loft. And what did he do but go off with our mattresses."

Xan. " Another trick of his."

First W. " Tell Cleon to come. He's my counsel."

Second W. " Mine is Hyperbolus, if you should see him."

First W. " Ah! you villain, how I should like to knock out those greedy teeth with which you ate up a poor woman's living, aye, and rip up your throat!"

Bac. "Curse me, if I am not very fond of Xanthias!"

Xan. "I know what you want. It is of no use your saying. I cannot possibly be Hercules."

Bac. "Don't say so, my dear fellow."

Xan. "But how could I be the son of Alcmena, 'a mere man, a mere slave'?"

Bac. "I know that you are angry, and I don't blame you. If you were to strike me, I could not object. But do take the things once more; and if I take them again, may I perish, I and my wife and my children and all that I have."

Xan. "I accept on these terms."

At this point Æacus reappeared with some attendants, and attempted to arrest the false Hercules for having stolen Cerberus. Xanthias, however, succeeded in beating them off, while Bacchus protested that it was monstrous that the culprit should add an assault to his former misdeeds.

Xan. "I protest that I have never been near the place in my life, much less stolen a farthing's worth of property belonging to it. But I'll tell you what I'll do, and it's really a generous offer. You may take my slave there and examine him by torture. If you can find out from him anything against me, then you can do what you like."[1]

Æacus. "What torture will you allow?"

---

[1] It was not lawful to examine a slave by torture, to support an accusation against his master. The false Hercules therefore appears to make a very liberal offer.

Xan. "Oh, any that you like. You may tie him to the triangles, or flog him with a cat-o'-nine-tails, or pour vinegar into his nostrils, or press him; in fact, do as you please."

Æ. "Very good; and if I happen to injure the fellow, of course I shall be liable to you for the money."

Xan. "Never mind about the money; take him away, and set to work."

Æ. " No, no; we'll have it here in your presence. Now then, my man, put down the baggage, and see that you tell no lies."

Bac. "I warn you not to touch me. I'm a god. After that, if you get into trouble, blame yourself."

Æ. "What do you say?"

Bac. "I say that I am an immortal god, Bacchus, son of Zeus. The slave is that fellow there."

Æ. "Do you hear this" (*to Xanthias*)?

Xan. "Yes; all the more reason for beating him, I say. If he is an immortal god, he won't be able to feel."

Bac. "Why shouldn't you be beaten, too, for you're an immortal god, you say?"

Xan. "That's only fair. Whichever of us shows any sign of being hurt, you will conclude that he is not the god."

Æ. (*to Xanthias*). "You really are a very fair-minded fellow. Strip, both of you."

Xan. "How will you manage to test us fairly?"

Æ. "Oh! easily enough; blow and blow about."
The first blow was dealt to Xanthias, and received
without a sign.

"I have struck you," said Æacus. — "No; did you,
really?" replied the man.

The next came to Bacchus. "When are you
going to begin?" said the god, after the stroke had
been administered. So it went on. The lashes
extorted, indeed, an exclamation or other sign of
pain, but the sufferers always contrived to account
for them. If Bacchus, for instance, was seen to
have tears in his eyes after a sharp stroke, "It was
the smell of onions," he said. After another, he
cried, "Apollo!" but the next moment went on
as if he were repeating a favourite passage : —

> "Apollo, whether on the Delphian steep
> Thou dwellest, or in Delos . . ."

At last Æacus gave it up. "I can't find out," he
cried, "which of you is the real god. You must go
into the palace. My master and Persephone will
know, for they are gods themselves."

"Quite right," said Bacchus, "but I wish you had
thought of it a little sooner."

Pluto and his queen were found to possess the
necessary power of distinguishing the god from the
slave. As they also satisfied themselves that it was
not the real Hercules that had come down to Hades,
the proceedings about the carrying off of Cerberus

were dropped, and Bacchus was hospitably entertained, while Xanthias was handed over to the care
of Æacus.

"That's a real gentleman, that master of yours,"
said the porter to his guest.

" I believe you," replied the slave, " he does not
know how to do anything but drink and amuse
himself."

Æ. " To think of his not hitting you when you
faced him out, pretending that you were the master,
when you were only the slave."

Xan. "He would have been sorry for it if he
had."

Æ. " You're the right sort, I see. That's just
the sort of thing that I like to say."

Xan. " You like it, do you ?"

Æ. " Yes ; but the best of all is to curse my
master when I am alone."

Xan. " And what do you think of muttering when
you have been well beaten and are going out of the
door ?"

Æ. " That's pleasant, too."

Xan. " What of making mischief ?"

Æ. " Better than anything."

Xan. " And listening at the door when they're
talking secrets ?"

Æ. " I'm simply mad on it."

Xan. " And gossiping out-of-doors about what you
hear ?"

Æ. " I can't contain myself for joy."

Xan. " Give me your hand, my dear fellow, and kiss me; you are my own brother. But tell me, what is all that noise˙and shouting and abuse about outside ? "

Æ. " Oh! that's only Æschylus and Euripides."

Xan. " What ? "

Æ. " There has been a tremendous disturbance and dispute among the dead people lately."

Xan. " What about ? "

Æ. " There is a rule down here that the best man in any art — I mean arts of the nobler sort — should have free entertainment in Government-house and a seat next to Pluto's own."

Xan. " I understand."

Æ. " But he has this only till some better man than he arrives. When that happens, he must give way. Well, Æschylus occupied the seat of honour among tragedians."

Xan. " And who occupies it now ? "

Æ. " When Euripides came down, he showed off to the robbers, and pick-pockets, and murderers, and burglars, — and we have a multitude of these gentry in Hades, — and they, when they heard his equivocations, and evasions, and turns, and twists, were beside themselves with delight, and declared that he was the best man that there was in his art. Thereupon he was so puffed up that he actually claimed Æschylus's seat."

Xan. " And was pelted, of course, for his pains."

Æ. " Not so; the mob cried out that there must be a trial to decide which was the better man."

Xan. " You mean the mob of scoundrels."

Æ. " Yes; and an awful noise they made."

Xan. " But Æschylus had his friends, too, I suppose."

Æ. " O yes! but good people are scarce down here, as they are up above."

Xan. " Well, what does Pluto mean to do ? "

Æ. " He means to have a trial which will show who is the better man."

Xan. " How about Sophocles ? Did he claim the seat ? "

Æ. " Not he : as soon as he came down he kissed Æschylus, and Æschylus made room for him on his seat. And now he means, if Æschylus should get the better in the trial, to stay where he is; but if Euripides, then to challenge him for the first place."

Xan. " And what sort of a trial are they going to have ? "

Æ. " A rare one, you may be sure. You'll see poetry measured by the pound weight, and rules, and compasses, and wedges. Euripides says he is going to take the plays to pieces."

Xan. " Æschylus takes it hard, I reckon."

Æ. " Yes indeed, he's like a bull going to charge."

Xan. " But who is to be the judge ? "

Æ. "Ah! that was the difficulty. Good judges are scarce. You know that Æschylus did not get on altogether well, even with the Athenians. However, they handed over the matter to your master. It was in his line, they thought. But we had better go in, or we shall catch it."

The two rival poets now appeared.

"I am not going to give up my claim to the seat," said Euripides, "so you may spare your advice."

Bac. "You hear what he says, Æschylus? Why don't you speak?"

Eur. "Oh! that's his solemn way that we used to have in his tragedies."

Bac. "Come, come, Euripides, be moderate."

Eur. "I know the man, with all his savage crew
Of heroes, and his rude, unbridled tongue,
And all his overbearing pomp of words."
Æschylus. "Son of the garden-goddess,[1] sayest thou thus?
Gleaner of gossip, with thy beggar train
And rags ill-patched together! Think not, knave,
To escape unpunished."
Bac. "Hold, Æschylus, nor vex thy noble soul
With rage beyond all measure."
Æsch.   "I'll not hold,
Till I have shown how poor a thing he is,
This maker of lame beggars."

---

[1] An allusion to the pursuits of Euripides's mother, who was said to have sold vegetables.

Bac. "A black lamb this moment,[1] my man; there's a hurricane coming. But I do beg you, my honoured Æschylus, to restrain yourself; and you, you unlucky Euripides. I advise you to get into shelter from the hail; a big stone might hit you on the head, and spill one of your precious tragedies. To both of you I would say that two poets ought not to abuse each other like a couple of bread-sellers."

Eur. "Well, I'm ready; I am not going to shrink from any test you like. Test my music, my language, my characters, anything that you please."

Bac. "And what say you, Æschylus?"

Æsch. "I had rather not be put to the trial down here. My poetry did not die with me; but this fellow's did. There he has the advantage. However, let it be as you will."

Bac. "Bring some incense and a red-hot coal. I should like to pray before they begin, that I may have the wit and taste to decide this matter aright. And each of you should say a prayer before you commence."

Æsch. "Grant, mighty mother, nurturer of my soul,
That I be worthy of your mysteries."

Bac. "Now, Euripides, it is your turn."

---

[1] Black victims were offered to the storms, and to malign powers generally. So we find in Virgil's *Æneid*, III. 119-20: —

A bull to Neptune, and a bull
To thee, Apollo hight,
A lamb to Tempest, black of wool,
To western winds a white.

Eur. " It is well ; I pray to quite another kind of god."

Bac. " I understand ; gods of your own, a new coinage, as it were."

Eur. " Just so."

Bac. " Pray away, then, to these particular gods of yours."

> *Eur.* " O air, fine nurturer of my soul, and thou,
> Quick-moving pivot of the tongue, and source
> Of keen perception, and the delicate power
> Of nostrils apprehensive, grant me grace
> That I may rightly form the words I try."

These preliminaries ended, the trial began. Euripides opened the attack. " Of my own poetry," he said, " I will speak afterwards. My first task will be to show what a braggart and cheat this fellow was. He found a silly audience used to the old-fashioned poets, and befooled it. First he put on the stage a figure muffled up and silent, that looked very tragical, but did not utter a syllable.[1] Meanwhile the chorus sang an ode of immeasurable length ; but from the hero not a word."

Bac. " And it seemed to me very fine, much finer than the chatter that I hear now."

Eur. " That was because you were an ignoramus."

Bac. " Perhaps you are right. But why did what's-his-name do it ? "

---

[1] A reader of Æschylus will remember the opening scene of the *Prometheus.* The demigod remains silent while the work of fastening him to the rock goes on.

Eur. "Out of sheer impudence. The spectator was to sit waiting till Niobe, or whoever it was, should say something. And so the play would get on."

Bac. "Oh, what a rascal! How he took me in!" (*To Æschylus*) "What is the matter with you, twisting about in that fashion?"

Eur. "It's because I'm finding him out. Then, after all this rubbish, when the play was about half-way through, our silent friend would mouth out some dozen words, each as big as an ox, and ugly as a bugbear, that none of the audience could understand."

Bac. (*to Æschylus, who had groaned*). "Be quiet there."

Eur. "A plain, intelligible word he never used."

Bac. (*to Æschylus*). "Don't grind your teeth."

Eur. "It was all about 'Scamander streams' and 'embattled trenches,' and 'shields embossed with vulture-eagles wrought in bronze,' and such neck-breaking words."

Bac. "'And I through weary hours of darkness lay,'[1] thinking what sort of a bird a 'tawny cock-horse' could possibly be."

Æsch. "It was the device on a ship, to be sure, you ignoramus." (*To Euripides*) "And pray, what were your inventions?"

Eur. "Not cock-horses, nor goat-stags, you may be sure, the sort of creatures you see on Persian

_____
[1] A parody of lines in Euripides.

hangings. No, I found my art swollen out with these heavy, pompous words, and I fined her down with verselets, and administered decoctions of chatter. Then I did not confuse my characters. My heroes began by giving their pedigree."

Æsch. "A better pedigree than your own, I should hope."

Eur. "Then from the very beginning there was no time wasted: wife, slave, master, maiden, old ⸤ woman, — all spoke in the same style."

Æsch. "That was a mortal sin."

Eur. "Not at all; a true democratic idea I call it. Then I introduced subtle rules of style, and fine finishing of verses, and twists and turns, and contrivances and suspicions."

Æsch. "Exactly what I say."

Eur. "And all this in matters of every-day life, things of daily use and wont, things which the audience know all about, and in which they are competent to judge my art. I did not try to drive them out of their sober senses with Cycnuses and Memnons, and battle steeds and clattering shields!

> "Then it was that I began
> With a nicer, neater plan:
> Logic by my art I brought
> Home to common men, and taught
> How to mind their own affairs,
> Most of all their household cares,
> Marking everything amiss;
> 'Where is that?' and 'What is this?'"

Bac. " Yes, now when a master comes in at his door,
He calls to his slaves, and examines his store.
' Now where is the pitcher? and some one has eaten
The head of the sprat, and has broken the bowl
Only purchased last year. As I live, he'll be beaten.
Half the olive is gone, of the garlic the whole;
So careful a watch of their substance they keep,
Who once were contented to slumber and sleep.' "

Æsch. " It makes me angry, it vexes me to the heart, to have to reply to such a fellow as this; still I will do it, lest he should say that he had got the better of me in the debate. Tell me now — What is most admirable in a poet ? "

Eur. " Righteousness and true counsel; the power of making our fellow-citizens better."

Æsch. " Then, if this is exactly what you have not done, if, instead, you found them honest men and left them villains, what do you deserve ? "

Bac. " Death, of course ; don't ask him."

Æsch. " Remember what our citizens were when they first came into your hands, fine tall fellows, who shirked no public duty, not cheats and scoundrels as now, but breathing spears and javelins and white crested helmets and breasts of seven fold hide."

Bac. " But, Æschylus, how did you do it ? "

Æsch. " By dramas that were full of war."

Bac. "Which, for instance ? "

Æsch. " The *Seven against Thebes;* no man could see that and not long to be a warrior."

Bac. " That's all very well; but you made the Thebans dangerously good soldiers."

Æsch. "Well, you might have made yourselves the same, but you chose other things. Then I exhibited *The Persians,* and I made them ever eager to conquer their foes. Yes, this is the function of the poet. And see how in all ages the really noble poets have discharged it. Orpheus taught us to worship the gods, and to keep our hands from blood; Musæus instructed us in medicine, and told us of the future; Hesiod sang of husbandry and the seasons; and for what is Homer famous, but that he sang of battle array, and noble deeds, and heroes arming for the fight? Then were trained such men as the hero Lamachus, and many another like him. But to think of the creatures that you have brought upon the stage, the foolish women, for instance! whereas I don't know that I ever introduced a woman in love."

Eur. "No, you did not know how."

Æsch. "No, and I don't want to know."

Eur. "But were they not true to life?"

Æsch. "I dare say; but that was no reason why you should put them on the stage. The poet should hide what is bad, not bring it forward. What the teacher is to the child, that is the poet to the youth."

Eur. "But what virtue was there in your huge-sounding phrases? Should you not use the common speech of men?"

Æsch. "Wretch, don't you know that noble ideas must be clothed in noble words? Demigods surely should use a loftier speech than ours, and wear a

more splendid vesture.   All this I set forth, and you
departed from it most villainously."

Eur. "But how?"

Æsch. "You clothed your kings in rags, to move
the pity of men."

Eur. "What harm did this do?"

Æsch. "It taught the rich men to shirk their duties.
They dress in rags, and whine about their poverty.
Then you taught men sophistry and lying.   You
emptied the gymnasia.   You made the young effemi-‐
nate and base.   You taught the seamen to answer
their officers, whereas in my time they knew no more
than to call for their porridge, and to cry, 'Pull
away!'"

So much, then, was said about matter and morals.
From this the competition passed on to style.   "Repeat one of your prologues," said Euripides.

Æschylus began: —

> "Be thou, I pray, my saviour and ally,
>   Who now have come to this my native land,
>   Come, and returned."

Eur. "See, the wise Æschylus has said the same
thing twice.   'Come' and 'returned' mean the
same."

Bac. "Yes, yes; just as if a woman were to say to
her neighbour, 'Use the kneading trough, and, if you
choose, the trough for kneading.'"

Æsch. "They are not the same; the thing is
quite rightly expressed."

Bac. " How ? Explain what you mean."

Æsch. " Don't you see ? A man that has been exiled not only comes to his own country, but returns, for he has been there before."

Bac. " Very good ! What do you say to that, Euripides ? "

Eur. " I say that Orestes did not return to his country; for he came secretly against the wish of the rulers."

Bac. " And that is good also; but I don't know in the least what he means."

Eur. " Now give us another."

Æschylus went on : —

> " From his sepulchral mound I call my sire
> To hear and hearken."

" Listen to him," cried Euripides, " ' to hear and hearken '; there's a repetition for you ! "

Bac. " Repetition ! Of course there is. Is he not speaking to the dead, to whom we call three times, and even then they do not hear us ? " [1]

Æsch. " And now let me see what I can make of his prologues. I'll spoil them all with a single flask of oil."

Eur. " What ! a flask of oil ? "

Æsch. " Yes; one little flask. For you, Euripides, compose them in such a way that one can always fit

---

[1] The dead were called three times, a custom which has survived to modern times.

in 'a little fleece,' or 'a little flask,' or 'a little wallet.'"

> *Eur.* "Ægyptus, — so the common story runs, —
> Father of fifty sons, the salt sea crossed,
> And reaching Argos —"
> *Æsch.*   "lost a flask of oil."

Bac. "Try another one."

> *Eur.* "Great Bacchus, who with wand and skin of fawn
> Equipped, while all around the torches blaze,
> Leads the loud revel —"
> *Æsch.*   "lost a flask of oil."

Bac. "Dear me! the flask has caught us again."

Eur. "I don't care. Now listen: here is a pro-logue, to which he won't be able to fit in his flask :—

> "'No man is found in all things fortunate.
> This, being noble, lacks the means of life;
> That, born ignobly—'"
> *Æsch.*   "lost a flask of oil."

Bac. "Try another, and do keep clear of the flask."

> *Eur.* "Cadmus, in olden time, Agenor's son,
> Sailing from Sidon —"
> *Æsch.*   "lost a flask of oil."

Bac. "My good man, buy his flask, or it will assuredly ruin your prologues."

Eur. "I buy it! Certainly not. Listen again :—

> "'The son of Tantalus, to Pisa bound,
> With fleet-foot horses — '"
> *Æsch.*   "lost a flask of oil."

Bac. " No, no ; you can't get rid of the flask. It sticks to your verses just like a sty on a man's eyelid.[1] We will go to something else."

Æsch. " I am for the balance and weights. Let that decide between us."

Bac. " Well, if you will have it so, though it seems odd to deal with the work of a couple of poets as a cheesemonger with his cheeses. Boy, bring out a pair of scales. Now, then, stand each of you by one of the scales, take a verse, but don't drop it till I say ' cuckoo.' "

Æsch. and Eur. " We are ready."

Bac. " Now, then ! "

Eur. " Would that the good ship Argon e'er had sped—"
Æsch. " Stream of Spercheius, and ye pasturing herds ! "

Bac. " Now, then, ' cuckoo'! See, Æschylus's scale is much lower."

Eur. " What is the reason of that ? "

Bac. " Why, he did what the wool-sellers do with their wool : he damped his verse with a whole river, while yours was a very airy affair."

Eur. " Let us have another trial."

Bac. " Very good. Are you ready ? "

Æsch. and Eur. " Yes."

Bac. " Go on, then."

---

[1] Aristophanes may be supposed to be ridiculing the monotonous cadences and unvarying pauses of Euripides's verse, as well as the commonplace character of his subjects.

Eur. "One only temple has Persuasion — Speech."
Æsch. "Alone among the gods Death loves not gifts."

Bac. "There it is; down again."

Eur. "I am sure that what I said about Persuasion was very fine."

Bac. "But Persuasion is a light thing, while Death is the heaviest of all evils. Well, you shall have one more trial, and this must be the last. Think, Euripides, of something solid to weigh him down."

Eur. "I have it : —

"'His right hand grasped an iron-weighted spear.'"
Æsch. "Chariot on chariot piled, and corpse on corpse."

Bac. "There, he has done you again!"

Eur. "How?"

Bac. "Why, by bringing in a couple of chariots and two corpses, more than a hundred Egyptians could lift."

Æsch. "Come, no more single lines. Let him put himself and his wife and his children and all his books and his ghost[1] to boot into the scale, and I will weigh them all down with a couple of verses."

---

[1] A "ghost" in artistic and literary slang is an unacknowledged assistant who does part or even the whole of an artist's or writer's work. He visits the study or the studio unseen, and works at the painting, the statue, or the book of which some one else is to get the credit. Cephisophon, who is named in the text, was accustomed to take the chief part in the plays of Euripides, and it was commonly said in Athens that he assisted the poet in the composition of them.

Bac. "Well, I don't think I can decide. One I think very wise, and the other I like; and I should not wish to be on bad terms with either."

Pluto. "And are you not going to do what you came for?"

Bac. "Well, if I do decide, what then?"

Plu. "You will take the one you choose and go. So you won't have come for nothing."

Bac. "Bless you for a good fellow. Then I'll try. I came down for a poet."

Eur. "With what object?"

Bac. "This: I want to have a prosperous Athens exhibiting tragedies as they should be exhibited; and so I mean to take back with me the man who can give the country a good piece of advice. What do you think about Alcibiades? Athens is having a hard time of it with him."

Eur. "And what does she feel about him?"

Bac. "She loves and she detests, yet longs to have."
Eur. "I hate the man that still is slow to help
  His country, quick to harm her, and contrives
  Much profit for himself and none for her."
Æsch. "Rear not a lion's cub within your walls;
  But having reared him, let him work his will."

Bac. "I am puzzled still. Try again. How would you save your country?"

Eur. "The counsellors you trust in, trust no more;
  The men you use not, use; so save your land."

Bac. "Now, Æschylus, what have you got to say?"

Æsch. "Tell me first, to whom does Athens go? To honest men?"

Bac. "No; she hates them like poison."

Æsch. "Then she likes the rogues?"

Bac. "Not she; but she is forced to employ them."

Æsch. "How save a city so perverse, that likes
Neither the noble's cloak nor beggar's mat?"

Bac. "Do think of something good, — that is, if you want to go back."

Æsch. "When they shall count their enemy's land their own,
Their own the enemy's, and in their ships
See their sole safety, and from hardship draw
Means of deliverance . . ."

Plu. "Now you must decide."

Eur. "Remember now the gods by whom you swore
To take me home, and choose the man you love."

Bac. "My tongue has sworn — yet Æschylus I choose."

Eur. "Villain, what have you done?"

Bac. "Done? Chosen Æschylus, to be sure. Why not?"

Eur. "And you are going to leave me here down among the dead?"

Bac. "It may be; death is life, and life is death."

Plu. "Now, Æschylus, in peace depart;
And with thy nobler poet's art
Enrich thy country as before,
And teach the fools — for many more
There are than were in days of yore."
Æsch. "So be it; and this seat of mine
To Sophocles, I pray, assign,
Till I return, if this should be;
He holds the second place to me.
And, mark me, keep that villain there
From sitting in my sacred chair."

VIII.

THE PARLIAMENT OF WOMEN.

This is one of the poet's later plays, having been produced in
392 B.C. The satire is, for the most part, social rather than political.
There is, indeed, a sarcasm on the passion for change and for novel
experiments in government, when the proposal for placing power in the
hands of the women is approved as being the only scheme which had
not yet been tried in Athens. But the general object of the satire is
woman, while there is doubtless a special reference to the fashion for
imitating Spartan manners. The Spartan women, it must be remembered, lived in a sort of comradeship, so to speak, with the men, which
was wholly unlike Athenian ways.

ONCE upon a time it happened in Athens that
every form of government having been tried to no
good purpose, and things getting worse and worse
instead of better, the women thought it would be
well to take affairs into their own hands. How they
managed this will be told; but first it should be said
that their leader in this revolution was a certain
Praxagora.

On the appointed day, while it was still dark,
Praxagora made her way to the place in the suburbs
where she had arranged to meet her fellow-conspira-
tors, and began by hanging up the lamp with which
she had lighted her way from home, and paying it
her respects. She said : —

> "Eye of the potter-moulded lamp, with whom
> Are shared the kindred honours of the sun,
> Let thus the splendour of thy faithful flame
> The sign concerted show. Faithful thou art,
> Knowing, yet not betraying; to thine eye
> Our toilet's secrets are revealed; thy help
> Is given, yet given in silence, when we take
> Toll from the treasuries of food and wine;
> Share, then, O lamp, the counsels of to-day.

"But how is this?" she went on, looking round about, "I don't see one of the friends whom I expected, although it is almost dawn, and the Assembly will soon be meeting. We must fill up the places first. Have they not been able to get the beards, or have they found it too hard to steal the men's clothes? But stay—I see a lamp approaching. I will just step out of the way in case it should be a man."

And now a number of women appeared. One declared that the cock did but crow the second time as she left her house; another said that her husband had been ill all night from having eaten too many pilchards, and that he had only just fallen asleep; a third had stood in the sun all the day before to give herself a manly brown; a fourth showed a formidable club which she had secured. A thrifty dame, who thought it would be well to save time by spinning while the place of Assembly was filling, incurred a severe rebuke, though she pleaded that she could listen just as well while she was at work, and that her poor children had nothing to put on. To spin would be fatally certain to betray them; whereas, if they would only sit in front, keep well muffled up, and show their beards, no one but would think that they were men. "A number of old women," said Praxagora, "have passed themselves off as men in the Assembly before now." The conspirators now proceeded to have a rehearsal of what they would have to do in the Assembly. For a time there was a doubt whether any one would be able to make a speech; but they comforted themselves by remembering that speech was the special gift of woman. One of the meeting began by proposing that vintners who kept a tank of water on their premises for weakening their wines should be severely punished. She made, however, the sad blunder of swearing by the two goddesses, an oath which women only were accustomed to use; and, when allowed to address the audience again, actually styled them "Ladies." Praxagora, hopeless of getting anything done by helpers so inefficient, resolved to carry the affair through by herself, and, having assumed the chaplet, addressed the meeting : —

"Gentlemen," she said, "the weal of this city is dear to me as it is to all of you, and it grieves me to see how ill its affairs prosper. Why do they prosper ill? Because you have no leaders. If a man behaves honestly for one day, he will be a scoundrel for ten. Make a change, some will say. Well, your new man will only do more mischief."

THE WOMEN'S CONSPIRACY.

"By Aphrodite! you speak well," cried one of the audience.

"By Aphrodite [1] indeed!" cried Praxagora, turning on the speaker.

"What a thing to say! Supposing that you had said it in the Assembly itself!"

"Oh! but there I should have been more careful."

"Well, be careful now. Then you are always blowing hot and cold. The allies of one day are the enemies of the next. Then you are not agreed. 'Man a fleet,' says the poor man, who is looking out for pay. 'No, no,' say the rich men, who don't want the taxes increased."

"That's a clever man," said the woman who had spoken before.

"Ah," cried Praxagora, "now that is the right sort of compliment. Well, gentlemen, the fault is in yourselves. The public wealth goes into private pockets. No man cares for the state; every man looks out for himself; and the country goes to ruin. What, then, is the remedy? Why, put the government into the hands of the women. They manage your houses; why not let them manage the state? Do you want to know why they are likely to do it well? I'll tell you. Because they keep to old ways, and do as their mothers used to do. They wash wool in hot water, for instance, after the old fashion. You won't see them trying new-fangled ways of

[1] Another woman's oath.

doing things. And an excellent thing it would be for Athens if it did the same. They bake bread sitting, as their mothers did; they bear loads on
/ their heads, as their mothers did; they make cheese-cakes, as their mothers did; they beat their husbands, as their mothers did; they keep titbits for them-selves, as their mothers did; they like good liquor, as their mothers did. I say, then, hand over the state to them; ask no idle questions as to what line of policy they will follow; think only of this: they are the mothers of our soldiers and they won't see them killed or starved; they are admirable providers; they are themselves so good at deceiving that no one will ever be able to deceive them. I need say no more: take my advice, and you will live happily ever after."

" But, my dear creature," cried one of the women who had been listening, "how did you learn to speak so well?"

"Oh!" replied Praxagora, "once when we had to
/ leave the country [1] I lodged with my good man close by the place of Assembly, and I learnt the trick of speaking by listening to the politicians."

Woman. "Very good! and you shall be our first prime minister. But how shall we manage to elect you? Tell us that."

Praxagora. "It won't be an easy matter, but still it can be done. Tuck up your tunics; tie on your

---

[1] During the annual invasion by the Spartan army.

sandals, just as you see the men do when they are going out. When this is done, fasten on your beards; put your husbands' cloaks, which I hope you have stolen, over all; take your staves, and march to the place of Assembly. You can sing, as you go, some old-fashioned ditty, and people will take you for voters from the country. And make haste. Mind, we must be there before dawn. Now let us be off, and sing a stave as we go."

The women accordingly marched away singing : —

> " Let us hasten away ;
> There's no time for delay,
> For the Archon has sworn
> That who wishes to-day
> To be sure of his pay
> Must be there before morn
> With our vouchers [1] in hand,
> An unanimous band.
> We will lift up our voice,
> Making excellent choice
> Of the women — nay, nay,
> Of the men, I should say ;

[1] The meaning of the song seems to be that the seats in the place of Assembly would be soon filled up, as it was only the first comers who received the ticket or voucher, which, when business was finished, was exchanged for the three *oboli*, or half-drachma. The greedy fellows who thought of nothing but their pay would soon come trooping in ; therefore the women must be beforehand with them to fill up their seats. From this it was a natural digression to regret the growth of the mercenary spirit, and to look back to the time when citizens were more disinterested and discharged their public duties without looking for reward.

We are all men to-day.
We must vote for, and mind
That the gain-hunting crowd
From the town be allowed
Not a sitting to find.
Ah! but once on a time,
In our fair golden prime,
Men had thought it a crime
To serve country for pelf;
But each brought for himself
Just a bottle of wine and a morsel to eat,
Bread with onions and olives may be for a treat;
But these fellows are patriots only for pay,
Like scavengers working for so much a day."

Meanwhile there was much perplexity and confusion in the houses which the women had left.
"Where in the world is my wife?" said one poor
man, who was Praxagora's husband. "I can't find
my shoes or my cloak; so I have had to put on her
mantle, and make shift to get my feet as far as they
would go into her Persian slippers. Fool that I was
to marry a wife at my age! However, I must be
going, if I am to get to the Assembly in time."

Just as he was outside the door, a friend met him.
"Can this be Blepyrus?" he cried. "Why have you
got that scarlet thing on?"

Blepyrus. "'Tis my wife's. I had to put it on."

Friend. "But where is your own cloak?"

Blep. "That I can't say. I have been looking for
it everywhere."

Fr. "But your wife — why did you not ask her?"

Blep. "She's not at home. She's gone some-where on the sly."

Fr. "Why, my dear sir, that is exactly what has happened to me. My wife has taken off my cloak; yes, and that is not the worst, but my shoes, too."

Blep. "My shoes are gone, too."

Fr. "Perhaps a friend has invited her to break-fast."

Blep. "Very likely; she is not a bad sort, after all."

Fr. "Well, I must be off to the Assembly; that is, if I can find my cloak, for I haven't got another."

Very soon afterwards another friend came in, Chremes by name. He had come, he said, from the Assembly. "What," asked Blepyrus, "is it dis-missed already?"

Chremes. "Yes, and almost before it was light."

Blep. "You got your pay, I suppose?"

Chr. "I wish that I had; as it was, I came too late."

Blep. "How was that?"

Chr. "A whole crowd of people, more than I ever saw together, came into the Pnyx; we thought, to look at them, they were a set of indoor artisans, they had such pale faces. However, they filled the place, and I could not get my money, and a good many more were in the same plight."

Blep. "Then I could not get it if I went now?"

Chr. "No, indeed; nor would you have got it, even if you had gone at second cock-crowing."

14

Blep. "Well, what, pray, was the business that brought all this crowd together?"

Chr. "The public safety. That was the question which the magistrates had prepared. One said one thing, and one another. The gentleman who seemed to have nothing over his tunic, though he declared himself that he had a cloak, proposed that the clothiers should be compelled to furnish cloaks to all persons in need. We should escape cold and pleurisy in that way. Any one who should refuse, and shut his door in the winter against an applicant, was to be fined three blankets."

Blep. "An excellent proposition; and if he had added that the corn-chandlers were to supply every poor man with three pecks of barley, under pain of death, he would not have found any one to vote against it."

Chr. "After that a good-looking young fellow, rather pale in the face, stood up and proposed that the management of affairs should be handed over to the women. At this all the artisans cried out, '*Hear! hear!*' while the country-folk shouted '*No! no!*'"

Blep. "And right they were, by Zeus!"

Chr. "Yes; but they were beaten. The young fellow said all kinds of good things about the women. They were choke-full of good sense; they made money; they could keep a secret; they could lend each other clothes, gold, silver, plate, and not cheat each other — no, not though there were no witnesses : whereas we were always defrauding each other."

Blep. "Yes, indeed, witnesses or no witnesses."

Chr. "They didn't inform against each other, nor prosecute, nor plot against the people: all this and other things too he said about the women."

Blep. "Well, what was the end of it all?"

Chr. "It was determined to hand over the management of affairs to them. You see, this is the only ⌐ thing that has never been tried in Athens."

Blep. "You mean that the law passed?"

Chr. "Yes."

Blep. "That the women are to discharge all our duties?"

Chr. "Exactly so."

Blep. "That my wife and not I is to try causes?"

Chr. "Yes; and your wife, not you, is to keep the house."

Blep. "This is all very alarming."

Chr. "Nay, nay; don't vex yourself. What says the old proverb?

> 'Though weak and vain our counsels, yet the gods
> Still overrule them to some happy end.'

But I must be going. Take care of yourself."

The women who had been passing this revolutionary vote now came hurrying in, looking about them as if they feared pursuit, and singing as they went : —

> "Is a man on our track? Look in front and look back,
> Keep a watch all around, and tramp hard on the ground;
> 'Twould be sad if a man should discover our plan.

Now we're near to the spot which first witnessed our plot;
Let us go one and all to the shade of a wall,
And away from all eyes doff our manly disguise."

They had scarcely finished when Praxagora appeared, calmly walking up to her house. Her husband naturally wanted to know where she had come
from.

Prax. "A dear friend who had been taken ill
sent for me in the night."

Blep. "But why not tell me that you were going?"

Prax. "Ought not I to have gone, then?"

Blep. "Gone — yes; but why did you take my
cloak?"

Prax. "It was so cold, and I am not very strong,
and I left you snugly wrapped in your blankets."

Blep. "But why my sandals and staff?"

Prax. "I was afraid, so I did my best to make myself look like you. I stamped with my feet, and
knocked the stones with the staff."

Blep. "Well, you've made me lose a peck of wheat
which I should have brought home from the Assembly."

Prax. "Never you mind about that; it was a very
fine boy."

Blep. "Whose boy? the Assembly's?"

Prax. "No; my friend's. But has there been an
Assembly?"

Blep. "Of course. Don't you remember that I
told you yesterday it was to be?"

Prax. "So you did."

Blep. "And don't you know what they have done?"

Prax. "Not I."

Blep. "They have handed over to you women the government of affairs."

Prax. "Spinning, do you mean?"

Blep. "No — ruling."

Prax. "Ruling? Ruling what?"

Blep. "Ruling everything."

Prax. "By Aphrodite, a very lucky thing for the country!"

Blep. "Why a lucky thing?"

Prax. "For many reasons; she won't be the prey of bad men any more. There will be no more per- juries, no more informers."

Blep. "Woman, what do you mean? Why, these are the things I live by."

Prax. "Silence, my good man, and let your wife speak. There'll be no stealing, no arguing, no nakedness, no poverty, no slander, no distraint for debt."

Blep. "That's all very fine if true."

Prax. "True! I'll warrant every word is true."

The women, who had assembled round their leader while this conversation was going on, now encouraged her to develop her plan for the better government of the city. They put their thoughts into verse : —

"Now befits thee to unfold
Skilful plan and counsel bold;
Now for friends and commonweal
Show how great and wise thy zeal.
Hope of better days impart,
Cheering weary mind and heart.
Time it is some skilful hand　　　.
Healed the sorrows of our land;
Only let thy wise intent
Some judicious scheme invent,
Such as ne'er before has been
Either thought of, heard, or seen;
Old things please not here, I ween."

Prax. "The first thing in my plan is that all should share and share alike. I won't have some rich and some poor; one man with a broad domain, and another with not ground enough for a grave; one man with many slaves, and another with not even one poor page. No. All the citizens shall fare alike. How shall I do it, do you ask? I shall make the land common property, and the money, and all that every man possesses. These things we women will wisely manage, apportioning to each what he wants."

Blep. "But what will you do with those who don't own land, but have a secret store of gold and silver?"

Prax. "We must bring them into the common stock."

Blep. "But suppose that the man swears that he hasn't got them?"

Prax. " Why should he ? 'Tis only poverty that makes men forswear themselves, and there will be no poverty here. Every man will have whatever he wants for the asking."

Blep. " But who is to cultivate the land ? "

Prax. " The slaves, of course. All that you will have to do will be to go nicely dressed to dinner when the dial shows the hour."

Blep. "And how shall we get new clothes ? "

Prax. " What there are now will serve for the present, and then we women will spin you new ones."

Blep. " Suppose there is a judgment against a man for a sum of money, how is he to pay it? Not out of the common stock, I suppose ? "

Prax. " But there will be no suits or judgments."

Blep. " No suits ! If any man owes money and denies the debt, how then ? "

Prax. " How did the creditor get the money to lend when everything is common ? "

Blep. " Good ! But tell me this : If a man is fined for assault, how then ? This will puzzle you, I take it."

Prax. " Not at all. He'll pay in pudding. Starve him a bit, and he'll learn not to be insolent."

Blep. " Then no one will steal ? "

Prax. " Why should he ? He'll be stealing his own property."

Blep. " Then there'll be no footpads ? "

Prax. "No; for all will have enough. And if a man should stop you with, 'Your coat or your life!' you'll only have to give it to him and go to the public store and get another."

Blep. "Will there be any gambling?"

Prax. "What should they gamble for?"

Blep. "And what is our fare to be?"

Prax. "The same for all. The city will in fact be one house."

Blep. "Where shall we dine?"

Prax. "We shall make the courts and the colonnades into dining-rooms. We sha'n't want them for purposes of law any more."

Blep. "And the speakers' platform,—what will you do with that?"

Prax. "We shall stand our mixing-bowls and water-pitchers on it. And the singing-boys shall stand on it and celebrate the deeds of the valiant, so that if by chance there should be any cowards they may slink away ashamed. Does this please you?"

Blep. "Excellently well."

Prax. "Now I betake me to the market-place,
Some shrill-voiced dame before me, who shall play
The herald's part, for there must I receive
The moneys flowing to the common purse;
For that same public voice that bade me rule
Hath laid these duties on me, and commands
That I should order well the sumptuous feasts,
Which with this day begin. And so farewell."

"Excellent, my dear," said Blepyrus. "I will come with you. How the people will stare at me, and say to each other, 'Look there! Do you know who that is? That is the husband of the lady in command.'"

IX.

PLUTUS.

There seem to have been two editions of the play entitled *The Plutus* (God of Riches). One was produced in 408 B.C.; the other in 388 B.C. According to the Argument or Introduction commonly prefixed, we have the second of these two editions. It is said to have been the last play which the poet exhibited in his own name. His career as a dramatist had then lasted thirty-nine years; his first comedy, *The Banqueters*, had been produced, though not in his own name, in 427 B.C. The character of *The Plutus* suits this position in the catalogue of the poet's works. It is mainly a comedy of morals, and in spirit resembles the dramas which are classed as the New Comedy, though the form is the same as that to which we are accustomed in the earlier plays; and . there is something of the same savage satire on individuals.

ONCE upon a time two travellers, a master, Chremylus by name, and his slave Cario, might have been seen painfully making their way from Delphi to Athens. The strange thing about them was that they were following the guidance of a blind man, a proceeding on which the master insisted, much to the annoyance of his slave. The latter bewailed the hard fate which compelled a sensible man to follow the caprices of a foolish one, blamed the god of the oracle, who, though he had the reputation of being both a physician and a prophet, had sent an inquirer away in a condition of madness. "For what," said the slave to himself, "could be a greater proof of

218

madness than for a man who can see to follow the
leading of one who is blind; and a fellow, too, who
won't answer a syllable to any question?" At last
the slave made up his mind to speak to his master.
" Tell me," he said, " who this man is that you seem
determined to follow. You know that I have always
done my best for you."—" That is so," said Chremylus, " that is so; I have always found you the most
faithful of my slaves—and the greatest thief. However, I'll have no secrets from you. You know that
I am a pious and honest man, and that I have always
been unlucky and poor."

Cario. " I know it perfectly well."

Chremylus. " And that robbers of temples, informers, politicians, and scoundrels of all sorts are
rich. Well, I went to consult Apollo about it. My
days, I knew, were pretty nearly over; but I wanted
to know about my only son. Was he to give up my
virtuous ways and turn into a villain, as it was only
the villains who prospered? The answer was this:
' Follow the first person whom you see after leaving
my temple; don't lose sight of him, but make him
go home with you.' "

Car. " And who was the first person you saw?"

Chrem. " That man there."

Car. " Well, master, that is very stupid of you.
Of course Apollo meant that you were to bring up
the boy as a villain. Everybody is a villain; therefore the first person you meet will be a villain; there-

fore you must follow a villain. Even a blind man
could see so much."

Chrem. "Apollo meant nothing of the kind, but
something much more serious. If we can only find
out who the man is, and what he wants, then we
should know what the god meant."

For a time the stranger refused to speak; at last,
under compulsion, and after a promise that he should
be released when he had answered, he revealed his
name and condition. "I am the god of wealth," he
said.

Chrem. "You the god of wealth! and in this miserable plight!"

Plutus. "That is easily accounted for. I am just
come from the house of a miserly fellow who never
went to the bath from the day of his birth, or let me
go either."

Chrem. "And how came you to be blind?"

Plu. "When I was a lad I said that I intended
to visit only the wise and good. Thereupon Zeus
made me blind, that I might not know them. He is
jealous of the wise and good."

Chrem. "And yet it is only they who honour him."

Plu. "It is so."

Chrem. "Tell me, now; if you could recover your
sight, would you keep to your intention, and avoid
the bad?"

Plu. "I certainly would."

Chrem. "And keep company with the good?"

Plu. "Certainly; it is many a long day since I saw one of that sort."

Chrem. "Just as it has been with me, and yet I can see."

Plu. "Now, then, you'll let me go."

Chrem. "Let you go indeed! No; we'll stick to you closer than ever."

Plu. "Ah! that is just what I feared."

Chrem. "My dear friend, don't leave me; you won't find a more honest man than I am to live with."

Plu. "So they all say; but as sure as ever I come to them, they turn into the worst rogues of all."

Chrem. "Ah! but you may trust me. And now listen to me, and I'll tell you what you will get by coming home with me; I hope, please the gods, to recover you of your blindness."

Plu. "No, no; I don't want to see."

Chrem. "Why not?"

Plu. "Because I am afraid what Zeus might do to me."

Chrem. "Don't be afraid of Zeus. You are a much greater power than he. Why do men pray to Zeus? For the sake of money, to be sure. Don't they pray for this in so many words? And could you not stop all this if you chose?"

Plu. "How could I stop it?"

Chrem. "Because no man could offer an ox, no, not even a barley-cake, without your good-will. You find the money for it. So it is clear that you have only to say the word, and the power of Zeus topples down."

Plu. "Do you really mean that I have all this to do with sacrifices?"

Chrem. "Yes, indeed; and everything on earth that has splendour or beauty about it comes from you; and you are the cause of every art and every craft that has ever been discovered. You make the cobbler squat, and the brazier hammer, and the carpenter ply his adze, and the goldsmith melt the gold — you give him the gold. Aye, and you make one man filch people's clothes from the bath, and another break into houses."

Plu. "Dear me! I knew nothing of all this."

Chrem. "You give all his glory to the Great King,[1] call together the Public Assembly, man the ships of war, pay the soldiers, make us bear Mr. Vulgar's manners and listen to Mr. Dryasdust's stories."

Plu. "Can I really do all this?"

Chrem. "Yes, indeed; and much more than this. You are the one thing of which men can never have enough. Of everything else they get a surfeit, — of love, for instance."

Car. "And of bread."

Chrem. "Of poetry."

Car. "And of sweetmeats."

---

[1] The king of Persia, — the only prince of whom the Greeks used the term "basileus."

Chrem. " Of honour."

Car. " And cheesecakes."

Chrem. " Of courage."

Car. " And figs."

Chrem. " Of glory."

Car. " And hasty-pudding."

Chrem. " Of office."

Car. " And pease-pudding."

Chrem. " But of you they never can have enough. If a man has thirteen talents, does he not straightway want sixteen? And if he gets sixteen, does he not want forty, if life is to be worth living?"

Plu. "You seem to be a very sensible man. But there is one thing I am afraid of. Tell me: if I get this power, shall I be able to keep it?"

Chrem. "They are quite right in saying that wealth is the most timid of creatures."

Plu. "Not timid at all. This was a slander that a burglar invented, when he got into my house and found everything locked up. Because I am cautious he said I was timid."

Chrem. "Well, never mind. Trust me, and I will make you keen-sighted as a lynx."

Plu. "But how will you contrive it? You're only a man."

Chrem. "I have good hopes that Apollo will help me."

Plu. " Does he know what you are doing?"

Chrem. "Yes; he does. I'll help you, if I die

for it, and so will all my friends and neighbours. Cario, go and call them; it is only right that they should have a share of my good luck. And now, Plutus, come into my house."

Plu. " I tell you that I don't at all like going into another man's house. I never got any good from doing it. If my host has been of the frugal sort, he has buried me in the ground; aye, and if a good fellow came to borrow a silver coin, has sworn that he has never set eyes upon me. If he has been one of the wild young fellows, then I am given over to bad company and dice, and turned naked out of doors at a moment's notice."

Chrem. " That is because you never happened to light upon a moderate man. I·like to save; no man more. And I like to spend, at the proper time. But come in; I should like you to see my wife and my son. He is my only son, you must understand; and I love him better than anything else in the world, — of course after you."

Meanwhile Cario had been inviting the neighbours to come to his master's house. They were not slow to answer the call, but left their work in the fields, and hurried up, followed by one Blepsidemus, who was the principal person among them. Blepsidemus was suspicious. His friend, he had heard, had become suddenly rich. This was in itself an unusual circumstance, and, put together with the mysterious answers which he got to his questions, inclined him to believe that his friend had committed some crime. When he heard that the god of riches was actually an inmate in his neighbour's house, his astonishment was great, nor was it diminished at being told that Chremylus's intention was to make his friends sharers in his good luck. He agreed with the notion that the god should, if possible, be cured of his blindness, but did not see how it could be done. This, indeed, puzzled both of the friends, till Chremylus suggested that the best plan would be to make him pass a night in the temple of Æsculapius. Scarcely had they resolved on this course when a strange visitor appeared, Poverty, a lean and spectral figure, from whom the two men fled in terror. However, they plucked up courage, and came back, wondering what it could be. " A Fury escaped from a tragedy, perhaps," said one of them. " It has a mad, tragical look."

" No," replied the other, " it hasn't got a torch."

" Who do you think I am?" said the figure.

Chrem. "The landlady of an inn, or an oyster-girl; you made such an uproar when no one had hurt you."

" I tell you," cried the Unknown, "that you are both intending to do a most villainous thing. Know that I am Poverty — your old inmate, Poverty."

Blep. "Good heavens! I'm off."

Chrem. " Coward, you are not going to run away ? "

Blep. " Yes, but I am."

15

Chrem. "What! two men run away from one woman?"

Blep. "Yes; but the one woman is Poverty, and a more terrible creature does not exist."

At last, however, Blepsidemus consented to stay, and the matter was argued out.

Chremylus argued on behalf of his plan for restoring eyesight to Plutus. He said: " Every one allows that good men ought to prosper, and that the bad and impious should fare ill. It has been our object to bring this about, and after much thinking we have devised a really good plan for doing so. If for the future Plutus should be able to see, and not wander about blindly, as he has hitherto done, then he will take up his abode with the good and shun the bad. So it will come about that all men will become good and pious. Is it possible to invent a better scheme than this? As for man's life, as it is at present, it is nothing but sheer, raving madness. Bad men enjoy the wealth which they collected by the most villainous devices, and the good are next door to starvation."

Poverty. " Now, you foolish old creature, listen to what I have got to say. Let Plutus divide his favours equally, and who would cultivate any art or knowledge? who would be a brazier, a shipwright, a tailor, a wheelwright, a shoemaker, a brickmaker, a dyer, or a skinner? who would sow and reap when he might sit at ease and enjoy himself?"

Chrem. "Our slaves would do all this for us."

Pov. "But where would you get your slaves?"

Chrem. "Buy them, to be sure."

Pov. "But who would take the trouble to sell them if he had money already?"

Chrem. "The slave-dealer, I suppose."

Pov. "Not a bit of it. Who would risk his life for money, when he could get it without? No; you will have to do all these things for yourselves. No more lying on couches, for couches there won't be; no more fine robes, for who will care to weave? no more perfumes, not even on your wedding day. And what will be the good of your riches without these things? But stick to me, and you will have the necessaries of life in plenty. It is I who stand by and drive men to work by my strong compulsion."

Chrem. "Oh, I know the sort of life you will give us, — bawling children, and cross old women, and buzzing gnats, and biting fleas, all bidding us get up and work; and rags instead of clothes, and rushes for feather beds, and a mat for a carpet, and a stone for a pillow."

Pov. "This is the way in which beggars live."

Chrem. "Well, is not Poverty sister to Beggary?"

Pov. "So you say; but then, you don't know the difference, I suppose, between Dionysius the tyrant, and Thrasybulus the patriot.[1] A beggar may live

---

[1] Thrasybulus restored a free constitution to Athens by upsetting the tyranny of the Four Hundred, which had been established after the capture of the city by the Spartans.

as you say, but a poor man lives frugally and sticks to his work."

Chrem. "Yes; happy man! and dies without leaving enough to bury him."

Pov. "Yes; you may laugh, but I make better men than wealth can make, — better in mind, better in body, not gouty, big-bellied, thick-legged creatures, but spare, and small-waisted, and terrible fellows to fight."

Chrem. "Spare enough, I dare say, for you starve them pretty well."

Pov. "And as for good manners, you find them with me; it is wealth that is insolent."

Chrem. "Oh, yes! excellently good manners — to steal and break into houses!"

Pov. "Then look at the politicians. While they are poor, they are honest; let them get a taste of the public money, and good by to their honesty."

Chrem. "I don't say that you're wrong here. Still this shall not help you."

Pov. "And how about Zeus? Isn't he poor? At the Olympic games, where all Greece meets every four years, what is the prize that he gives to the conquerors? A wreath of wild olive. If he had been rich, would it not have been of gold?"

Chrem. "He satisfies them with a trifle, and keeps the riches to himself."

All Poverty's arguments having proved to be unavailing, she was driven away, though not without warning her adversaries that it would not be long before they sent for her.

The next thing was to cure Plutus of his blindness. The story of how this was done was told next morning by Cario to his mistress.

"The first thing that we did was to take him down to the shore and bathe him in the sea. After that we went up to the temple, offered on the altar the usual sacrifices, and then laid Plutus down, every one of us at the same time making his own bed. He was not the only suppliant. Indeed, I noticed another blind man, who, however, is a cleverer thief than most people with eyes, and there were other persons suffering from all manner of diseases. Then an attendant came round, put out the light, and bade us go to sleep, telling us to be silent in case we should hear any noise. As for me, I could not get to sleep; there was an old woman near me, and a little way off from her head was a pitcher of porridge, for which I had quite an inspired longing, so good did it smell. And when I opened my eyes I saw the priest snatching the pastry and figs from the holy table, and then going the round of the altars to see if there was a cake left on any of them. Whatever he found he consecrated into a wallet that he had. When I found that this was a devotion practised in the place, I crept up to the porridge-pitcher. The old woman heard me coming, and put out her hand to hold the porridge, and I

hissed like a serpent, and bit it. Thereupon she
drew it back, and covered her head with the bed-
clothes. As for me, I had a good meal from the
porridge, and lay down in my bed. After a while
Æsculapius himself came round with his two daughters, Recovery and All-Healer,[1] followed by a boy
who carried a stone mortar, a pestle, and a small
chest. I was very much frightened and covered
myself up; still I could see what was done through
a peep-hole in my cloak — I had a good choice of
peep-holes. The god began by making an ointment
to plaster on the eyes of that blind thief I spoke
of; he mixed together three heads of garlic, fig-tree
sap,[2] and mastic, and moistened it with vinegar.
Then he turned the fellow's eyelids out — to hurt
him more, you understand. The thief roared like
a bull, and ran out of the temple. The god laughed
and said, ' There, there; now you may learn not to
forswear yourself.' After this he came and sat
down by Plutus. The first thing that he did was to
stroke his head; then he took a clean napkin, and
wiped his eyelids with it. Next, All-Healer covered
his head with a purple kerchief. Then the god
whistled, and two huge serpents came out of the
sanctuary. These put their heads under the kerchief, and, I imagine, licked the eyelids; and — in

[1] Iaso and Panacea are the Greek names.
[2] This was an acrid fluid used by the Greeks instead of rennet to
curdle milk for cheese-making.

AESCULAPIUS.

less time than you could drink a pint of wine —
Plutus stood up seeing as you or I. I clapped my
hands for joy, and woke my master; the god and
his serpents vanished into the sanctuary, and we all
wished Plutus joy of his recovery, and watched till
the day broke. And now he is coming with a great
crowd of people after him rejoicing and singing."

The slave had scarcely finished his narrative when
Plutus appeared, and returned thanks in solemn fashion for his recovery : —

> "First the great Sun I reverence; then the plain,
> The famous plain where holy Pallas dwells,
> And Cecrops' hospitable land, my home.
> The past I do remember sore ashamed,
> In what ill company I spent my days,
> Unknowing; how all ignorant I fled
> From worthier friends, unhappy that I was!
> Choosing the bad I erred; I erred no less
> The good refusing. But this self-same hour
> I changed my ways in all things, so that man
> May know me to have sinned against my will."

And indeed the change was something marvellous.
Chremylus, who had not been popular in the days of
his poverty, now found himself the object of admiring
attention from friends without number. In his house
everything was changed. The bin, in old times generally empty, was full of the finest flour, the jar of
delicious wine, the coffers of gold and silver. The
well was brimming over with oil, and the oil-cruse
with perfume. The fish-platters, once of wood and

half-rotten, were found to be silver, the dresser was
ivory; the very slaves played at odd and even with
gold pieces.

Not less wonderful was the crowd of visitors that
came to pay their respects to the god. The first arrival was a good man, who had been poor. He had
been left a comfortable fortune, he explained, by his
father, and had thought that the best use he could
make of it would be to help his friends. If he should
come to need, of course they would help him. Naturally he had not been long in reaching the bottom
of his purse, and then he found that his friends could
not so much as see him. Thanks to this change in
the god, he was now well off, and he was coming to
dedicate to him the ragged cloak and worn-out shoes
which he had worn in the days of his poverty. The
next comer was as much disgusted at the new order
of things as his predecessor had been pleased. He
was an informer, and came in a condition of frantic
hunger; his business had failed him, and he threatened the most fearful penalties against those who
had ruined him. All the satisfaction he got was to
be stripped of his fine clothes, have the good man's
cloak wrapped round him, and the shoes fastened on
his forehead. Next came an elderly lady, who had
lost the suitor who had paid her attentions on account
of her wealth, but now, being rich himself, had trans-
ferred them elsewhere. She too got nothing by her
visit. The succeeding visitor showed that the influ-

ence of the revolution had reached to heaven itself. Hermes presented himself, complaining that since Plutus had recovered his sight, no one had offered to the gods so much as a grain of frankincense, a twig of laurel, or a cake. " I," said the god, "am a peculiar sufferer. You know that I am a little friendly to rogues, and these, in return, used to give me some perquisites. That is all over now; I go hungry all day long. Give me," he went on, addressing the slave Cario, "a loaf and a piece of the flesh."

Car. "I can't. The things are not to be taken out."

Hermes. "Ah! my man, don't you remember how I used to help you when you filched anything of your master's?"

Car. "Yes, but only on condition of having your share."

Her. "Which share you always ate yourself."

Car. "And very right. Who got the stripes, if I was found out?"

Her. "Well, well, let's have an amnesty now that the battle is over.[1] For heaven's sake, make me one of your household here!"

[1] Literally, "now that Phylæ is taken." The reference is to a memorable event in Athenian history. The "Thirty Tyrants," put in power by the Spartans after the capture of Athens and their overthrow by Thrasybulus, have been mentioned in the introduction to this story. The first step which Thrasybulus and his followers took was to seize the frontier fort of Phylæ. The end of the struggle was the proclamation of an amnesty.

Car. "What! you going to leave the gods and stay here!"

Her. "Yes; you seem to be much better off."

Car. "A deserter is a mean sort of creature."

Her. "Listen:—

"My country is the land where best I fare."

Car. "But what good will you be to us?"

Her. "I will be your turnkey."

Car. "We want none of your turns."

Her. "Your merchant, then."

Car. "We are rich; we want no huckstering."

Her. "Your master of craft?"

Car. "We want no craft; simple ways are the fashion now."

Her. "Your guide?"

Car. "The god has his sight, and will want no more guiding."

Her. "Your Chief of the Sports? for, of course, he will do well to have musical competitions and games."

Car. "What a thing it is to have a number of titles! At last he has hit upon some capacity in which he may be useful to us. Well, go to the spring and wash these haunches for me, that you may learn to make yourself useful and handy."[1]

---

[1] Hermes pleads the various capacities which he was supposed to have. He was the Porter of the Hall of Heaven, the Patron of Trades, the God of Council, the Guide, as conducting the Souls of the Dead, etc., and the Patron of Sports.

A priest now came, with the same complaint that Hermes had made, — he was starving. No one wanted anything; therefore, no one offered sacrifices. He was glad to take service with the new deity.

A procession was now organized to conduct Plutus to his temple. The elderly lady who had come back in very gay attire was induced to carry the pots of boiled pulse,[1] on the promise that her suitor should return to her, and the god of wealth was solemnly enthroned as the one and only deity thenceforward to be worshipped in Athens.

[1] Commonly carried by young girls, who wore gay-coloured robes, at the dedication of an altar or temple.

PART II.

STORIES FROM THE NEW COMEDY.

PHILEMON, DIPHILUS, MENANDER,
APOLLODORUS.

I.

THE BURIED TREASURE.

[*From* PHILEMON. *Translated by* PLAUTUS.]

CHARMIDES, a citizen of Athens, being compelled to go abroad on business, intrusted the charge of his affairs to his old friend Callicles. Among the matters which he put in his friend's hands was an important secret, nothing less than the fact that he had buried under the floor of one of the rooms in his house a treasure of three thousand gold philips.[1] This he had done to provide a dowry for his daughter, in case she should be sought in marriage during his absence. His son, Lesbionicus by name, he could not trust, so extravagant was the young man. And indeed what happened after his departure seemed to prove that he had been right. Lesbionicus went from bad to worse, squandered everything that he could lay his hands on, till at last nothing was left him but the house and a small farm outside the city. The house he promptly advertised for

---

[1] This was a coin first minted by Philip II. of Macedon (the father of Alexander the Great), and called after his name. It contained gold to the value of fifteen shillings (as reckoned by our standard).

sale.[1]   Callicles, dismayed at the thought that it was going to pass into other hands, and that the new purchaser might discover, even if he were not legally entitled to, the buried treasure, determined to buy the property himself.   But this proceeding did not satisfy everybody.   Some of his friends and acquaintances suspected him of having taken advantage of the young man's folly, and made a good bargain for himself.   Accordingly, no sooner had he taken possession of his new purchase than a friend, Megaronides by name, presented himself and told him what people were saying.

Megaronides. "You're in bad repute, my friend. People do not scruple to call you a vulture.   ' Friend or foe,' they say, ' it is all one to him, as long as he makes his meal.'   This vexes me, you may believe, very much."

Callicles. "Well, I can't prevent people talking ; but whether they are right is another matter."

Meg. " Tell me, was Charmides a friend of yours?"

Cal. " He was and is.   If he had been anything else, would he have handed his affairs over to me, when he sailed for Syria, charging me with the care of his grown-up daughter — his wife, as you know, is dead — and that spendthrift of a son ? "

Meg. "Ah! it was about the son that I was going

---

[1] Plautus, or Philemon, whom he translates, does not tell us how the son could sell his father's property.   Audiences, it is probable, did not criticise details of this kind.

to speak. Have you endeavoured to reform him? Would you not have done better to try to make a respectable man of him than to abet him in his bad courses?"

Cal. "How have I abetted him? What have I done?"

Meg. "Behaved like a rascal, to speak plainly."

Cal. "That's not my way."

Meg. "Did you not buy this house from the young man? Why don't you answer? I mean this very house in which you are living."

Cal. "I did buy it. I paid the money to the young man, two hundred pounds down."

Meg. "You paid the money?"

Cal. "Certainly. I see nothing to be ashamed of in that."

Meg. "Well, then, I say that you betrayed your trust. You gave the young fellow a sword to kill himself with when you supplied him with the means of crowning the edifice of his folly."

Cal. "Oughtn't I to have paid him the money?"

Meg. "You ought not to have had any buying and selling with him. See how the thing stands. The young man is put in your charge, and you get possession of his house. On my word, you are a fine trustee!"

Cal. "My friend, when you talk to me in this fashion, I have no choice but to tell you a secret that I was charged to keep strictly to myself. Can I trust you?"

16

Meg. " Implicitly."

Cal. " Can anybody overhear us ? "

Meg. " No one."

Cal. " Then listen. When Charmides was on the point of leaving Athens, he showed me a treasure which he had buried in a room in this house — you are sure there is no one listening ? "

Meg. " There is no one near."

Cal. " As much as three thousand philips. He begged me not to let his son know anything about it. If he comes back safe, I shall give it up to him ; if anything should happen to him, then I have the means of finding a dowry for his daughter."

Meg. " Good heavens ! this is quite another story. But go on."

Cal. " Well, I happened to go away for a week, and, without saying a word, my young friend advertises the house for sale."

Meg. " Ah ! the old story. The wolf watches till the dog is asleep, and then makes a meal of the whole flock."

Cal. " So he would have done, but the dog was beforehand with him. But tell me, what was I to do ? Was I to inform him of the existence of the treasure, when his father had specially charged me to say nothing about it ? Or was I to let a stranger become the owner of the house ? Of course not. I had to buy it myself, not for my own profit, as you see, but for my friend. So I did ; I paid the money out of my own pocket. Well, if that is behaving like a rascal, as you put it, I plead guilty."

Meg. "You are right; I have nothing to say."

Cal. "And now I want you to help me."

Meg. "I am at your service. But tell me, where does the young man now live?"

Cal. "When he sold the house, he kept back this little building in the rear, and he is living there now."

Meg. "And the daughter?"

Cal. "She is in my house. I treat her just as I do my own child. Good by, my friend, and don't be so ready to believe all that these busybodies say. They know everything: what the king whispers in the queen's ear, what Zeus has to say to Heré, in short, everything that is, and a great deal that is not."

Meanwhile, a conversation was going on elsewhere in the city which promised to produce a new complication. A young Athenian named Lysiteles has fallen in love with the daughter of Charmides. The difficulty was that the girl was probably without a dowry. Her father was abroad, no one knew where; her brother, who was the most notorious young spendthrift in Athens, could not be expected to do anything for her. The young man was in great doubt whether Philto, his father, could be induced to consent to his marriage with a portionless girl. Anyhow, he would see what could be done. Accordingly he proceeded to pay the old gentleman a visit. He found him in a moralizing mood. "My son," said

the old man, "as you love me, don't have anything
to do with the worthless fellows who are to be found
everywhere nowadays. This is an awful time that
we are living in. I know it well; there is robbing
and lying everywhere; nothing is sacred to these
fellows. I can't sleep for thinking of it. I positively weep to think that I have lived to see such
days. My dear son, do mind what I say to you. Do
as I do; that is the good, old-fashioned way of living;
keep to that, and you'll never get into trouble."

Lysiteles. " My dear father, I have always felt
that, freeman as I was, I could not do better than be
your slave."

Philto. " The great question with a young man is
this : are his inclinations to master him, or is he to
master his inclinations? If you get the better in
this conflict, it will be all right with you ; if you are
worsted, it will be all wrong."

Lys. " I have always done my best to keep myself
from harm. I have shunned bad companions; I
have kept good hours ; I have avoided anything that
could vex you ; I have followed your precepts to the
utmost of my power."

Phil. " Don't reckon up your goodness in that
fashion. My days are pretty well over ; it is you
whom these things concern, and I take it that a
really honest man is never very well satisfied with
himself."

Lysiteles now saw that his protestations of filial

piety and rectitude were not likely to do him much good, and thought it better to go straight to the point. " I have a great favour to ask you, my dear father," he said.

Phil. " What is it? I shall be glad to do anything I can."

Lys. " There is a young friend of mine, of an excellent family I should say, who has not managed his affairs very prudently. I should like to help him."

Phil. " With your own means? "

Lys. " Certainly; I suppose I may say that what is yours is mine. I am sure that all that is mine is yours."

Phil. " Is your friend poor? "

Lys. " He is poor."

Phil. " Had he any property? "

Lys. " He had."

Phil. " How did he lose it? By farming, or the taxes, or by trade ventures? "

Lys. " No, no; by nothing of that kind."

Phil. " How was it, then? "

Lys. " By his lazy ways, and a certain habit he had of pleasing himself."

Phil. " Well, you are certainly a candid friend. You don't mince matters, — a poor fellow that never did anything that he ought, and yet is in want. Somehow I don't care that you have friends of this kind."

Lys. " There is no harm in him, and I should like to give him a little help."

Phil. "You don't really help a beggar by giving him something to spend in eating and drinking. You lose what you give him, and only prolong his misery. However, I don't mean this to apply to your friend. I don't like, in fact, to refuse anything in reason. Tell me what it is you want. Speak freely to your father."

Lys. " Lesbionicus, who lives there — "

Phil. "Oh! that is the man, is it? The fellow who has eaten up all that he had and all that he hadn't. However, what do you want to give him?"

Lys. " Nothing at all, father ; only you must not hinder him from giving me something, if he wants to."

Phil. " How you're to help him by taking something from him I cannot see."

Lys. " Perhaps I can show you. You know what family he belongs to ? "

Phil. " Yes ; it's as good as any in Athens."

Lys. " He has a grown-up sister. I want to marry her without a dowry."

Phil. " Without a dowry ! "

Lys. " Yes, father ; it won't make us worse thought of."

Phil. " Well, let it be so, if you will have it."

Lys. " One thing more ; would you mind asking for her ? "

Phil. "This is a pretty business I have let myself in for. However, it has to be done. What is the use of trying to cross one's son? It only breeds trouble for oneself, and does no sort of good. But here comes the young man himself in the nick of time."

And, indeed, Lesbionicus had just come out of his house in consultation with his slave Stasimus. " Stasimus," he said, " it is just a fortnight since Callicles paid me two hundred pounds for my house. Is it not so?"

Stasimus. " I do remember something about it."

Lesbionicus. "Well, what has become of the money?"

Stas. " Eaten away, drunk away, bathed away; the fishmongers, bakers, cooks, butchers, green-grocers, poulterers have got it. They are like so many ants with a poppy-head."

Les. "I don't think they had more than five and twenty pounds."

Stas. " Then there are the presents you made."

Les. " Put them down at as much more."

Stas. " Then there is what I cheated you of."

Les. "Ah! that is more than either."

Stas. "Then you had to pay fifty pounds to the bank for Olympias, the money you were surety for."

Les. "Ah! poor fellow, I could not refuse to help. I was so sorry for him."

Stas. " I wish you would be sorry for yourself."

At this point Philto came up. He courteously introduced the business which he had in hand. Lesbionicus could not believe him to be serious. It was not like him, he said, to make fun of an unfortunate man. Philto protested that he had no thought of the kind in his head; but only to be met with the reply that the two families were not in the same position. The daughter of an impoverished house could not marry into one so wealthy. " I had hoped," said the old man, " for a kinder answer. It is not wise to refuse a friendly offer."

Stas. " The old man is right."

Les. (*to the slave*). " Hold your tongue, or I'll knock your eye out."

Stas. " I don't care. If I had only one eye I should say the same."

Phil. " You say our position is not the same. Well, consider this. You are next to a rich man at a public dinner. Something is served to him which you like; would you eat it with him, or go away dinnerless ? "

Les. " I should eat it with him, if he did not object."

Stas. " So should I, whether he objected or not. We must have no false shame about eating. It is a matter of life and death. I will make way for a man in the street or the footpath; but when it comes to eating — no; in these hard times a dinner is not to be despised."

PHILTO AND LESBIONICUS.

Phil. " My dear Lesbionicus, what are the odds between one man and another? The gods are great and rich, but we mortals — what are we? Just a breath of air; that gone, the rich man and the beggar are just the same. And now to show you that we have no feeling of superiority, I ask you to give your sister to my son without a dowry. Heaven prosper the match! May I consider it settled? Pray say, ' I promise.' "

Stas. "The other day he was ready enough to say, ' I promise'; now when he ought to, he won't."

Les. " Philto, I am greatly honoured by your high opinion of my family. However, though things have not gone very well with me, I have still a little farm, near the city. That I will give as my sister's dowry."

Phil. " I assure you that I do not want a dowry."

Les. " I am resolved to give it."

Stas. (aside to his master). " What are you doing? Giving away our only subsistence? How are we to live now? "

Les. (to the slave). " Hold your tongue! Am I going to give account to you? "

Stas. "We are undone, unless I can contrive to stop it somehow."

He drew Philto aside, and whispered to him, " Let me have a word with you."

Phil. " Speak on."

Stas. " For heaven's sake, never allow that farm

to become yours or your son's. When we plough it, the oxen cannot get through five furrows without dying. The wine gets rotten before it is ripe. Sow corn, and you'll get just a third of it back."

Phil. " Ah! that should be just the place to sow bad habits."

Stas. " Every one to whom that field has belonged has come to a bad end. Some have been banished; others are dead and gone ; some have hanged themselves. The man to whom it now belongs is utterly ruined."

Phil. " I'll have nothing to do with it."

Stas. "Ah! you would say that if you knew all. Every other row of trees is struck with lightning. The sows die of suffocation. The sheep get scabby; they are as smooth as my hand. And as for men, the Syrians, who, as you know, are the hardiest labourers there are, can live there only six months. Now don't say that I told you, but the fact is that my master wants to get rid of the place."

Phil. " Well, I promise you it shall never be mine."

Stas. (aside). " Ah! I've frightened the old gentleman off. How in the world we should have lived without that farm is more than I can say."

Phil. " How about our matter, Lesbionicus?"

Les. " What was that fellow talking to you about?"

Phil. "Oh! it seems he wants to be free, and hasn't got the money."

Les. "Just as I want to be rich, and I haven't got the money. Now, Stasimus, go to Callicles's house, and tell my sister what has been settled."

Stas. "I will go."

Les. "And give her my congratulations."

Stas. "Of course."

Les. "And tell Callicles that I should be glad to see him."

Stas. "Hadn't you better go, sir?"

Les. "To settle about the dowry."

Stas. "Pray go!"

Les. "I have quite made up my mind that she must have a dowry."

Stas. "Now do go!"

Les. "Of course I can't let her be injured —"

Stas. "Pray go!"

Les. "By my carelessness."

Stas. "Pray go!"

Les. "It is only fair that if I have done wrong—"

Stas. "Now do go!"

Les. "I should suffer."

Stas. "Go, go!"

Les. "Father, father, shall I ever see you again?"

Stas. "Go, go, go!"[1]

Les. "Well, I am going. See that you do what I told you."

---

[1] The slave is anxious to get his master out of the way.

Stas. "At last I have got rid of him. If I have
saved the farm, there is something done, for we have
got a good husband for the young mistress. But I
don't feel quite easy; and if the farm goes, then
it is all over with my neck. I shall have to carry
shield, helmet, and knapsack; for the young master
will be off as soon as the wedding is over. He will
go soldiering to some accursed place, and I shall
have to go with him. But now for my errand,
though I hate the sight of the house, since we have
been turned out of it."

Callicles was not a little surprised at the news
which Stasimus communicated — Lesbionicus's sister
was to be married to Philto's son, and without a
dowry. He was more than surprised; he was scan-
dalized. The idea was monstrous; such a thing
could not be permitted. Finally, he made up his
mind to ask the advice of Megaronides, his censor,
as he called him, and went off for that purpose.
"Ah! my friend," said Stasimus, as soon as his back
was turned, "I see what you are after. You mean
to turn the poor fellow out of his farm as you did
out of his house. O my poor master Charmides,
what havoc they are making with your property!
How I should like to see you come back and punish
these false friends, and reward your poor, faithful
Stasimus!"

The slave's prospects continued to have a gloomy
look. A conversation which he overheard between

his young master and the son-in-law that was to be did not reassure him. The young spendthrift was determined not to let his sister go portionless into another family. He roundly accused his friend of unwittingly desiring to do him a great injury. The friend retorted that all the injury that he had suffered had been done by himself. His father and his grandfather's exertions had laid an honourable career open to him, and by his idleness and folly he had lost the opportunity.

"I want," said Lysiteles, "to leave you this farm as something to begin with. As an utterly penniless man you would have no chance of retrieving your position."

Lesbionicus had no hesitation in acknowledging that he had been grievously to blame. "Only," he said, "what you want to do would send me down from bad to worse. I should be poor, if I do as I propose, but I should not be dishonourable. To let my sister marry without a dowry would be to disgrace her and myself; for you to take her would, indeed, redound to your credit, but in exactly the same degree it would be discreditable to me."

"Redound to my credit!" cried Lysiteles, "it would do nothing of the kind. I know what you are going to do. The marriage once celebrated, you mean to fly from your kinsfolk, friends, and country. And what will people say of me? Why, that my greed had driven you away."

Stasimus could not contain himself at this, so admirable did the argument appear. "Good! good! Lysiteles," he cried, "your play gets the prize."

Les. "What brings you here?"

Stas. "My feet, to be sure, and they are going to take me away. Ah!" he went on, as the two young men walked away, unable to come to an agreement; "what will become of me? There is nothing left for me but to strap up my knapsack and throw my shield over my shoulders. However keen the fighters I may fall in with, I warrant I shall be quite as keen — in running away. Fit me out with a bow and arrows in my hand, and a helmet on my head, and I'll be as good as any man, as far as sleeping in my tent is concerned. However, there is that talent that is owing me. I will go and get it; that will give me something for my journey."

Meanwhile Callicles had asked his friend's advice in the matter of the marriage portion. That the girl should go without a dowry when there was money at hand was impossible, as well as for other reasons. Callicles could not pay it out of his own pocket. People would be sure to say that he was giving a part only of what the absent father had provided. The marriage could not be put off, for the young man might change his mind; and the secret of the treasure could not be revealed, in view of the father's strict injunctions to the contrary. Under these circumstances the friend's advice was to this effect: Make every one believe that the girl's father has sent home a messenger with a thousand gold philips for his daughter's dowry. The money you can supply yourself, repaying it out of the treasure when the proper time comes. The supposed messenger you can find in one of those fellows who are always glad to do any kind of job for a consideration. Dress him up in some outlandish fashion, and tell him to say that he comes from Charmides in Seleucia; that the old man is well, and means to return very shortly; meanwhile, he sends his love and this money. He must have with him two letters, one to his son, one to you. These we shall have to make up. The letters must desire the gold to be given to you; as a matter of fact, you will pay it over to the husband when the wedding is over. The son will think it comes from his father; and you can repay yourself out of the treasure when all is quiet. There may be a difficulty about the seal on the letters. The young man probably knows his father's device, and will wonder that the new documents did not bear it. That, however, may easily be accounted for. Charmides might have lost his seal, or the letters might have been opened in the custom-house.

This plan did not altogether commend itself to Callicles, who did not like the idea of so elaborate a plot. However, he agreed to do his part and proceeded to hire a messenger.

Meanwhile Charmides himself had landed, and was making his way to his home. It so happened, indeed, that he and his own pretended messenger came at the same time into the street in which his house stood. His attention was attracted by the man's curious dress, the most conspicuous feature of which was a huge hat resembling a mushroom. A closer inspection did not make him like the man's look any more. "That's some swindler or cutpurse," he said to himself. "He's probably examining the house, and means to pay them a visit some night." When the next moment he saw the stranger knock at his own door, it seemed to him high time to interfere. "Ho! young man," he cried, "what do you want? What are you knocking at that door for?"

Messenger. "I want a young man of the name of Lesbionicus, and an old gentleman, Callicles by name, who has a white head like you."

Charmides (aside). "Why, he is asking after my son, and the friend to whom I entrusted my family and my property."

Mes. "Can you tell me where these gentlemen live?"

Char. "You tell me first who you are, what is your family, and where you come from."

Mes. "That is a great number of questions to put all at once. I don't know which to answer first. Put them quietly one by one, and I'll tell you my name, what I have done, and where I have travelled."

Char. "Very good; begin by telling me your name."

Mes. "You're beginning with something very difficult."

Char. "Why so?"

Mes. "I have so many names that, if you began at dawn, you would not reach the end before midnight."

Char. "Your first name, then?"

Mes. "'Pax.' That is my every-day name."

Char. "Well, what business have you with these people whom you are asking after?"

Mes. "The father of this young friend of mine, Lesbionicus, gave me two letters."

Char. (aside). "Well, I have got him here. He says that I gave him two letters. I'll have a fine game with the fellow."

Mes. "The old gentlemen said that I was to hand one of the letters to his son Lesbionicus, and the other to his friend Callicles."

Char. "Where was he?"

Mes. "He was quite well."

Char. "But where?"

Mes. "In Seleucia."

Char. "Did he give you the letters himself?"

Mes. "Yes, with his own hands."

Char. "What sort of look had he?"

Mes. "Oh, a foot and a half taller than you."

Char. "There's a hitch here — it seems that I am taller there than here. Do you know him?"

Mes. "What a question! Do I know the man that I used to dine with?"

Char. "What was his name ? "

Mes. " Name ?   An honest man's name."

Char. "That makes me want more to hear it."

Mes. " His name was — was — " (*Aside*) " Here's a piece of bad luck ! "

Char. "What is the matter ? "

Mes. " I had it on the tip of my tongue."

Char. " You don't seem to know him very well."

Mes. " Not know him !   I know him as well as I know myself.   But it is always the way — the thing you know best you are apt to forget.   However, I can make it out letter by letter.   I know it begins with a ' C.' "

Char. " Callias ? "

Mes. " No."

Char. " Callippus ? "

Mes. " No."

Char. " Callidemides ? "

Mes. " No."

Char. " Callimenes ? "

Mes. " No."

Char. " Callimachus ? "

Mes. " It is of no use ; and indeed it does not matter in the least."

Char. " Well, there are many men of the name Lesbionicus here, and unless you know the father's name you may not be able to find the young man. See whether you can guess it."

Mes. " Well, it was something beginning with ' Char.' "

Char. "Chares? or Charides? or was it by any chance Charmides?"

Mes. "Ah! that was it. Confound the fellow!"

Char. "Why confound him?"

Mes. "Because the villain kept giving me the slip."

Char. "How did you come across him?"

Mes. "Oh! in the course of my travels."

Char. "Where did you travel, then?"

Mes. "First I sailed to Arabia in Pontus."

Char. "Oh! Pontus is in Arabia, is it?"

Mes. "I don't mean the place where the frankincense grows, but the wormwood country."

Char. (aside). "This is a pretty kind of liar! But what a fool I am to ask him these questions; still, I want to see how he'll get out of it." (*To the messenger*) "Well, where did you go after Arabia?"

Mes. "Oh! to the river that rises in heaven under the throne of Zeus."

Char. "Under the throne of Zeus?"

Mes. "Just so."

Char. "Rises in heaven, did you say?"

Mes. "Yes, in heaven, in the middle of it."

Char. "So you've been up to heaven?"

Mes. "Just so; we sailed up-stream in a skiff."

Char. "And did you see Zeus?"

Mes. "No; the other gods said that he had gone to his country-house to serve out his slaves' rations. But would you point out to me the persons who ought to have the letters?"

Char. "If you were to happen to see this Charmides, do you think you would know him again?"

Mes. "Know him again? Do you take me for a fool not to know the man that I have lived with? And do you think that he would have trusted me with a quantity of gold—a thousand philips, nothing less—unless we had known each other perfectly well?"

Char. "Now, if I could but swindle the swindler! A thousand philips indeed! and I would not trust him with one brass farthing—no, not if it were a matter of life and death! Come, Pax, a word with you."

Mes. "Three hundred, if you like."

Char. "Have you got that money you talked of?"

Mes. "Yes, of course; a thousand gold pieces."

Char. "And you received it from Charmides himself?"

Mes. "From whom should I receive it? Not from his father or his grandfather, who are dead, I take it."

Char. "Then hand over the gold to me, my young friend."

Mes. "Hand it over to you! Why?"

Char. "Because you said that I gave it you. I am Charmides."

Mes. "You Charmides? Not you!"

Char. "I tell you I am Charmides."

Mes. "It is no good, my friend; you are too

clever. When I mentioned the gold, you made yourself Charmides; now you may unmake yourself."

Char. " But who am I, if I am not Charmides?"

Mes. "What is that to me? You may be anybody
but he."

And the man went off to tell his employer the
curious adventure he had met with.

Stasimus, who had been trying to drown his cares
in drink, now returned, talking to himself about the
degeneracy of the times. For a while Charmides
listened to his soliloquy without knowing who he
was, but when the slave happened to turn his face,
he recognized him. " Ho! Stasimus," he cried. —
"Order your own servant," was the answer. — "Well,"
said Charmides, "you are my servant, for I certainly
bought you." The slave, who was scarcely sober,
continued to make impertinent answers, till his master said, " Look at me; I am Charmides."

Stas. "Who spoke of that good man Charmides?"

Char. " The good man himself."

Stas. " Heaven and earth! Is it the man himself,
or is it not? It is he; it certainly is! O my dear,
dear master!"

Char. " Are my children well?"

Stas. " Very well indeed."

Char. " Both of them?"

Stas. " Yes; both of them."

Char. "Well, I have a hundred things to talk
about. Come in here " (*pointing to his old house*).

Stas. " Where are you going ? "

Char. " Where should I go ? "

Stas. " That's not your house now ; your son sold it for two hundred pounds in ready money."

Char. " Good heavens ! and who bought it ? "

Stas. " Callicles, your fine friend whom you trusted."

Char. " And where does my son live ? "

Stas. " In the little place at the back."

Char. " To think of this, after all I have done for him ! It kills me. Hold me up, Stasimus."

It was not difficult, however, to console the old man. Callicles, who was actually digging up the treasure at the time, came running out in the street, just as he was, on hearing his friend's voice, and explained what had happened. While he was talk-ing Lysiteles appeared, and after listening a while to the conversation of the two friends, introduced him-self, was warmly greeted, and had his betrothal confirmed by the father of the lady himself. Only he was given to understand he must be content to take the dowry as well as the girl. To this he could make no objection ; and, the engagement ratified, he proceeded to ask a favour on his own account. Would Charmides forgive his spendthrift son ? The old man hesitated a moment. "I hardly think it right," he said, "and yet I should not like to refuse your first request. Let it be as you wish." Les-bionicus, accordingly, was summoned, and greeted

his father with no little confusion of face. "Father,"
he began, "if you have suffered — " he stammered
out. — "Oh ! it has been nothing," said the old man,
"if you would only turn over a new leaf." Lesbionicus was profuse in his promises of amendment.
"Then," said his father, "suppose you marry the
daughter of our friend Callicles here."

Les. "Certainly, my dear father, her and any one
else you please to mention."

Char. "No, no. I was angry with you, and not
without good reason; but, after all, one plague is
enough, even for you."

Les. "I am going to reform."

Char. "So you say ; let us hope you will do it."

Lys. "Is there any reason why I should not be
married to-morrow ? "

Char. "None whatever; and you, my son, be
ready to be married the day after."

II.

THE GHOST.

[*From* PHILEMON. *Translated by* PLAUTUS.]

PHILOLACHES, a young Athenian gentleman, had
been left by his father, during the latter's absence
on mercantile business in Egypt, with considerably
more liberty than was good for him. The business
had kept the old man away for as much as three
years, and during that time the son had run through
no small amount of money, and had committed a
variety of follies. His adviser and abettor in these
had been a certain slave, Tranio by name.

One evening he was about to sit down to dinner,
when a friend, Callidamates by name, came in with
some companions. The new arrival had already
been drinking deeply at another entertainment, but
growing weary of his host, had thought fit to change
the scene. "Philolaches," he said, "is always the
best of fellows and the pleasantest of hosts. I will
go and see him." It was no easy task for his friends
to pilot him through the streets, for more than once
he manifested a decided inclination to lie down.
When at last he arrived, he could do nothing but
go to sleep. A few minutes after, the slave Tranio

came bustling in with some very alarming news. He had been sent by his master down to the harbour, with instructions to buy some fish. When the young man saw him, he only supposed that the errand had been accomplished. " Ah ! " he said, " Tranio at last ! Now we shall be able to dine." — " Philolaches ! " cried the man, breathlessly, for he had been running as fast as he could.

Philolaches. " Well, what is it ? "

Tranio. " You and I — "

Phil. " What about you and me ? "

Tra. " Are undone."

Phil. " What do you mean ? "

Tra. " Your father has come back."

Phil. " Where is he ? "

Tra. " At the harbour."

Phil. " Who saw him ? "

Tra. " I did, with my own eyes."

Phil. " Well, if that's true, it is all over with me."

Tra. " True ! of course it is true. What should I tell a lie for ? "

Phil. " But what am I to do ? "

Tra. " Get rid of your company here in the first place. Who is that asleep on the couch there ? "

Phil. " That is Callidamates. Wake him," he went on, speaking to another of the guests.

Guest. " Callidamates, Callidamates, wake up ! "

Callidamates. " I am awake. Give me something to drink."

Guest. " Wake up, I say. Philolaches's father has come back from abroad."

Cal. " Bother his father ! "

Phil. " For goodness' sake, wake up ! My father has come."

Cal. " Your father has come ? Then make him go away again ; what business has he to come bothering here ? "

Phil. " What can I do ? My father will be here directly and find pretty goings on. It's a bad business. I can't think what is to be done. It is like beginning to dig a well when one is dying of thirst. And see, that fellow there has dropped asleep again. Wake ! I say. Don't you know that my father will be here in a minute ? "

Cal. " Your father, do you say ? Give me my shoes and my sword ; I'll kill your father."

Tranio now rose to the occasion. He bade his master cheer up. He would keep, he said, the old man from coming into the house. The guests need not go ; they might continue to enjoy themselves ; only the house must he shut up ; there must be no noise, and if there was a knocking at the door, there must be no attempt to reply. To make assurance doubly sure, he would take the precaution of locking the door from the outside. These arrangements had scarcely been made, when the father, whose name was Theopropides, arrived, followed by his slaves. Reaching his house, he stood awhile to return thanks to Poseidon for having allowed him to come back safe. "But," he went on, "I don't trust you again. If I do, I give you leave to do what you please."

Tra. (aside). "Poseidon, you made a great mistake when you allowed this fellow to come back."

Theopropides. "Three years have I been away in Egypt, and my household, I hope, will be glad to see me back again. But what is the meaning of this? The door shut in the daytime! Ho, there, open the door!" (*Knocks.*)

At this point Tranio came up, and was recognized by his master. After mutual greetings, the old man expressed his astonishment that he could not get any one to open the door, or even to make any answer. He had already almost broken in the door. Wasn't there any one at home?"

Tra. "Have you really touched the house?"

Theo. "Why shouldn't I touch it? Touched it indeed! I have pretty nearly broken the doors in."

Tra. "You have actually touched it?"

Theo. "Yes; touched it and kicked it."

Tra. "That's a bad business."

Theo. "What is the matter?"

Tra. "I can't say what a terrible thing you have done."

Theo. "What?"

Tra. "For heaven's sake, come away, come nearer to me. Did you really touch the door?"

Theo. "Touched it? I tell you I kicked it."

Tra. "Then you have utterly ruined you and yours. But tell those men to go away, and I'll explain. For seven months past, ever since we left it, no one has set foot inside that house."

Theo. "But why?"

Tra. "Listen. But first, can any one hear me?"

Theo. "No, no. It's all safe."

Tra. "Look again."

Theo. "There is no one; go on."

Tra. "A frightful murder was once done in that house. The crime was committed many years ago, and had been forgotten. We only lately came to know of it."

Theo. "What was it? Who did it?"

Tra. "In that house a host murdered his guest,— I fancy it was the man who sold the house to you,— possessed himself of his victim's money, and buried the body somewhere in the house."

Theo. "What makes you suspect that such a thing happened?"

Tra. "I'll tell you: listen. One night your son came home after dining out. He went to bed, and so did we all. It so happened that I had forgotten to put out one of the lamps. All of a sudden he cried out—"

Theo. "Who cried out, my son?"

Tra. "Hush! don't say a word. He said that the dead man had appeared to him in his sleep."

Theo. " In his sleep, you say ? "

Tra. " Certainly. How could he have appeared to him when he was awake, seeing that it was sixty years since the man was killed? You are sometimes extraordinarily stupid, my master."

Theo. " I say no more."

Tra. " What the dead man said to him was this: ' I am a stranger from over the sea, Diapontius by name. I dwell here. The regions below would not receive me because I was slain before my time. I was treacherously murdered by my host in this house, and within these walls. I was thrust into the earth without due burial rites. All this the villain did for the sake of gain. Depart thou hence. This is a wicked house; it is under a curse.' This is what the ghost said. As for the horrible things that happen here, it would take me a year and more to tell them. Hush ! "

At this point a noise was heard from within. The party had forgotten their situation, and were becoming uproarious.

Theo. " Good heavens! What is it ? "

Tra. (speaking to the ghost). " It was he that knocked, not I."

Theo. " Oh, dear! the dead man will carry me off alive ! "

Tra. (aside). " These fellows will spoil the whole business with their noise."

Theo. " What are you talking to yourself about ? "

Tra. " Come away from the door, I implore you. Come to me. I am not afraid. I am on good terms with the dead."

A voice from within cried, " Tranio ! "

" Don't call me," said the slave. " I tell you it wasn't I that knocked; it was my master."

Theo. " Whom are you talking to ? "

Tra. " Was it you that called ? On my word, I thought it was the dead man remonstrating with me because I had knocked at the door. But come away. Cover your head and fly."

Theo. " Why don't you fly ? "

Tra. " I am on good terms with the dead."

Theo. " I thought you seemed very frightened."

Tra. " Never mind about me; I can take care of myself."

A new danger now presented itself. A money-lender, who had supplied the young Philolaches with a considerable sum, appeared on the scene, and loudly complained, after the habit of his kind, of the very unlucky year he had had. He loudly demanded his money, while Tranio vainly endeavoured to get rid of him. If he would come back a little later he should have it without fail. The money-lender, however, preferred to stay. He had been put off several times before, and would wait no longer. Meanwhile Theopropides returned. He had been to see the person of whom he had bought the house, and had told him the whole story. He had been met with a flat contradiction, and he now returned to make further inquiries. The clamour made by the money-lender attracted the attention of Theopropides. "Who is this fellow," he said, "that is making all this uproar? He seems to have some complaint against my son."

Tra. "Oh, throw the money in his face, the horrid wretch!"

Money-Lender. "Throw away; I don't object to being pelted with silver."

Tra. "Do you hear what he says? A regular usurer all over."

Theo. "I don't care who he is, or what he is. I want to know about this money."

Tra. "Well, if you must know, your son Philolaches owes him something."

Theo. "How much?"

Tra. "One hundred and sixty pounds, or thereabouts. You don't think that very much."

Theo. "A mere trifle, of course."

Tra. "Then there is a little matter of interest, say ten pounds more. Say that you will pay him, and send him off."

Theo. "I am to say that I will pay him?"

Tra. "Yes, you. But listen. It is all right. Say you will."

Theo. "Tell me this — what has been done with the money?"

Tra. "It's all safe."

Theo. "If it's safe, why don't you pay for it yourselves ? "

Tra. " The fact is, your son bought a house."

Theo. " A house.? "

Tra. " Yes, a house."

Theo. "Good, good! He is a chip of the old block; he has an eye to business. You say a house?"

Tra. " Yes, a house; but what kind of a house, do you think ? "

Theo. " How can I tell ? "

Tra. " Where ? "

Theo. "What do you mean ? "

Tra. " Don't ask me."

Theo. " Why ? "

Tra. " I tell you it's a perfect picture."

Theo. " Well done ; but what does he give for it ? "

Tra. " Four hundred and eighty pounds, and has paid the hundred by way of deposit. You see, when he found out how it was with the other house, he bought a new one for himself."

Theopropides was so pleased with his son's smartness that he made no difficulty about promising the money-lender that he would pay the debt. " And now," he said, turning to Tranio, " tell me where the house is." The question perplexed Tranio. " A lie," he said to himself, " is best served up hot, I have heard. I must say the first thing that comes uppermost." (*To Theopropides*) " It was our next door neighbour's house that he bought."

Theo. " Really ? "

Tra. "Yes, really, if you are going to pay the money ; but not really, if you don't."

Theo. "Well, I should like to see it."

Tra. (*to himself*). " Here is another trouble. I'm no sooner off one shoal than I am on to another."

Theo. "What are you stopping for ? Call some one."

Tra. " But, sir, there are ladies there ; and we ought to find out whether they are willing to have the house seen."

Theo. "Very good ; go and inquire. I will wait for you here."

Tra. " Confound the old man ! how he ruins all my little schemes. But here comes our neighbour Sinio himself. Sinio, my master is very anxious to see your house."

Sinio. " But it is not for sale."

Tra. " I am quite aware of that ; but the old man wants to build apartments for the women, with a bath and a colonnade."

Sin. " What is he dreaming about ? "

Tra. " You see he wants his son to marry as soon as may be. So he is anxious to build a new women's apartment. He has heard an architect say that your house is astonishingly well built, and he wants to make his on the same pattern. It is a capital place in summer, he hears."

Sin. "Oh, indeed! I know the sun is like a

dun; we never get rid of him. As for shade, there
is none, except you get into the well. However, if
he wants to see the house, he is quite welcome, and
to copy it, too, if he pleases."

Tranio now went to fetch his master, who had
been waiting impatiently for him. The vendor, he
explained, had been busy, and he had to wait till
he was at leisure. "There he is," he went on,
"standing at his door and waiting for us. See how
sad he is about having sold his house. He begged
me to persuade your son to give up the bargain." —
"Give up the bargain!" said Theopropides. "No,
no; every man for himself. If he made a bad bargain, we are not going to give it up. If one gets a
little bit of advantage, one must keep it."

Sinio received his visitor very politely, begging
him to walk over the house as if it were his own.
"As if," said Theopropides, half aloud.

"Don't, don't!" interrupted Tranio; "say nothing
about having bought the house. Don't you see how
gloomy he looks?"

As a matter of· fact, Sinio's gloom had been
caused by a naturally bad temper and a quarrel
with his wife.

Theopropides now went over the house, criticising
this and that detail, but admiring it on the whole,
while Tranio pointed out its beauties, and felt not a
little relief when the owner, pleading business elsewhere, left the two to inspect the remainder of the

house by themselves. The result of this inspection was a thorough satisfaction on the old man's part with the bargain that his son had made. " I would not take fifteen hundred pounds for the place, money down," he said, when he had finished his survey. Tranio promptly claimed credit for his share in the transaction. " I advised it," he said; " I made him borrow the money for the deposit." Theopropides declared his intention of concluding the business the next day by paying up the balance that remained to be paid, and directed Tranio to announce his arrival to his son, who, he had been given to understand, was at his farm outside the city.

A slave of Callidamates now made his appearance. He had come to fetch his master, who would probably be unable by that time to make his way home alone. Theopropides, who was surveying his new possession, as he supposed it to be, from the outside, seeing him knock at the door, and hearing him call for Tranio, asked him his business.

Slave. " I have come to fetch Callidamates."

Theo. " But why knock at that door ? "

Slave. " Because my master is drinking inside."

Theo. " Nonsense, young man. No one lives here."

Slave. " Doesn't Philolaches live here ? "

Theo. " He used to live here, but he has moved."

Slave. " You are very much mistaken, my dear sir; unless he moved yesterday or to-day, he certainly lives here. The fact is, that since his father went abroad, he has been keeping it up here with his jolly companions."

Theo. "Who has been keeping it up, do you say?"

Slave. "Philolaches."

Theo. "What Philolaches?"

Slave. "Why, the Philolaches whose father is named Theopropides."

Theo. "You say Philolaches has been in the habit of drinking here with your master?"

Slave. "Just so."

Theo. "And you are sure that you haven't come to the wrong house?"

Slave. "I know what I am about. This is the house, and Philolaches is the young gentleman's name. He has been borrowing lately —"

Theo. "Borrowing what?"

Slave. "A hundred and sixty pounds."

Theo. "And you say that he has been keeping it up with your master?"

Slave. "Just so."

Theo. "Didn't he buy this next house?"

Slave. "I never heard of it."

Sinio, who had finished his business, now came back, and Theopropides questioned him about the house. "You received," he said, "a hundred and sixty pounds from my son Philolaches." — "Never a shilling," Sinio replied. — "Well, from Tranio the slave." — "No, nor from him." A few more ques-

tions sufficed to show the old man that the whole
story was a fiction from beginning to end. "Well,"
said he to his neighbour, "lend me two stout slaves
and a whip or two; that is all you can do for me,
for I have been most abominably cheated."

Tranio had succeeded in clearing his master's
house of its inconvenient inmates, and was meditating what was best to be done, when he saw his
master approach. A brief conversation followed,
and Tranio soon understood that his game was up.
The slaves were not to be seen, for Theopropides
had told them to keep in the background till he
should call them, but the culprit was perfectly well
aware that a very severe punishment awaited him.
His only resource was to flee for protection to the
family altar. This he at once did, and no persua-
sions could induce him to leave it.

Affairs were in this situation when Callidamates,
who had by this time slept off his drunkenness,
appeared upon the scene. Tranio, impudent to the
last, bantered his master on having been cheated so
grossly. "A man with white hair ought," he said,
"to have known better. If you have a friend among
the comedians, you could not do better than tell him
the story of how a slave has taken you in." Callidamates here intervened. "You must know that I
am your son's closest friend. After what has happened he is ashamed to show himself. Pray pardon
his youthful folly. Young men will do such things,

and I am just as much in fault as he is.   As for the
money, I will pay it, capital and interest, out of my
own pocket."

"Very good," said Theopropides; "as you are so
liberal, I will forgive him.   But as to that scoundrel
there, I will be the death of him."

" No, no, replied Callidamates; "pardon him, for
my sake."

" Pardon him ! " cried the old man, "a likely thing
indeed ! "

"You may as well," said Tranio, from his place of
refuge.   " You won't lose anything by it.   You may
be certain that I shall do something as bad to-morrow,
and then you can punish me to your heart's content."

Theo. "Well, well; I'll excuse you this once,
but you have to thank my friend Callidamates for
your escape."

III.

THE SHIPWRECK.

[*From* DIPHILUS. *Translated by* PLAUTUS.]

"THAT was a terrible storm we had last night, my man," said Dæmones to his slave Sceparnio.

"True, master," replied Sceparnio; "I never knew a worse. It has made more windows in the poor old cottage than the builder ever meant there to be."

"Yes, indeed," Dæmones went on. "And look at the roof! It has as many holes in it as a sieve."

Dæmones was a worthy Athenian who, though he had not a single vice, had contrived to ruin himself as effectually as if he had been the veriest spendthrift in the city. Nobody was more generous, and nobody more unlucky. At last things came to such a pass that he was obliged to leave Athens, and settle down, with the few pounds that he had been able to save out of the wreck, on a little farm which a kinsman had left him near Cyrene. He was now ruefully contemplating the damage which had been done to the old farmhouse by the wind. Looking round he saw a handsomely dressed young man, who

had come up unobserved. His name was Plesidippus, and he lived at Cyrene.

"Good morning, father," said the stranger respect-
fully. — "Father!" muttered the old man to himself.
It was a common mode of address from the young
to their elders, but poor Dæmones could never hear
it without emotion. It reminded him of what had
been a far greater trouble than the loss of his fortune. He had been robbed years before of his only
child, a sweet little girl of three years or so. She
had wandered out alone one morning, while her maid
was busy with some work, and had never been heard
of again.

"Good morning, my son," he replied, recovering
himself. "What can I do for you?"

Plesidippus. "Have you seen a slave dealer, an
old rascal with curly white hair?"

Dæmones. "Old rascals I have seen in plenty, or
else I should not be here."

Ples. "He had two girls with him, and he was
going to sacrifice in the temple of Aphrodité here.
It was to have been to-day, or possibly it was yesterday, though I think not."

Dæm. "There has been no one here on that
errand, I am sure. The fact is, that no one comes
to sacrifice without my knowing it. They are always
wanting water, or fire, or dishes, or knives, or something. My things belong much more to the goddess
than to me. No, my young friend, you may be

sure that no one has been here for several days past."

Ples. "Dear me! This is a bad business."

Dæm. "He asked you to dine with him after the sacrifice?"

Ples. "He did."

Dæm. "And hasn't come?"

Ples. "Exactly; but there is more than that. He has cheated me most shamefully."

Dæm. "Stop! I see two men over there, by the sea; possibly your friend may be one of them."

Ples. "Where? where?"

Dæm. "There; to the right."

Ples. "I see; I hope it is the scoundrel."

And the young man set off, running as fast as he could.

He had hardly been gone a minute, when Dæmones's slave, Sceparnio, who had been standing by, listening to the conversation, cried out, "Look, master!"

"What is it?" said Dæmones.

Sceparnio. "The boat! the boat! to the left there."

Dæm. "It is too far, I can't see anything."

Scep. "There are two women in it by themselves, poor things. Good heavens! how the sea is knocking them about! Ah! they're on the rock. No; the wave carried them clear — a pilot couldn't have done it more cleverly. But what an awful sea! I have never seen anything so bad in my life. Ah!

there's one of them tossed right out of the boat!
She is lost! No, she's not! she's in shallow water,
and has got upon her feet. Capital! And now the
other has jumped on shore; silly thing, she does not
see her friend, and is going the wrong way."

Dæm. "Well, my man, now that you have seen
them safe on shore, perhaps you wouldn't mind going
on with your work; you are *my* servant, not theirs.
Come with me."

Scep. "Very good, master, I am coming."

And the two went off to fetch what was wanted
for repairing the house.

While they were thus employed, one of the two
shipwrecked girls came along. She was in a terrible
state of distress, poor creature, for she had lost
everything she had in the world except what she
stood up in, and she believed that her friend had
been drowned.

"Dear! dear!" she cried, wringing her hands.
"Why am I so dreadfully unlucky? I am sure that
I have always tried to be a good girl. I loved my
dear father while I had one, and I used to go regu-
larly to the temples; and yet, if I had been the
wickedest girl in the world, I could not have been
worse off. No food, no shelter, nothing left but
what I have on; and my dear Ampelisca drowned!
I could have borne it if she had been with me."

And she sat down and cried as if her heart would
break. So overwhelmed was she with distress that

she never caught sight of the cottage or the temple, but fancied that she had been thrown ashore at some uninhabited place.

Things, however, were not as bad as she feared. Ampelisca had not been drowned, and, though she had missed her friend on first getting to land, had afterwards wandered along the shore in the same direction, looking for her, and very unhappy because she could not find her.

" I am sure I don't want to live if everything is going to be wretched," she said to herself. " My darling Palæstra is lost, and there is nobody to ask whether they have seen her. I shouldn't have thought that there was such a lonely place in all the world as this seems to be."

She said this out loud, almost without knowing it, and Palæstra, who was not far off, caught the sound. " Is that some one speaking ? " she said.

Ampelisca heard her, and cried, " Who's there ? "

" It sounds like a woman's voice," said Palæstra.

" It must be a woman," answered the other.

" Is it you, Ampelisca ? "

" Is it you, Palæstra ? "

There was a sort of thicket between them, and the girls did not find it easy to get through it. At last they managed it, and rushed into each other's arms, and kissed each other.

" Now, Palæstra dear, what are we to do ? " said Ampelisca. Palæstra always took the lead.

"Walk along the shore," answered Palæstra; "we must come to some place sooner or later."

Amp. "What! with these dripping clothes?"

Pal. "There is no help for it."

Amp. "Stay! stay! don't you see the temple there?"

Pal. "Where?"

Amp. "To the right; and a very pretty temple it seems."

Pal. "Well, if there is a temple, there must be people about. Let us go there."

So the girls went and fell on their knees in the porch, and prayed : "Dear god or goddess, whoever thou art, hear us, and help two unhappy women."

The priestess, who was sitting inside, heard them and came out.

"Good morning, mother," said the girls.

"Good morning, my children," answered the priestess. "But how is it you come in such a sorry plight? We expect our visitors to be dressed in white, and to bring offerings with them."

"Yes, dear mother; but then we have been ship-wrecked, and had nothing to bring, and nothing to wear but what you see. Do help us, pray, and give us something to eat."

"So I will, poor creatures," said the priestess, making them get up from their knees. "We are very poor here, you must know," she went on; "I serve Aphrodité, but I get nothing for it : I have to keep myself."

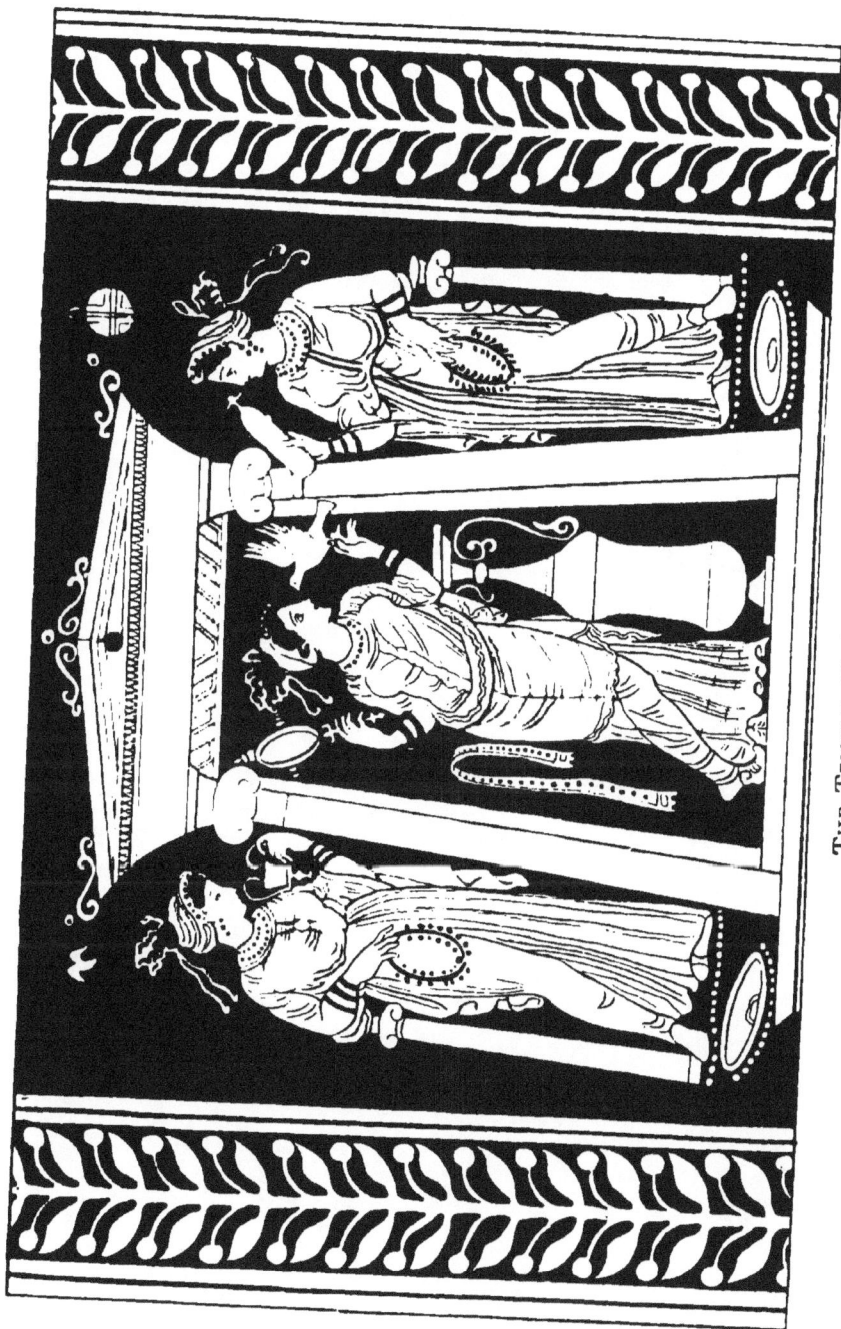

THE TEMPLE OF APHRODITE.

"What!" said Ampelisca; "is this a temple of Aphrodité?"

"Just so, and I am the priestess. But come along, and I will do the best I can for you."

Just as the three women disappeared into the temple, Plesidippus's servant, Trachalio, came running along the beach, looking for his master, who had said he should be at the temple at noon. It was now past noon, but he was not there. Some fishermen, slaves of Dæmones, were just getting their nets ready, and Trachalio spoke to them. " Have you seen my master," he asked, " a fine, bold young fellow, with a fresh-coloured face?"

"No," said one of the men, "no one of the kind."

"Well, have you seen an old wretch with a huge stomach and arched eyebrows, for all the world like a satyr, who had two rather pretty girls with him?"

"No," replied the fishermen, "we haven't seen either your good-looking young man, or your ill-looking old one."

"Well," said Trachalio to himself, "I will go and inquire at the temple."

Just at that moment Ampelisca was coming out with a water-can in her hand. She was going to fill it at the cottage.

"Good heavens!" cried Trachalio, "why, it is Ampelisca herself!"

"Why, it is Trachalio, Plesidippus's valet," said the girl, equally surprised.

"How are you getting on, my dear Ampelisca?"

Amp. "Only poorly. But where's your master?"

Trachalio. "What a question! Of course he is inside there."

Amp. "Inside! I have never seen him."

Trach. "I suppose the dinner is about ready?"

Amp. "What dinner?"

Trach. "Why, the sacrifice dinner, to which your master Labrax invited my master."

Amp. "I see, I see! He has cheated the man, and he has cheated the god. There is no sacrifice, and no dinner. Just like him!"

Trach. "Explain, explain!"

Amp. "Listen, then. After he had made the appointment with your master to meet him here, old Labrax took Palæstra and me, and every stick of property he had, and set sail for Sicily. He was going to sell us there."

Trach. "The scoundrel!"

Amp. "Well, the ship was wrecked, and everything went to the bottom."

Trach. "Good Poseidon! But what became of Labrax?"

Amp. "He died of drinking — salt water."

Trach. "Aha! very good. Poseidon sconced him to some purpose. But you — how did you escape?"

Amp. "Why, we jumped into a boat when we saw that the ship was drifting on to the rocks, and after being terribly knocked about, got to land more dead than alive."

Trach. " Just so, my dear. That's Poseidon's way. He's very particular. Give him a bad piece of goods, and he's sure to throw it up."

Amp. " You're an impudent rascal ! "

Trach. " And so Labrax tried to carry you off. Well, it is exactly what I knew he would do. After this I'll let my hair grow, and set up for a prophet."

Amp. " But if you knew it, my friend, why didn't you take care, your master and you, that he did not run off ? "

Trach. " But how ? "

Amp. " Ask how, and he a lover ? Why, watch the girl night and day. Fine care he has taken of her, indeed ! "

Trach. " Well, well; this watching is not so easy as you think. You see, the thief knows the honest man, but the honest man doesn't know the thief. But where is Palæstra ? I should like to see her."

Amp. " You will find her in the temple. She is crying, poor thing."

Trach. " But why ? "

Amp. " Because she has lost the casket that had her tokens in it. I mean the tokens by which her parents were to recognise her. You know she was free-born. She had put the casket into a little trunk, and now it has gone to the bottom."

Trach. " I dare say some one has dived down and recovered it. Anyhow, I will go in and try to cheer her up."

Amp. "Very good; and I will go and fetch the water. What a good, kind creature the priestess is! If we had been her own daughters, she could not have treated us better."

While she went on her errand, who should appear on the scene but Labrax himself. The old villain had not been drowned after all. As may be supposed, he was in a towering rage.

"Well," he said, stamping his foot on the ground, "if a man wants to be a beggar, let him venture on the sea. This is the sort of plight that he comes home in! But where is the old fool who let me in for all this? Ah! I see him."

The "old fool's" name was Charmides. He was in Labrax's employment, and it was he who had advised the voyage to Sicily.

"What are you in this deadly hurry about?" cried Charmides, who was an old man, when, with much panting and puffing, he came up with his employer. Labrax turned upon him sharply.

"Oh, it's you, Charmides, is it? I wish you had been crucified in your dear Sicily before ever I set eyes on you."

Charmides. "And I wish I had lodged in a jail rather than with you."

Labrax. "What in the world possessed me to listen to you? It has ended in my losing every farthing I had."

Char. "No wonder: ill got, soon gone."

Labr. "Yes; and you told me that I should make my fortune in a trice in that precious island of yours."

Char. "And you thought, I suppose, that you were going to swallow the place whole."

Labr. "I tell you what, Charmides, some whale has swallowed the trunk in which I had packed all my gold and silver."

Char. "The very same, I fancy, Labrax, that has gobbled down my little pouch full of coin."

Labr. "And the end of it is that I am reduced to this tunic and cloak."

Char. "Well, we can go into partnership, for my capital is just the same as yours."

Labr. "If only the two girls had been saved, I should not have minded. But now — and there's Plesidippus, who paid me a deposit for Palæstra: if he catches sight of me, there will be a pretty piece of business."

The truth was that Plesidippus had caught sight of the girl as she was going back to her master's house from a music lesson, and had fallen in love with her. Somehow he contrived to get a few words with her, and finding that she was free-born, had arranged to buy her and make her his wife. Part of the purchase-money he paid down, but he had to wait till the rest was remitted to him from Athens. Meanwhile, the old villain, Labrax, had taken up the idea of making off from Cyrene and going to

l)

Sicily, where he would get a high price for his slaves, and put Plesidippus's deposit into his pocket besides. The very day the purchase was to be completed, he had set sail, having fooled the young man by making an appointment at the temple.

Labrax, of course, had no idea that what he said about the two girls being saved could possibly be true. He was sitting very disconsolately on the ground, when he overheard the slave of Dæmones talking to himself. The man had been so charmed with Ampelisca, who was a very pretty and lively girl, that he had drawn the water which she had come to fetch, and had carried it for her into the temple. What he saw there so astonished him that he could not help talking about it when he came out.

"I never saw such a thing in my life," he said. "Two girls sitting with their arms round the statue of the goddess, as if they were afraid of being dragged away."

Labrax pricked up his ears. "What do you say, young man?" he asked. "Two girls! Where?"

"In the temple, to be sure," said the man.

"Charmides," cried Labrax, "they must be mine. I will go in and see."

Just as he went in, Dæmones came out of his cottage, talking to himself.

"What fools the gods make of us. Even at night they don't let us sleep in peace. Last night I had the strangest dream. I thought I saw an ape trying to climb up to a swallow's nest. The beast could not manage it, so he came and asked me to lend him a ladder. I said 'No; I am an Athenian, and the swallows are my kinsfolk; for the first swallow was an Athenian princess. I can't have you hurt them.' The ape was furious, and threatened me with all sorts of trouble. Thereupon I got angry, caught the beast round the middle, and shut him up in a prison. Now what in the world can be the meaning of such a dream as that? But, hark! What's all this uproar in the temple?"

Almost as he spoke, the slave Trachalio rushed out of the temple door, shouting, "Help, help, everybody! Don't allow such abominable things to be done! They are carrying off some poor creatures who have taken sanctuary. Make an example of the scoundrels! Help, help!"

"What in the world is the matter with you?" said Dæmones.

Trach. "I beseech you, old man, by your knees, whoever you are — "

Dæm. "Never mind about my knees. Tell me what you are making all this noise about."

Trach. "I beseech you, as you hope for a good crop of garlic — "

Dæm. "Is the fellow mad?"

Trach. "I beseech you, as you would have your assafœtida — "

Dæm. "I beseech you, as you would *not* have a
good crop of birch twigs about your legs, to tell why
you are making all this uproar."

Trach. "Well, sir, there are two poor girls in the
temple here, who want your help; and the priestess,
too, is being shamefully knocked about."

Dæm. "Knocked about! The priestess! Who
could have dared? Who is the man, and who are
the girls?"

Trach. "The man is a slave-dealer; the girls, both
of them by rights free, had their arms round the
goddess; he tried to drag them away, and when the
priestess wanted to stop him he nearly strangled
her."

Dæm. "Strangle the priestess! I'll strangle him.
Ho, there!"

Two stout fellows came hurrying out at the call.

"Quick!" said the old man; "quick, into the
temple with you! There is a fellow there who has
hold of two girls. Drag him out by the heels like a
dead pig."

While this was going on the girls had wrenched
themselves from the hands of the slave-dealer, and
came rushing out of the temple by another door into
the court outside. Dæmones had followed his men,
and was inside.

"We'll kill ourselves sooner than be carried off,"
cried both the girls.

"Don't talk nonsense about killing yourselves,"

said Trachalio. " I'll see that you come to no harm.
Go and sit on the altar there."

" The altar!" said Palæstra. " How will the altar
help us any more than the image?"

" Never you mind; sit you down. I will take care
of you."

The girls did as they were told, and began to
sing : —

> " Goddess, hark to our cry,
> Where thou sittest on high;
> From all mischief defend;
> At thy altar we bend;
> And excuse us, we pray,
> This unseemly array;
> Nor, though squalid our garb, turn away from our prayer,
> 'Twas Poseidon, thy uncle, that stripped us so bare."

When they had finished, Dæmones, with his men,
came pushing Labrax out of the temple. " Out with
you, you scoundrel!" he cried.

" You shall suffer for this," said the slave-dealer,
as soon as he could get his breath.

Dæm. "What! You threaten me?"

Labr. " Yes, I do. Those two girls are my slaves,
and I'm not going to be robbed of them for
nothing."

" Slaves!" cried Trachalio, interrupting. " Your
slaves! Touch one of them with your little finger
and you'll see."

Labr. " See what?"

Trach. " Why, see that I'll beat you into a jelly."

"I'm not going to talk to this gallows'-bird of a slave," said Labrax, turning to Dæmones. "I tell you, these girls are my slaves."

"And I tell you," cried Trachalio, "that they are your betters, real Greek girls, none of your colonists. One of them, I know, was born at Athens."

"What do you say?" said Dæmones, more interested than ever, when he heard Athens mentioned.

"I say that this one here," and he pointed to Palæstra, "was born at Athens of free parents."

Dæm. "What? A countrywoman of mine?"

Trach. "Why, I thought you were a Cyrenean."

Dæm. "No, no. I was born and brought up at Athens."

Trach. "Well, then you are bound to help your countrywoman."

Dæm. "Yes, yes. How the girl reminds me of my dear little daughter: she was three when I lost her, and she would be just of this girl's age if she were alive."

"This is all nonsense," said the slave-dealer. "I bought these girls with my own money, and I don't care a brass farthing whether they were born at Athens or at Thebes."

A long dispute followed, things being brought to a point by Labrax declaring that if he could not drag the girls from the altar, he should burn them out. This was more than Trachalio could stand. "Look after them," he said to Dæmones, "and I will run and tell my master."

"Run," replied the old man; "they shall not come to any harm."

When the slave was gone the dispute waxed fierce again, Labrax declaring that he would carry off his own property in spite of all the gods of Olympus, and Dæmones bidding him lay a finger on either of them at his peril. It ended by the old man going away, and leaving the two slaves in charge. "Stand here," he said; "if that fellow touches either of the girls, or if he offers to go away himself, then use your sticks to him. Stop till Trachalio and his master, Plesidippus, come back; then you can go home." They had not to stop long. The two came hurrying back, talking as they went. "What!" he cried; "did the scoundrel try to drag my dear Palæstra from the altar? Why did you not kill him at once?"

Trach. "I did not happen to have a sword handy."

Ples. "Why not with a club or a stone?"

Trach. "They would hardly have served."

Labrax recognized his voice. "Good heavens!" he cried, "here is Plesidippus! It's all over with me!"

The next moment the young man rushed into the court.

"Good morning," said Labrax, as coolly as he could.

"Bother your good morning! You have got to have a rope round your neck and go before a magistrate."

Labr. " But what have I done?"

Ples. "What have you done? Why, you took a deposit for Palæstra, and then ran off with her."

Labr. "I didn't run off. I wish I had " (*aside*). "Didn't I agree to meet you here? and here I am."

Ples. "Hold your tongue, you villain! Here you go!"

And in a trice he had a rope round the fellow's neck, and dragged him off, in spite of his protests and appeals, to which, indeed, no one, not even his friend Charmides, would listen for a moment. As soon as he was gone the two girls, and the slaves who had been set to keep guard over them, went into the cottage.

Meanwhile, one of the fishermen to whom Trachalio had spoken, Gripus by name, had drawn up something in his net that promised to be much more valuable than fish — a little travelling trunk, which was so heavy that he felt sure it must have something inside it.

"It must be gold," he said to himself, as he walked along the shore, dragging his new treasure after him by a rope. "Gripus, you have got your chance at last, and you must not lose it. First, I must buy my freedom; I shall have to be careful how I manage that. Of course the old man must know nothing about this, or else he will run up the price. Well, suppose that is done, and I am free. First, I shall buy an estate. Then I shall make a great fortune in trade. When I am rich I shall build a town all for myself. Gripus I shall call it, and be the first king myself. Yes, Gripus, a king — nothing less; but just now I wish that I had something better for breakfast than bread with a dash of salt, and a draught of master's very small beer."

He had got so far in his day-dreaming, when he heard some one calling out, "Ho! stop there!"

"Stop!" he cried, "why should I stop?"

The new-comer was Trachalio, who recognized the trunk as that which Palæstra had lost.

Trach. "I should like to help you with the rope. It's always a pleasure to help a good fellow."

Gripus. "Do you know you are very tiresome?"

Trach. "That may be; meanwhile you are not going away."

Grip. "But why not?"

Trach. "Because I am going to keep you. Now listen. I saw a man steal something. I know whom he stole it from. I go to him and say: 'Give me half and I'll say nothing about it.' Don't you think that I ought to have it?"

Grip. "Yes, indeed; and more. If he won't pay, tell his master."

Trach. "Very good; I quite agree. Now listen. You are the man."

Grip. "I?"

Trach. "Yes, you. I know the person to whom that trunk belongs. I know how it was lost."

Grip. "Well, I know how it was found; I know to whom it belongs now. Don't think for one moment that any one will get it."

Trach. "What! Not its owner?"

Grip. "It has got no owner but me, for I caught it."

Trach. "Caught it?"

Grip. "Yes; just as I catch the fishes. When I have caught them they are mine. No one claims them. I sell them as my own in the market."

After a long argument, at the end of which they were no nearer agreeing than at the beginning, Trachalio caught hold of the other end of the rope, and there was very nearly a fight. At last the two slaves agreed to refer the matter to the arbitration of Dæmones.

Just as they reached the cottage the old man came out, and they put the case before him. When Gripus had had his say, claiming the trunk because he had fished it out of the sea, Trachalio began : —

"The trunk is not mine. I don't claim it, no; nor any part of it. But it has got in it the girl's casket — her, I mean, who I said was free-born."

"What!" cried Dæmones, "do you mean my countrywoman?"

Trach. "The very same. She had her old toys in a casket that was in the trunk. They can be of no

use to this man, and she can't find her father and
mother without them."

Dæm. " He shall give them up."

" Give them up ? " said Gripus, " I shall give up
nothing."

Trach. " I want nothing but the casket and the
toys."

" I dare say," Gripus replied ; " but what if they
are gold and silver ? "

Trach. " You shall have what they are worth by
weight : gold for gold, silver for silver."

Grip. " Let me see the gold, and you shall see
the casket."

" Hold your tongue," broke in Dæmones, getting
out of all patience. " And you tell me exactly what
you want," he went on to Trachalio.

" Well, the case is this," said Trachalio. "These
two girls are free by right; the one, Palæstra I
mean, was stolen when she was a little child at
Athens, and the proof of it is in that trunk there."

" I understand," said Dæmones. " Now, Palæstra,
tell me, is that your trunk ? "

" Yes, it is," said the girl. " And there is a
wooden casket in it, and in the casket the toys which
I had when I was a child. I can describe them all.
If I am wrong, there is nothing more to be said.
If I am right, then pray let me have them back."

" So you shall," said Dæmones. " That's simple
right."

"I say it's simple wrong," cried Gripus. "Suppose she's a witch, and so knows what to say? Am I to lose what I found because she's a witch?"

"It's all nonsense about witches," said Dæmones. "Open the trunk."

The trunk was opened, and a casket, which Palæs-tra at once recognized as hers, was found inside. Dæmones told her to turn her back and describe its contents.

"First," said the girl, "there is a little gold sword, with letters on it."

Dæm. "What are the letters?"

Pal. "My father's name. Next, there is a little hatchet, also of gold. That has not my father's name on it."

Dæm. "But stay. Your father's name — what was it?"

Pal. "Dæmones."

"Dæmones!" cried the old man, astonished. "Still, that is a common name enough. It might not be the same. What was your mother's?"

Pal. "Dædalis."

Dæm. "She must be my daughter. But tell me what else there is in the casket."

Pal. "A little sickle in silver, and two hands clasped, and a necklace which my father gave me on my birthday."

Dæm. "Ah! so I did. I remember it, and here it is again, the very thing! It is my own child!

Kiss me, my darling! And now come and see your mother."

Dæmones and his wife had scarcely finished rejoicing over their newly-found child, when young Plesidippus came up, and told his story, and explained who he was.

"So you fell in love with our little girl," said Dæmones, "when you did not know who she was? Very good; you shall have her."·

"I owe you something for what you have done," said Plesidippus to his slave, Trachalio. "I shall set you free."

"A thousand thanks, master!" said Trachalio. "But there is something else, if I may make so bold. There is Ampelisca."

"All right," said Dæmones. "I will buy her of her owner, and you shall marry her."

"And what am I to have?" said Gripus. "If I hadn't fished up the trunk, where would you all have been?"

"Of course you will be satisfied with seeing everybody happy," said his master.

Poor Gripus's face fell.

"Cheer up, my man," cried Dæmones, "you shall have your freedom, and something to start in business with."

IV.

THE BROTHERS.

[*From* MENANDER. *Translated by* TERENCE.]

THE two brothers Demea and Micio were men of very different tempers. Micio was an easy-going person, self-indulgent and good-natured, · living an idle life in the city ; Demea was hard-working, frugal, and severe, allowing himself little pleasure, and not expecting others to take it. Demea was married, and had two sons, Ctesipho and Æschinus. Ctesipho lived at home, and was supposed to emulate the virtues of his father ; Æschinus had been adopted by his uncle Micio, who treated him with the utmost indulgence. The old man's only thought was to make his nephew love and trust him. " Other young men," he would say to himself, "keep secrets from their fathers ; I am sure that Æschinus will never do so, for the simple reason that I never find fault with him. My brother," he went on, " doesn't approve of this method, and accuses me of spoiling the young man. He pursues a quite different plan with Ctesipho, and, in my judgment, is far too severe. I am convinced that the obedience that is rendered for fear is worthless. Take away the restraint and the young man will show himself in his true colors."

It was not long before this theory of education was put to a severe test. Demea arrived in a high state of indignation : " You have heard this about Æschinus ? " he said.

Micio. " What has he done ? "

Demea. " What has he done ? He seems to have neither shame nor fear. As for law, he supposes himself to be above it. I am not talking of any old story now, but of what he has just done."

Mi. " What is that ? "

De. " He broke down a man's door, rushed into his house, beat the owner and his household almost to death, and carried off a woman he was in love with. Everybody is talking of it. I don't know how many mentioned it to me as I came along. How different from his brother ! There is a sober, hard-working fellow. You never find him doing anything of this kind ! And what I say of Æschinus, Micio, I say of you ; it is you who are ruining him by your foolish indulgence."

Mi. " I don't agree with you. There is no real harm in a young man's wildness. If you and I never indulged in such things it was because we were too poor. If you had any human feeling about you, you would let your Ctesipho have his fling now while he is young. If he puts it off till he is old, when he has buried you, it will be ten times worse."

De. "Well, if you are not enough to drive a man mad! It is no crime forsooth for a young man to do such things!"

Mi. "Listen to me. Don't go on hammering in the same thing over and over again. You allowed me to adopt your son. He is now my own. If he goes wrong, it is my lookout. If he is extravagant, I find the money — so long as I choose. He has broken in a door; it shall be repaired. He has torn a man's coat; it shall be mended. Thank heaven! I have the wherewithal; and at present I am content to supply it. Really, when you talk in this way, you seem to be repenting of having made him over to me."

De. "Well, well; let him be as extravagant as he pleases; it does not matter to me. But if I ever say another word — "

Micio, to tell the truth, was somewhat uneasy at this fresh outbreak on the part of his adopted son. The young man had promised to reform, and had even expressed his intention of looking out for a wife and settling down, and this violent proceeding of his was a great disappointment. Nor, indeed, was it long before the severe Demea also began to feel uncomfortable. A rumour reached him that the model young man Ctesipho had taken part with Æschinus in his scandalous proceedings. He was thinking where he was likely to find his son when he spied Micio's favourite slave, Syrus. "Ah!" he said, "I'll

MICIO AND DEMEA.

find out from him. He is one of that rascally crew indeed, and if he fancies that I am looking for my son, the scoundrel will never tell me. I won't let him know what I want." Syrus was busy with some cooking, and was talking to a fellow-slave, and pretended not to see the new-comer. He was telling, with much apparent satisfaction, how Micio had taken the news of Æschinus's recent exploit. "We told the old man the whole story of what had happened. I never saw any one more delighted."

De. (*aside*). "Good heavens! what a fool the man must be!"

Syrus. "He praised his son. He thanked me for having suggested the scheme. He counted out the money on the spot, — you know we paid the dealer what the girl had cost him, — and he gave me two pounds for myself. I shall know how to spend that."

De. (*aside*). "Well, that's a nice fellow to trust anything to!"

Sy. "Oh! Demea, I did not see you. How are things going on?"

De. "I can't sufficiently admire your way of proceeding."

Sy. "Well, it is foolish and unreasonable, to speak the truth. Dromo, you may clean the other fish, but let the big conger play in the water a little time; when I come home I will bone him; but don't do it before."

De. "That there should be such wickedness!"

20

Sy. "I don't like it at all. Stephanio, see that this salt fish is properly soaked."

De. "Does he really think that it will be to his credit if he ruins his son? I see a day coming when the poor wretch will be a beggar and will have to enlist."

Sy. "O Demea, this is true wisdom in you, that you see not only what is before your eyes, but also what is coming."

De. "Tell me; is the singing-girl in the house?"

Sy. "Certainly."

De. "And is going to stop there?"

Sy. "Of course; he has married her; the more fool he!"

De. "To think that such a thing should be possible!"

Sy. "Well, his father is foolishly easy with him."

De. "Oh! as for my brother, I am thoroughly ashamed and disgusted with him."

Sy. "Ah! Demea, there is far too much difference between you. You are nothing but wisdom from top to toe; he is the most frivolous creature. You would not allow your son to do such things!"

De. "Allow him indeed! If he had had a notion of any such thing, I should have smelt it out six months ago."

Sy. "Oh! I know that you keep your eyes open."

De. "There is no fear of him going wrong."

Sy. "Yes, yes; a son always is what his father would like him to be."

De. "What about him? Have you seen him to-day?"

Sy. "Your son, you mean?" (*Aside*) "I'll send the old fellow off into the country." (*Aloud*) "I think that he had some business in the country."

De. "You are sure?"

Sy. "Oh, yes; I saw him go myself."

De. "Very good; I was afraid he might be hanging about here."

Sy. "And a pretty rage he was in!"

De. "Why so?"

Sy. "He had a regular quarrel with his brother, in the market-place, about the singing-girl."

De. "You don't say so!"

Sy. "Ah! but he had, and didn't spare him. He came in unexpectedly, just as the money was being counted out. 'O Æschinus,' he cried, 'to think that you should do such shameful things, so unworthy of our family!'"

De. "Did he speak like that? I could cry for joy."

Sy. "He went on: 'It is not your own money, it is your own self you are losing.'"

De. "Bless him! He is like those who have gone before him."

Sy. "Hem!"

De. "Syrus, he is stocked with maxims of that kind."

Sy. "Ah, yes; he has a teacher at home."

De. "I do my best; I lose no chance. I accustom him to this kind of thing. I tell him to look into his neighbours' lives, as he might into a looking-glass, and to learn by others. 'Do this,' I say."

Sy. "Excellent!"

De. "'Avoid that.' 'This is to a man's credit; that is set down against him.'"

Sy. "Good, good!"

De. "Then I go on —"

Sy. "Excuse me, but I haven't time to listen. I have got just the fish I wanted, and I must take care they are not spoilt. It is as much a crime among us to do this, as to do the things you talk of among you; and as far as I can, I instruct my fellow-slaves in this fashion: 'This is too salt,' I say; 'that is burnt; this is not quite clean; that is very good.' I advise in this way to the very best of my capacity. In a word, Demea, I tell them to look into the dishes as they would into a looking-glass, and tell them what they ought to do. These are but trifles, Demea, that we busy ourselves about; but what would you have? Can I do anything for you?"

De. "I wish you a better mind; that's all. However, I shall go straight to the farm, as my son, on whose account I came, is there. He is my own, at all events. Let my brother look to the other."

But Demea had not yet heard all Æschinus's misdemeanours. This young man had actually broken off his engagement to a girl, poor, indeed, but of good family, in order, as it appeared, to marry this singing-woman. A friend and kinsman of her father, Hegio by name, had taken up her cause, and appealed to Demea to help him. Demea, now doubly indignant, at once set about finding his brother. This, much to his annoyance, he was unable to do. He searched for him all over the town, but to no purpose; and while he was so engaged, he happened to come across a man from the farm, and heard from him that his son had not been there. His wanderings brought him back to the point from which he had started, — his brother's house; and he had no choice but to ask the help of "that scoundrel Syrus," as he called him. "My good fellow," said he, "is my brother at home?"

Sy. "Good fellow indeed! I am pretty nearly killed."

De. "What is the matter?"

Sy. "That Ctesipho of yours nearly beat me to death."

De. "What do you say?"

Sy. "See there, how he cut my lip!"

De. "Why did he do it?"

Sy. "Because I was the cause, he said, of the singing-girl having been bought."

De. "But didn't you say that he had gone out to the farm?"

Sy. "So he did; but he came back in a fury. He wasn't ashamed to beat an old man who dandled him when he was only so big."

De. " Excellent! excellent! Ctesipho, you take after your father."

Sy. " Excellent, you call it! Well, he had better keep his hands off me in future."

De. " I say that he couldn't have done better. He felt, as I do, that you were the prime mover in the whole affair. But is my brother at home?"

Sy. " No."

De. " I want to find out where he is."

Sy. " I know, but I don't mean to tell you."

De. " What is that you say?"

Sy. " That I sha'n't tell you."

De. " I'll break your head, if you don't."

Sy. " Well, I don't know the man's name where he is, but I know the place."

De. " Tell me the place, then."

Sy. " Do you know the arcade, and the market down below?"

De. " Of course I know it."

Sy. " Go straight up that street. After that, there is a slope right in front of you. Go down that. On the left hand there is a chapel, and an alley close by."

De. " In which direction?"

Sy. " Where there is a large wild fig-tree. Do you know it?"

De. " Yes, I know it."

Sy. " Well, go up the alley."

De. " But it isn't a thoroughfare."

Sy. "True; well, we all make mistakes. Go back to the colonnade. There is a much nearer way. Do you know the house of the rich Cratinus?"

De. "Yes."

Sy. "When you reach that, go up the street to the left. When you come to Diana's temple, turn to the right. Before you come to the gate, there is a mill by the pond, and a workshop exactly opposite. He is there."

De. "What is he doing?"

Sy. "He is having some couches made."

De. "For you to lie on and drink, I suppose."

Sy. (*when Demea is out of hearing*). "Go, you old skeleton! I'll give you a nice little walk. And now, I think, I may take a little something to drink."

Syrus did take the little "something," and the consequence was that when Demea came back, fuming after his fruitless walk, for of course he did not find his brother, and even the shop was imaginary, he was not able to cope with the situation. "What annoys you?" he asked, when he saw the old man.

De. "Oh, you scoundrel!"

Sy. "Ah, old wisdom overflowing again!"

De. "Oh, if you belonged to me!"

Sy. "You would be a rich man. I should have set your affairs on a sound footing."

De. "I would make an example of you."

Sy. "Why, what have I done?"

De. "Why, not to mention anything else — in all this confusion you have been drinking as if everything was all right."

At this moment one of Syrus's fellow-slaves called out to him from within, "Syrus, Ctesipho wants you!"

De. (catching the name). "Who is talking of Ctesipho?"

Sy. "It is nothing."

De. "You scoundrel! is Ctesipho here?"

Sy. "Certainly not."

De. "Then why did I hear his name?"

Sy. "Oh, that was quite another person, one of Micio's hangers-on. You must know him."

De. "Well, I'll find out."

Sy. (catching hold of the old man). "What are you about? Where are you going?"

De. "Let me go."

Sy. "I won't."

De. "I'll break your head, if you don't."

So saying, he broke loose from the slave's grasp. "Ah!" said Syrus, "he will not be a welcome addition to their little party."

The fact was, that it was for Ctesipho that Æschinus had carried off the singing-girl; it was the steady Ctesipho, as his father thought him, that had made this not very reputable marriage; and now, after being put off more than once, the old man had found it out. Things, being at their darkest, now began to lighten. Æschinus was, it turned out, perfectly ready

to fulfil the engagement which he was thought to
have broken off; and Micio was willing to start his
other nephew in life with a handsome present of
money. Demea, finding that amiability and com-
plaisance were the order of the day, determined to
fashion his own behaviour accordingly, though he
slyly contrived to make his good-natured brother
bear the burden of the general benevolence. Syrus
was to receive his liberty as an encouragement to
honest servants; Hegio, who had taken up the cause
of Æschinus's neglected bride, was to have his poverty relieved by the present of a little farm. Finally,
the young lady's mother was to be provided for, and
in view of this object, what could be a more convenient fact than that Micio was a bachelor?
"Brother," said Demea, "there is your daughter-in-
law's mother, a very reputable lady."

Mi. "So I am told."

De. "A little advanced in years, and a lone
woman."

Mi. (*aside*). "What is the man after?"

De. "Don't you think that you ought to marry
her?"

Mi. "I marry when I am sixty-five years old, and
marry an old woman! Is that what you want?"

Æschinus. "Oh, do, father! In fact, I have promised you would."

Mi. "You have promised I would! Keep your
breath to cool your own porridge, my son."

De. " Now, do it."

Æsch. " Don't make any trouble about it."

Mi. " Well, it is absurd ; it is quite contrary to all that I have ever done and said. Still, if you are so anxious for it, I will."

Then Demea explained himself. " I wanted to show you, Micio," he said, "that all your easiness and good-nature did not come from true kindness, but from a lazy habit of giving way to others. If you, Æschinus, persist in disliking me because I do not choose to approve of everything that you do, be it good or bad, let it be so ; go your way, you and your brother, waste and spoil as much as you please. But if you think that after all it would be well that, where you, in your youth and inexperience, fail to see clearly, and are ready to buy your pleasures too dearly, I should step in, advising and criticising, while not failing to give way on proper occasions, I am at your service."

" You are right," said Æschinus ; " you know far better than we do what ought to be done. And how about my brother ? "

" I forgive him," replied Demea. " Now that he is married, he will, I hope, behave himself respectably."

V.

THE GIRL OF ANDROS.

[*From* MENANDER. *Adapted by* TERENCE.]

Terence tells us himself that he had used two comedies of Menander in constructing this play, and that he had been blamed for so doing by some critics. The two seem to have borne the titles of *Andria* (the girl of Andros) and *Perinthia* (the girl of Perinthos). An early commentator informs us that it is the first part of the play that is borrowed from the *Andria*.

Simo, an Athenian citizen, happening to be present at the funeral of a lady with whom he had had a slight acquaintance, witnessed a spectacle which caused him no little anxiety. Among the women who were attending as mourners was a young girl of singular beauty. This, and the manifest depth and sincerity of her grief, so excited the old man's interest that he inquired who she was, and was told in reply that she was a sister of the deceased. The corpse was placed on the funeral pile, and this was lighted in due course. When the flames were at their fiercest, the young girl rushed forward, as if intending to throw herself into them. So near did she come that she seriously imperilled her own life, which, indeed, would probably have been sacrificed, had her clothes caught fire. At this point, Simo saw

a young man, in whom he recognized his own son
Pamphilus, run out from among the crowd of spectators and catch the girl round the waist. The next
moment he heard him remonstrating with her. " My
dear Glycerium," — these were his words, — " what
are you doing? why do you try to kill yourself?"
The girl turned at the sound of his voice, and fell
into his arms in a passion of tears. It was evident,
Simo thought to himself, that this was not the first
time that they had met. And all the time Pamphilus
was betrothed to Philumena, the daughter of an old
friend, Chremes by name. It was a desirable match
in every way, and Simo was greatly troubled at the
thought that it might be broken off.

This indeed seemed not unlikely to happen.
Others besides Simo had witnessed the scene at the
funeral, and one of them had carried the report to
Chremes, Philumena's father, with the result that he
came in a great rage to his friend, and declared that
he should not think of allowing his daughter to
become the wife of a young man whose affections
were evidently bestowed elsewhere, and who, indeed,
was possibly married already.

Simo now resolved, by way of bringing matters to
a crisis, to tell his son that the marriage with Philumena was to take place that very day. If the young
man made no objection, all was well. The foolish
engagement to the girl seen at the funeral would be
broken off, and it would not be difficult to induce

Chremes to withdraw his objections. Simo's freed-
man Sosia was charged with the duty of announcing
to Pamphilus the arrangements for his marriage.
This he proceeded to do, and his report to his patron
was that the young man made no objection, but that
he and his confidential slave Davus were evidently
disturbed.

Before long Davus made his appearance. He was
talking to himself, unaware, it was evident, of his
master's presence.

Davus. " I wondered what was going to happen.
The master's good humour was suspicious. The
match broken off and not an angry word to any
one ! It was too good."

Simo (aside). " Well, you'll hear plenty of angry
words soon, my man."

Da. "We were to think it all blown over; and
then he would spring this upon us. The cunning
old fellow ! "

Si. (not hearing). "What does he say ? "

Da. " Good heavens! there is the master, and I
never saw him ! "

Si. " Davus ! "

Da. " Yes, sir ! "

Si. "I am told that my son has made a foolish
engagement."

Da. " People will talk, sir."

Si. "A young man so situated would not like
marrying the wife his father had chosen for him."

Da. "It is possible, sir."

Si. "He might have had advisers who would encourage him in this feeling."

Da. "I don't understand."

Si. "Not understand?"

Da. "No, sir; I am Davus, not Œdipus."[1]

Si. "Then you want me to speak plainly?"

Da. "If you please, sir."

Si. "Listen, then; if you try any tricks to hinder this match, you will be well flogged and sent to the treadmill till you die. Is that plain enough?"

Da. "Certainly, sir."

Si. "Well, don't say that you have not been warned."

But there was another complication. Though Pamphilus had no thought of Philumena, his friend Charinus was deeply in love with her, and the news of the intended wedding struck him with despair. He hurried, on hearing of it from his slave Byrrhia, to see whether anything could be done. "O Pamphilus," he cried, as soon as he saw his friend, "are you going to be married to-day?"

Pamphilus. "So they say."

Charinus. "Then you have seen the last of me."

Pam. "Why so?"

Char. "I am ashamed to say." (*Turning to his slave*) "Tell him, Byrrhia."

Byrrhia. "The truth is, my master is in love with your betrothed."

---

[1] Œdipus — famous as having guessed the riddle of the Sphinx.

Pam. "That is more than I am."

Char. "I beseech you not to marry her."

Pam. "I will do my best."

Char. "If you can't help yourself, or if, after all, you really wish to marry her, at least give me a few days to get out of the way, so that I may not see it."

Pam. "My good fellow, I don't want to make any merit of it, but it is the simple truth that I hate the idea of the marriage quite as much as you do. Do all you can to get the girl, and I will help you. But here comes my clever Davus; he is the man to advise us."

Char. "Is he? This fellow Byrrhia is no use at all."

Davus had good news to tell. The marriage was all an invention. "I suspected something of the kind," he said, "and went to Chremes's house. There wasn't a sign of anything festive. No one was going in or out. There were no signs of preparation. Then I met his man as he was going away. He had a few vegetables and half a dozen anchovies for the old man's supper. That did not look like a wedding."

Char. "Excellent! excellent!"

Da. "But, my good sir, it does not follow that you will get the young lady because she is not to be married to Pamphilus here to-day. Bestir yourself, or you will lose her as sure as fate."

Charinus promptly departed to take counsel with

his friends. This was what Davus wanted. " And
now, sir," he said to his master, as soon as the young
man had disappeared, " I should recommend you to
go to your father, and say that you have no longer
any objection. If you don't, he will find some way
of doing a mischief to Glycerium, — will get her
banished from Athens, it may be, for he has interest
with the government. Don't be afraid of anything happening. Whatever your father may wish,
Chremes is quite resolved that you sha'n't marry his
daughter." Pamphilus was persuaded, and, meeting
his father soon afterwards, let him know that he was
ready to fulfil the engagement. As luck would have
it, he was overheard by Byrrhia, who had been
strictly charged by his master, Charinus, to watch
the movements of the bridegroom. Byrrhia went
off to tell the news, Davus meanwhile making Simo
uncomfortable by representing that he wasn't treat-
ing his son very well in the matter. " You keep
your purse too close, sir," he said, " for a father who
is going to marry his son. That's what he feels.
Why, he can't even ask his friends to the wedding."

Simo now conceived the happy idea of turning the
feint into a reality. The marriage which he invented
to test his son's feeling might actually take place.
Only he must persuade Chremes to withdraw his
veto. This he set about doing. The alliance had
been a cherished scheme with both of them for
many years. The young man and the girl had been

intended for man and wife ever since they lay in their cradles. Simo implored his old friend to give way. For a time Chremes stoutly refused. The young man had set his affections elsewhere, and the marriage would turn out badly. This argument Simo answered by an assurance that the old engagement was at an end. Pamphilus and Glycerium had quarrelled; so Davus, his son's confidential slave, assured him. Overborne by his old friend's entreaties, Chremes gave way, and consented that the marriage should take place. Davus, who happened to be passing, was summoned to hear the good news. " Davus," said Simo, " I have had hard work to persuade my friend Chremes, but he consents. Pamphilus is to marry Philumena."

Da. " We are all undone."

Si. " What did you say ? "

Da. " I said that it was well done of you."

Si. " Now, Davus, I feel that this marriage is really your work. Pray do your best to keep my son straight; and if he is a little discontented just at first, do represent things in the best light."

" Here is a pretty state of things ! " said the unlucky slave to himself. " I have cheated my old master, entrapped my young one into a marriage that he hates, and all because I would be so clever ! I am simply ruined. I only wish there was a precipice here for me to throw myself down."

Things were indeed come to a terrible pass. The

21

fact was that Pamphilus had been really married to
Glycerium for nearly a year, and what was more,
that very day his wife had borne him a son. And
here he was in a fearful strait. His wife crying out
to see him, for somehow she had heard of the new
marriage; his friend Charinus furious at being, as
he thought, deceived; and the preparations for a
second wedding going actively on!

Davus, who had had a great deal to do with bringing about this state of things, now came to the
rescue. He got hold of the new-born baby, and
persuaded Mysis, Glycerium's nurse, to lay it down
in front of his master's door. "Why don't you do it
yourself?" said the woman. "Because," he replied,
"I may have to swear that I didn't do it." Just as
this had been done, Chremes arrived. He had been
making preparations for the marriage, and was now
come to invite the bridegroom's friends. "But what
is this?" he cried, seeing a bundle on the threshold.
"On my life, it is a child! Woman," he went on,
turning to the nurse, "did you put it here?"

The woman was too much flustered to answer, but
looked round for Davus, who had disappeared as
soon as he caught sight of Chremes. But when
Davus returned he promptly denied all knowledge of
the matter, and pretended to know as little where the
child came from as did Chremes himself. "Whose
child is it?" he said to the nurse in a threatening
voice.

The Nurse. " You mean to say you don't know ? "

Da. " Never mind whether I know or not; answer my question."

Nurse. " Why, it is the child of your own — "

Da. " My own what ? "

Nurse. " Your own master Pamphilus."

Da. " Oh! I dare say. I know where it came from. Take the brat away, or it will be the worse for you."

Nurse. " Is the man sober ? "

Da. " The next thing will be that we shall be told that the mother is Athenian born."

Chremes. " A pretty mess I have nearly been getting into ! "

Da. (*pretending to become aware of his presence*). " O Chremes! you here ? What ought to be done to this wicked woman ? "

Chr. " I know the whole story. Is Simo at home ? "

Saying this, he entered the house. As soon as he was out of sight Davus explained his action to the nurse. " Don't you understand," he said, "that this is Philumena's father? This was the only way of frightening him off the new marriage."

Chremes meanwhile had finally broken off the match. " I was willing," he said, " to do the best I could for your son. I risked my daughter's happiness on the chance; but knowing what I know, I can't go on. The young man has another attachment, and I hear, too, that the woman is a native Athenian. Consider the other affair is at an end."

Davus now made his appearance. The news he had to communicate brought Simo, already furious with disappointment, to something like madness. "A stranger," said the slave, "has just come, a most respectable looking man, who declares that Glycerium is a free-born Athenian woman."

Simo deigned to make no answer. "Dromo," he said to another of his slaves, "carry this scoundrel off to prison. He shall learn not to play tricks on his master; aye, and I have something to say to Master Pamphilus himself." In vain did Chremes remonstrate. The old man was quite beside himself with passion, and the unlucky Davus was hurried off to punishment.

Pamphilus was the next to come in for a share of the old man's wrath. To a certain extent he contrived to turn it away by a soft answer. At least Simo was persuaded to hear what the stranger had to say about the parentage of Glycerium. At first, the interview seemed to promise little good. Simo roundly accused the stranger, whose name, by the way, was Crito, of having invented the whole story, in the interests of Pamphilus. Thus challenged, Crito spoke out, and told the whole story; not, however, without being interrupted by exclamations of incredulity from the angry old man. "Some years ago," he said, "an Athenian citizen was shipwrecked near Andros, but managed to escape to land. He had with him a little girl, the same person, I have discovered, as the

THE WRATH OF SIMO.

Glycerium of whom I have been told since my arrival at Athens. Both were received in the house of a relative of my own, from whom indeed I heard the story. There the man died; the girl was always regarded as a daughter of my kinsman."

"What was the name of this Athenian?" asked Chremes.

Crito. "Phania."

Chr. "Good heavens!"

Cri. "At least I think it was, Chremes. I know he was a native of Rhamnus."

Chr. "Did he say that the girl was his daughter?"

Cri. "No; he said she was his niece, his brother's daughter."

Chr. "Phania was my brother. I left him in charge of my child. War broke out, and he followed me to Asia, and I now learn was shipwrecked on the way."

All was now happily settled. Pamphilus brought his wife and child home with the full consent of his relatives, receiving at the same time a substantial portion from his newly-found father-in-law. At the same time, the faithful Charinus was rewarded with the hand of Philumena.

VI.

PHORMIO.

[*From* APOLLODORUS.   *Translated by* TERENCE.]

DEMIPHO and Chremes were brothers, respectable
and well-to-do citizens of Athens.   Both had occasion to leave their homes on business at the same
time, Demipho going to Cilicia, where a friend had
promised to find a profitable investment for him,
Chremes to Lemnos, where his wife Nausistrata had
a property, the rents of which he was accustomed to
collect.   Each brother had an only son; and both of
the young men took the opportunity of their fathers'
absence to get into formidable scrapes.

Chremes's son Phædria fell violently in love with
a music-girl.   Really she was a free-born Athenian,
but she was supposed to be a slave, the property of
a villainous dealer, Dorio by name, who refused to
sell her for less than a hundred and twenty pounds.
Phædria, who was bent on buying the girl and making her his wife,[1] obtained the man's promise that
if he could find the money, she should not be sold
to any one else.   For the present, however, he was

---

[1] This would have been something like a morganatic marriage.   As
a matter of fact, the girl being of Athenian birth, the marriage would
have been perfectly regular.

penniless. All that he could do was to wait at a barber's shop which happened to be opposite the music-school where she was receiving lessons, and accompany her to her owner's house. One day, as he was looking out for her, his cousin Antipho being with him, a young man of their acquaintance came up, who had a story so piteous to tell that it moved him to tears as he spoke. "I have just had a proof," he said, "what a terrible thing poverty is. Hard by here I saw a girl mourning for her mother, who had just died. The corpse was laid out opposite the door of the house, and the poor creature had no kinsman, or friend, or acquaintance with her except one old woman; a very beautiful girl she was, too." They were all touched by the story, and Antipho said at once, "Shall we go and see her?"—"Good," said Phædria, "let us go; take us to the house." They went, and found that the girl, whose name was Phanium, was certainly beautiful. There was nothing to set her off; her hair was dishevelled, her feet bare, her clothing of the meanest. Phædria, his head full of the music-girl, said nothing more than, "She is pretty enough," but with Antipho it was love at first sight. The next day he paid another visit. The girl he did not see, but the old woman, who turned out to be her nurse, told him that she was a free-born Athenian, of good family. Antipho at once made up his mind to have her for his wife. But how was it to be managed? He was afraid to do such a thing in his father's absence, and yet he knew perfectly well that, were his father at home, he would never consent, for the girl of course had not a penny of dowry. He confided his difficulty to an acquaintance, Phormio by name, a man without either occupation or means, who contrived to pick up a living by his wits. Phormio at once contrived an audacious scheme. "The law directs," he told Antipho, "that when a citizen dies, leaving an orphan daughter, the next of kin must marry her, or provide her with a dowry. I will pretend to be a friend of her father, and will bring a suit against you. We will go into court. There I will invent a name for her father, a name for her mother, and her relationship to you. Of course you will offer no defence, and I shall win the suit." This was actually done; the suit was brought, Antipho was ordered by the court to marry the girl, and, as may be supposed, readily obeyed.

From what has been said, it will be evident that both the young men were in no small trouble; Phædria was afraid that his lady-love might be sold before he could find the money, of which indeed he saw little prospect; Antipho dreaded his father's return. The two were discussing the situation, when Geta, a confidential slave in whose charge the young men had been left, made his appearance in a state of great agitation. "Your father has arrived," he cried, when he caught sight of Antipho; "I saw him at the har-

PHAEDRIA AND THE MUSIC GIRL.

bour." Antipho was in despair. His cousin and Geta implored him to screw up his courage to the point of meeting his father. "Your only chance," they told him, "is to put a bold face on it." Antipho made an effort to pluck up his spirit. "Brazen it out," said Geta, "that you were compelled by the court to contract the marriage. Do you understand? But who is that there?" he went on, looking down the street that led to the Piræus. "It is he!" cried Antipho, following the direction of Geta's eyes. "It is my father himself. I can't stand it. I am off." And in spite of all remonstrances, he disappeared. In a few minutes Demipho made his appearance. He was in a towering rage. "So Antipho has married without my leave! What audacity! And Geta, too! a pretty counsellor, indeed! Of course I know what he'll say, 'I did it against my will; the law compelled me.' Ah! but did the law compel you to give up the case without a word?"

Phædria (aside). "That's a poser!"

Geta (aside). "I'll answer him. Trust me."

Demipho. "I am so annoyed that I can't bring my mind to consider what's to be done. It is always the way. When everything seems to be going well, then we must look out for trouble. A son goes wrong, a wife dies, a daughter falls ill. These are the things we must expect. Anything that doesn't happen one must count as clear gain."

Ge. (aside). "See, Phædria, how much wiser I

am than my master. I thought of all I should have to put up with when my master came back, — work at the mill, a good beating, my feet in the stocks, set to work at the farm; there is nothing that I haven't reckoned on. And whatever doesn't happen that I shall count as clear gain. But, Phædria, why don't you go forward and speak to him?"

Phæ. (advancing). "How do you do, my dear uncle?"

Dem. "How do you do? But where is Antipho?"

Phæ. "I am delighted —"

Dem. "Where is he?"

Phæ. "At home and quite well. I hope that all is right."

Dem. "Right indeed! A pretty match you made up between you while I was away."

Phæ. "But surely you are not angry with him."

Dem. "Very angry indeed, and I'll let him know it, when I see him."

Phæ. "But he has given you no cause."

Dem. "Oh! yes; you are all tarred with the same brush. He gets into mischief, and you stand by him."

Phæ. "My dear uncle, if Antipho had done wrong, if he had wasted his money, or lost his character, I should not say a word against his suffering for it. But if a designing fellow plotted against his youth and innocence and got the better of him, who was to blame, he or the judges? They, as you know, are always jealous of the rich, and in favour of the poor."

Ge. (aside). "Upon my word, if I didn't know the facts, I should think he was speaking the truth."

Dem. "But what was a judge to do when the defendant doesn't say a word?"

Phæ. "Your son could not say what he had prepared. His modesty struck him absolutely dumb."

Ge. (advancing). "Very glad to see you, master!"

Dem. "You scoundrel! you who were to take care of my house!"

Ge. "Now, this is unjust. A slave is not allowed to plead, or give evidence."

Dem. "That is all very well. But he was not compelled to marry the girl. Why did he not pay the dowry, and let her find another husband?"

Ge. "But where was the money to come from?"

Dem. "He might have found it somewhere."

Ge. "Where? It's easy enough to say."

Dem. "He might have borrowed it."

Ge. "That is good. Who would have lent it while his father was alive?"

Dem. "Anyhow, I won't allow the marriage to stand, no, not for a day. But where is that fellow?"

Ge. "You mean Phormio?"

Dem. "Yes, the woman's advocate."

Ge. "Oh! he'll be here soon, I warrant."

Dem. "Well, tell Antipho I want to see him. I shall look up some friends, and have it out with this fellow Phormio."

Geta lost no time in finding Phormio, and telling
him of the old man's fury.   The adventurer was
very little concerned at the prospect.   " I have nothing to lose," he said.   " Suppose he gets a verdict
against me,˒and puts me in prison.   Well, he'll have
to keep me, and I have an excellent appetite."

" Ah ! " said Geta, " he's coming, and in a fine
rage."

*Phormio (to Geta, but speaking loud that Demipho,
who has come in with his friends, may hear him).*
" And he positively asserts that Phanium is not a
relative ! "

Ge. " He does."

Dem. (to his friends). " I do believe that he is
talking about me.   Come a little nearer."

Phor. " And that he does not know who her
father was ? "

Ge. " Just so."

Phor. " Because the poor girl was left without
money, her father is forgotten and she herself neglected.   See what the love of money does ! "

Ge. (who pretends to be indignant). " Don't abuse
my master, or it will be the worse for you."

Dem. (aside). " Why, the fellow is absolutely abusing me ! "

Phor. " I have nothing to say against the young
man for not knowing my old friend.   He was an
elderly man, always busy, and seldom coming to
town.   He rented a farm of my father.   He used

to tell me, I remember, that his kinsman Demipho took no notice of him. But what a man he was! The very best fellow I ever saw!"

Dem. (advancing). "Young man, I have just a question to ask you. Tell me who this friend of yours was, and how he was related to me."

Phor. "As if you didn't know!"

Dem. "I know!"

Phor. "Of course you know."

Dem. "I declare that I don't."

Phor. "Not know the name of your own cousin?"

Dem. "Tell me yourself."

Phor. (in a whisper to Geta). "I have forgotten. What was it?"

Ge. (in a whisper). "Stilpho."

Phor. "Well, if I must tell you, it was Stilpho."

Dem. "What did you say?"

Phor. "Stilpho; do you know the name?"

Dem. "I never heard of the man, and certainly never had any relative of the name."

Phor. "But if he had left three thousand pounds —"

Dem. "Confound you!"

Phor. "I warrant you would have had his whole pedigree at your fingers' ends."

Dem. "But you haven't told me how the girl was related to me."

Phor. "I explained the matter quite satisfactorily to the right persons, — that is, the judges. If it was not true, why did not your son disprove it?"

Dem. " My son, indeed ! the poor fool ! "

Phor. "Very good ; if you are so wise, go to the court, and ask for another trial. You are master here ; and though no one else can have a cause tried twice over, you must have your own way."

Dem. " Well, I know that I've been cheated. Still, to save trouble, I will suppose that the girl is related to me. Take her away, and I'll pay twenty pounds."

Phor. " A pretty story, indeed ! A girl is married, and you propose to give her a paltry sum of money, and send her away ! "

Dem. " Well, I'll manage it somehow, and not rest till I have."

Phor. " Demipho, I have nothing to do with you. It is your son that is concerned, not you. You are too old to marry."

Dem. " I shall turn him out of my house, if he objects."

Phor. " My dear sir, would it not be better to put up with what can't be undone ? Let us be friends."

Dem. " Friends ! As if I wanted to be friends with you ! "

Phor. " Make it up with her, and she'll be such a comfort to your old age. Remember your years, my dear sir."

Dem. " She may comfort *you ; I* don't want her."

Phor. " Don't be angry ! "

Dem. " Enough of this ! Except you take the

woman away immediately, I'll turn her out of doors. That is my last word, Phormio."

Phor. "Lay a finger on her, and I'll have you up before the court. That is my last word, Demipho."

The old gentleman now proceeded to ask his friends what they thought about the matter. The first thought that what had been done in Demipho's absence might be considered null and void; the second that a legal decision once given could not be invalidated; the third suggested that the matter should be postponed. Demipho was no wiser than before, and resolved to refer the matter to his brother, who was hourly expected to return.

Meanwhile Phædria's love affair had gone wrong. The music-girl's owner had received a good offer for her, and declared that he should accept it. "You," he said, brutally, to the young man, "are all tears and no money. I have found some one who is all money and no tears. You must give way to your better." Nothing could persuade him. "Pay the money to-morrow, or she'll be sold," was his last word as he turned away. Phædria was in despair; without the girl, he felt life was not worth living. The only scrap of comfort he got was that Geta declared that, by hook or by crook, he would get the money for him.

While this was going on, Chremes had returned from Lemnos. It must be here explained that, some years before, he had contracted a secret marriage in that place, and had had a daughter born to him. His brother knew all about it, and it had been arranged between the two that Antipho should marry his unknown cousin. Chremes had intended to bring the girl home on the present occasion, but found that she and her mother had disappeared. They had gone to Athens, so he heard from their neighbours, to look for him. This was disturbing news, and it was met by the equally unwelcome intelligence which Demipho had to communicate, that the intended bridegroom had made another match.

While they were considering what should be done, Geta approached. He had been talking, he said, with Phormio, and that ingenious adventurer had devised a scheme which would get rid of the difficulty and at the same time be of advantage to himself. "I long wanted " — this was the substance of Phormio's words, as the slave reported them — " to marry the daughter of my old friend. I saw how unsuitable it would be that a penniless girl should enter a wealthy house such as your master's. But to tell you the truth, I wanted a wife who would bring me something to set me free from sundry difficulties. I have my eye upon a girl who would suit me; but if Demipho will make it worth my while, I will throw her over and marry Phanium. I have mortgaged a little property that I have for fifty pounds."

At this point Demipho broke in impatiently:

"Well, I don't mind so much. I will give him the fifty pounds."

Geta went on with his report: "Then I have a house mortgaged for so much more."

Dem. "That is too much."

Chremes. "Hush! He may look to me for this fifty."

Geta continued : "My wife must have a maid. I shall want a little more furniture. Then the marriage expenses will be something. Suppose we say fifty pounds more."

Dem. "The scoundrel! Let him do his worst!"

Chr. "Do be quiet. If only Antipho marries the girl that you and I mean for him, it will be well. I'll pay this fifty, too. Happily I have some money of my wife's in hand. I'll tell her that you wanted it."

Unluckily Antipho had overheard the dialogue, and was furious at the thought that he was to be robbed of his wife. No sooner had the old gentleman disappeared than he rushed at Geta, and struck him. The slave had no little difficulty in pacifying him. "It's only a scheme for getting the old men's money," he said. "The marriage will never come off ; of that you may rest assured." With this assurance Antipho had to be content.

While this was going on a mutual recognition had taken place. Phanium's nurse, Sophrona, had heard of Demipho's indignation at his son's marriage with her charge, and was terribly alarmed at the prospect of trouble that seemed in store for the young bride. Her only hope was in finding the missing father. At this moment she heard her own name softly called. It was Chremes. " Look at me," he said.

Sophrona. " Is that Stilpho ? "

Chr. " No."

Soph. " You deny it ? "

Chr. " Come away ; never call me by that name again."

Soph. " What ? are you not what you always said you were ? "

Chr. " Hush ! "

Soph. " Why do you look at that door ? What are you afraid of ? "

Chr. " I have an angry wife inside there. I called myself Stilpho over at Lemnos, lest the affair should reach her ears."

Soph. " And so that's the reason why we could never find you."

Chr. " Where are they ? "

Soph. " Your daughter is alive. Her mother died a little time ago."

Chr. " That is a bad job."

Soph. " What was I to do ? I had nothing ; nobody knew me ; I married your daughter to the young man who is master of the house there."

Chr. " What ? to Antipho ? "

Soph. " Yes — his name is Antipho."

Chr. " Has the fellow two wives, then ? "

Soph. " No ; certainly not."

Chr. " What about the other — the cousin, then ? "

Soph. " Why, it's the same person. That is your daughter Phanium."

Chr. " Heaven be thanked ! That's exactly what I wanted, and it has all come to pass without my doing anything."

Demipho had by this time paid the money agreed upon to Phormio. The arrangement only half pleased him. " We encourage these fellows to be scoundrels by our easiness," he said. Still, he could only hope the best. The next thing he had to do was to persuade Chremes's wife Nausistrata to undertake the unpleasant task of breaking the thing to Antipho's young wife. She had already helped him more than once, and this would be another act of kindness.

" You are very welcome," replied Nausistrata ; " I only wish I could have done more, but my husband is a very poor man of business. He does not manage things as my father did. He used to get nearly five hundred pounds out of the property, and that when prices were much lower than they are now."

" Five hundred pounds ! " said Demipho.

" Yes," said Nausistrata, " I only wish that I had been born a man. I would show them."

As she spoke she saw Chremes, who was, of course, greatly excited by the identification of his missing daughter with the orphan girl whom Antipho had married.

"Have you paid the money?" he asked his brother.

Dem. "Yes, I have."

Chr. "I wish that you had not. Ah! there is Nausistrata."

Dem. "But why not?"

Chr. "It's all right."

Dem. "How about the girl?"

Chr. "She can't be sent away. The young people love each other too much."

Dem. "But what does that matter to us?"

Chr. "Very much. She is a relative, after all. There was a mistake about the father's name."

Dem. "What? she did not know her own father?"

Chr. "Oh! she knew it."

Dem. "Then why did she say something else?"

Chr. "Don't you understand? You are ruining me."

Nausistrata. "What is it all about?"

Dem. "I am sure I don't know."

Chr. "If you must know, as I am alive, she has no nearer relatives than you and me."

Dem. "Good heavens! Let us go and see her. We all ought to know whether this is true or not."

Chr. "Stop! stop!"

Dem. "Well, what is to be done about our friend's daughter?" [1]

---

[1] By "our friend's daughter," Chremes's own daughter is meant. Nausistrata was not to know who was meant.

Chr. "All right."

Dem. "We are to drop her?"

Chr. "Yes."

Dem. "And the other girl is to stop?"

Chr. "Certainly."

Naus. "I think that would be best, for she seemed a very ladylike young person, when I saw her."

So saying, Nausistrata disappeared into the house. Chremes made sure that the door was shut, and then turning to his brother, exclaimed : "It is an interposition of Providence; Antipho's wife is my daughter Phanium."

Geta had contrived to overhear what had been going on, and was not long in telling the news to Antipho. The only difficulty that remained, concerned the money that the two old men had paid to Phormio as a consideration for marrying the girl whom, before they knew who she really was, they had been so anxious to get rid of. Phormio, true to his character, took the bull by the horns. He called at Demipho's house, and inquired for the master.

Dem. (coming from behind). "Ah, Phormio! we were just on our way to you."

Phor. "I dare say on the same business that brought me here. Well, gentlemen, I am a poor man, but I have always kept my promises. I came to say that I am quite ready to marry."

Dem. "Well, to tell the truth, we have thought it over again. It might have been done before the girl was married to Antipho, but it would hardly do to turn her out. Just what you said yourself, you remember."

Phor. "This is pretty treatment, gentlemen."

Dem. "How so?"

Phor. "Because now I have lost the other girl. How can I go back after I have jilted her?"

Dem. "The truth is that my son won't give up the girl. To cut it short, I want you to pay back the money."

Phor. "If you are ready to hand over to me the wife you promised me, very good; I will marry her. Failing that, I keep her dowry. It is only fair, because I gave up for her another girl who had just as much."

Dem. "Pay me the money, you scoundrel!"

Phor. "Give me the wife."

Dem. "Come along to the magistrates."

Phor. "Now, if you are going to be troublesome, I have something to say. I know a lady whose husband—"

Chr. "How!"

Phor. "Had another wife at Lemnos."

Chr. "I am undone!"

Phor. "And had a daughter by her."

Chr. "For heaven's sake, don't say anything about it."

Phor. "Oh! you are the man, are you?"

After some more angry parleyings, the two old

men caught hold of Phormio, and tried to drag him away; Phormio, on the other hand, struggled to get to the door of Chremes's house. Finding that the two were too strong for him, he shouted out, " Nausistrata!" at the top of his voice. "Stop the villain's mouth!" cried Chremes. " I can't," said Demipho, " he's too strong."—" Nausistrata!" shouted Phormio again, and Nausistrata appeared. "Who calls me?" she asked, "and what is all this disturbance about?" Phormio told the story, Chremes cowering in abject fear. Demipho's intercession and her husband's misery, along with the reflection that what was done could not be undone, did something to mitigate Nausistrata's wrath; but before she had brought herself to forgive the culprit, Phormio thought it well to secure himself and his young friend Phædria. "Nausistrata," he said, "I got one hundred and fifty pounds from your husband by a trick, and gave them to your son. He spent them in buying a wife."

Chr. "What do you say? Buying a wife?"

Naus. "Pray why not? If an old man has two wives, may not a young one have one?"

Dem. "He will do what you like."

Naus. "Well, I sha'n't forgive him, till I hear what my son has to say. He shall decide. And you, sir, what is your name?"

Phor. "My name is Phormio; a friend of your family, madam, and a particular ally of your son Phædria."

Naus. " Phormio, rely on my doing hereafter all I can for you."

Phor. " I am greatly obliged to you, madam."

Naus. " The obligation is with us, sir."

Phor. " Would you do something that would please me and make your husband's eyes smart? "

Naus. " Certainly."

Phor. " Then ask me to dinner to-day."

Naus. " I shall be happy to see you, sir."

Dem. " Let us all go in."

Chr. " But where is Phædria, who is to be my judge? "

Phor. " He'll be here before long, I warrant."